D0343983

C334577689

Aftershocks

Also by Nadia Owusu

So Devilish a Fire

Aftershocks

Dispatches from the Frontlines of Identity

NADIA OWUSU

SCEPTRE

First published in Great Britain in 2021 by Sceptre
An imprint of Hodder & Stoughton
An Hachette UK company

1

Copyright © Nadia Owusu 2021

A CIP catalogue record for this title is available from the British Library

Hardback ISBN 9781529342864
Trade Paperback ISBN 9781529342871
eBook ISBN 9781529342888

Printed and bound in Great Britain by Clays Ltd, Elcograf S.p.A.

Hodder & Stoughton policy is to use papers that are natural,
renewable and recyclable products and made from wood
grown in sustainable forests. The logging and manufacturing
processes are expected to conform to the environmental
regulations of the country of origin.

Hodder & Stoughton Ltd
Carmelite House
50 Victoria Embankment
London EC4Y 0DZ

www.sceptrebooks.co.uk

For mad black women everywhere;
and for my father, Osei Owusu

I am the history of the rejection of who I am.

June Jordan

—Name?
—Fela.
—Just Fela?
—Yeah, jus' Fela.
—Address?
—My house.
—Where?
—Right here, in Surulere, man, yeah!

**Fela Kuti, in conversation
with his arresting officer**

Contents

The Blue Chair

Faults

Mainshocks

Faults

The Blue Chair

Author's Note

A note about truth and time

I write toward truth, but my memory is prone to bouts of imagination. Others remember events differently. I can only tell my version. This does not mean I do not also believe theirs.

Names have been changed. Time, for me, is not linear. I have written for meaning rather than order. I have blurred some lines between people and places.

First Earthquake

Rome, Italy, Age 7

My mother's hair is long, straight, and black. It blows behind her in the wind. She is walking away again. In the moonlight, she is a phantom ship, drifting out on obsidian waters, toward the place where the sky and ocean meet, disappearing over the curvature of the earth, and the moment is so evanescent, so intangible, that I am already wondering, a wisp of her still in sight, if she was ever there at all. She does not turn to see me in the doorway. I am seven years old, bundled up in a pink sweater and down-stuffed coat, my bobbled hat pulled down past my eyebrows. My white socks are dingy and damp from the rain that seeped into the black canvas shoes I insist on wearing no matter the weather. I want to call out to her but am afraid she will not turn around. Or, worse, that she will, but still won't choose me. She gets into the passenger seat of the blue Fiat her husband borrowed from an acquaintance. They are passing through Rome for a day, on their way back to Massachusetts. They vacationed in Venice.

Earlier, before my mother arrived without sign or signal, I woke up to the sound of rain. It was dark outside, so dark I thought it might still be night until I smelled pancakes. My father makes pancakes on Saturday mornings.

As I ate my breakfast, face buried in a shabby copy of *Little Women*, my father fretted. He tapped his foot, peeped at his watch, pushed his glasses up the bridge of his nose. I wondered what was making him anxious and hoped that whatever it was wouldn't require him to sit at his desk all weekend. He had just returned from a work trip to Dhaka. I wanted him to myself. The radio, always perched on the kitchen counter next to the toaster, its bent antenna somehow finding the BBC World Service, brought news of a catastrophic earthquake in Armenia. Tens of thousands of people were killed; hundreds of thousands lost their homes and everything in them. A city called Spitak was destroyed. A new city, the woman on the radio said, would have to be built over the ruins. Soviet leader Mikhail Gorbachev asked the world for help. On my pancake, I spread butter and sprinkled sugar.

"Does Mama have family in Armenia?"

My father flinched, then looked at me with wide eyes magnified by Coke-bottle glasses.

"No," he said. "Her family are Armenian, but they lived in Turkey. They are all in America now."

We usually avoided the topic of my mother, but the BBC said this was an emergency. Rules are suspended in emergencies.

I am half-Armenian but was not sure if the earthquake had anything to do with me. My Ghanaian father, stepmother Anabel, sister Yasmeen, and I live in Italy. This was the first I'd heard of the Caucasus Mountains, the fault rupture point that caused the event. I asked my father what an aftershock was. He said they are tremors in the earth that follow an earthquake. They are the earth's delayed reaction to stress.

The doorbell rang just as I was about to go upstairs to brush my teeth. Yasmeen, who had stumbled into the kitchen rubbing her eyes, jolted awake and scampered after me to see who it was. We hoped our friends from next door had come to play.

Our mother was on the front porch with two red balloons and shaking hands. I stared at her. Remembering my voice, I shouted for my father to come. We hadn't seen my mother in three years, not since I was four. My father nodded hello and sent Yasmeen and me to get dressed. When we came downstairs, my parents were still standing in the hallway. They weren't speaking. My mother's hands were in her pockets. She had let go of the red balloons and they had floated up to the ceiling. Her head dropped. My father's shoulders were drawn back, his legs spread apart.

"Your mother is going to take you for a drive." My father opened the closet and pulled out our puffy coats. I could feel him on the other side of the front door when he closed it behind us, as though to say he would be there, exactly where we left him, when we returned.

My mother's husband drove, silent while my mother chattered. Our half sisters were dying to see us. She would bring them next time. Venice was a magical place. She could hardly believe it was real. Our grandparents bought us a kite in the shape of a fish. Our father could show us how to fly it in the spring.

Despite the drizzle, my mother's husband dropped us off in Piazza Navona. An artist drew a funny sketch of us, together, with bulbous heads and startled eyes. We ate at a café—plates of spaghetti al pomodoro. All of us requested lots of parmesan cheese. My mother asked about school and said she liked our house, even though, as far as I knew, she had only seen the hallway. I asked her about the earthquake. She hadn't heard the news.

"Someday, we'll all go to Armenia," she said. It sounded like half question, half statement, so I said, "Yes," even though I didn't believe her.

As we left the restaurant, a juggler swept over, grinning. His hands seemed to barely move, but his blue, yellow, and red clubs hurtled high above his head. He caught two in one hand and one in the other and bowed deep. My mother clapped. Yasmeen and I, always tentative around strangers, considered the cracks in the paving stones. My mother pressed a few gold and silver thousand-lire coins into the juggler's hand. She also gave one each to Yasmeen and me to toss into the Fontana dei Quattro Fiumi. I told my mother what my father told me about the fountain—about how the four figures in it are the gods of four rivers on four continents: the Nile, the Ganges, the Danube, and the Rio de la Plata. Above the gods is an obelisk, topped with a dove. The obelisk represents the Catholic Church. The river gods are powerful, but they prostrate themselves before the Vatican.

"The fountain is a symbol of colonialism," I whispered, echoing my father, who speaks to me like I was a grown-up. Colonialism, as I understand it, is white people stealing land from black and brown people, white people beating and killing black and brown people, white people forcing black and brown people into slavery and servitude. My father, I know, was born in the last year of colonial rule in what was then the Gold Coast. He says being born as Ghana was being born was the beginning of his good fortune, of our good fortune. I liked that my mother laughed and told me I was smart. When I threw my coin into the water, I closed my eyes tight and listened to my mother's laughter sing with the sound of water. That sound was the wish I dared not shape into words because words could be misconstrued.

Now, I watch my mother get into the blue Fiat. Her husband starts the ignition. To see her more clearly, I squint. She rests her head against the window and I imagine, or perhaps hope, she is crying. The car pulls away, absorbed by the night. I sniff the air for exhaust or perfume, for any remnant of my mother's presence. But I smell only wet limestone and garlic. My stepmother, Anabel, is cooking dinner. Piazza Navona seems far away now. We live in EUR, a neighborhood known by an acronym for the Esposizione Universale di Roma—a world's fair that never happened because of the onset of World War II. EUR was built by Mussolini to celebrate twenty years of Fascist Italy, and to expand the city to the sea. Unlike the rest of Rome, EUR is an orderly place. Its buildings are solid, polished white, and arranged around a grid of right angles. Usually its predictability makes me feel safe, but now it feels inhospitable, spiritless.

Somewhere in the house, my sister shrieks. She does not want to take a bath. Her anger, I know, is about something else entirely. With a last deep breath, I inhale whatever particles of my mother remain, and close the door behind me.

In the hallway, I remove my shoes. The marble floor is cold against my thin socks. Above me, the bulb my father keeps forgetting to change flickers from light to dark then light again. Between my thumb and fingers is the Polaroid my father took of my mother, Yasmeen, and me minutes ago. All of us blinked.

Later, as I am about to walk into my father and Anabel's room to say goodnight, I overhear my father venting.

"She can't even bother to spend time with her daughters," he says. "A few hours are all she could spare for them? That's why I didn't even want to tell them she was coming. She's never going to change." He drank a lot of red wine at dinner and his voice is louder than usual. It rises above the hiss of the radiators and the near-human yowls of the stray cats that beg under trattoria tables by day and hunt mice in the city's sewer system by night.

I knock on the cracked-open door and enter, trying to walk normally, resisting running into my father's arms. My lips quiver and I purse them to keep from crying as my father pulls me into a long hug. My head on his shoulder, I nuzzle into the soapy smell of his neck. He holds me like this every night until we vibrate to the same rhythm. Our heartbeats say he is mine and I am his. He kisses my forehead and reminds me to dream sweet dreams, reminds me that tomorrow will be ours. We can read together all day and maybe, in the evening, we will listen to highlife music and dance in our pajamas. These reminders, I know, are meant as consolation. He wants me to forget my mother was here.

The following week, I take the caricature by the artist in Piazza Navona and the Polaroid picture of my mother, Yasmeen, and me to school for show-and-tell. I do not tell my father.

I attend an international school on Via Cassia. My classmates are from all over the world, but I am one of only two black students. Sarah Brennan, an English girl with green eyes, wants to know why my mother and I are different colors. There is no malice, only curiosity, in her voice, but I feel embarrassed. I can only say I don't know why. As I return to my seat, my face burns.

At lunchtime, Miss Rossi, my teacher, sits next to me and asks if I enjoyed spending time with my mother. Tears pool in my eyes as I nod. She takes me by the hand and leads me into the bathroom, where she helps me wash my face. She asks what is wrong. How do I tell her about the trembling that leads to ripping, then to violent rupture; to whole lives and whole cities disintegrating; to piles and piles of rubble; to displacement and exile? How do I tell her that a day that begins with pancakes for breakfast can end in disaster; that, in an instant, an earthquake or a mother can arrive and change everything? How do I tell her that even when the earth stops shaking, cracks in the surface spread silently? Pent-up forces of danger and chaos can be unleashed at any time. I don't know how to explain any of this, so I tell her I am afraid of the aftershocks.

Resettlement Registration Form

Name: Nadia Adjoa Owusu
Alias Name(s): N/A
Date of Birth: February 23rd, 1981
Age: 28
Gender: Female
Marital Status: Single
Citizenship: United States of America; Ghana
Religion: Atheist? Agnostic?
Education: BA, MS (in progress)
Occupation/Skill: Waitress, Graduate Student, Writer
Name of Father: Osei Owusu
Name of Mother: Almas Janikian

Ethnic Origin: Black. Biracial. Indo-European? Central Asian? Although I identify as Black, I am more literally Caucasian than most people who call themselves Caucasian. My mother is ethnically Armenian, and Armenians are from the Caucasus region between Europe and Asia. Her grandparents escaped Turkey during the Armenian genocide of 1915-1917. They eventually settled in Watertown, Massachusetts, where my mother was born. My father belonged to the Ashanti tribe from the Kumasi area of southern Ghana.

Preferred Language: English is my first language. I used to be fluent in Italian. I still speak it, but my vocabulary has dwindled. I also speak conversational French and some Swahili. But, my preferred language is Twi—my father's native tongue—even though I don't speak but a few words of it. When I walk by people speaking it on the streets of New York, I slow my pace, listen for a while. The sound warms me from the inside, like groundnut soup and fufu. This is probably not what is meant by "preferred."

Country of Origin: I was born in Dar es Salaam, Tanzania, but that is only because my father happened to be stationed there at the time. He worked for a United Nations agency.

My mother is an American citizen, so I became American at birth. However, I did not live in the United States until I was eighteen. Much of America felt familiar to me when I arrived. America is experienced everywhere in the world. But calling myself American doesn't feel quite accurate.

I also hold a Ghanaian passport. I've never used it, as far as I can remember. It's much easier to travel with the American one. But it was important to my father that I was officially Ghanaian.

I have never been to Armenia or Turkey (except for a layover in the Istanbul airport once).

For my father's job, we moved a lot. I lived in Tanzania until I was three. At three, I moved to England to live with my aunt Harriet for two and a half years. I lived in England for a second time at age twelve for a term at boarding school in Surrey. From ages five to eight, I lived in Italy. I moved back there for three years at age thirteen. Between the ages of eight and ten, I lived in Ethiopia. From ten to twelve, and then again from sixteen to eighteen, I lived in Uganda.

My stepmother, Anabel, is from a small village on the Tanzanian side of Mount Kilimanjaro. My mother's second husband was Somali. So I have two half sisters and a half brother who are Armenian-Somali-American. And my half brother on my father's side, Kwame, is Ghanaian and Tanzanian.

When I turned eighteen, I moved to New York, where I have lived for my entire adult life. New York is a kind of home.

Confused? Me too. I never know how to answer the question of my origin.

Country of Asylum: There are three relevant definitions of the word *asylum*: 1. Protection from arrest and extradition given especially to political refugees by a nation or by an embassy or other agency enjoying freedom from what is required by law for most people. 2. (antiquated) An institution for the maintenance and care of the mentally ill, orphans, or other persons requiring specialized assistance. 3. Any secure retreat.

Though my application seems to relate to the first, I am seeking the kind of place described by the second and third definitions. I am seeking a place to wait out the aftershocks.

FORESHOCKS

Foreshock:

a relatively small earthquake that precedes a greater one by a few days or weeks and originates at or near the focus of the larger earthquake

Note:

The terms *foreshock*, *mainshock*, and *aftershock* have no strict scientific definition. They are used to distinguish the largest shock in an earthquake sequence from the events that preceded and followed it. If an aftershock is larger than the event before it, we rename it the mainshock and the previous earthquakes in the sequence become foreshocks. The story is reshuffled. In the sequence, we only know what goes where in retrospect.

Unwelcome Reunion

When I was twenty-eight, my stepmother Anabel came to New York on vacation. She was living, at the time, in Pakistan, where she worked for a UN agency. At a restaurant a few blocks from my Chinatown apartment, we ate noodle soup and drank red wine. That night, Anabel told me my father did not die of cancer as I believed. He died, she claimed, of AIDS.

I don't remember why neither my sister Yasmeen nor my half brother Kwame joined us for that dinner—they both lived in New York at the time. Yasmeen worked the counter at a taco shop in Red Hook. Kwame was a sophomore in college.

My father had died fourteen years earlier, when I was weeks away from my fourteenth birthday. The argument that culminated in Anabel telling me he died of AIDS was over nothing of consequence:

"After dinner, let's go see some live music," Anabel said.

"I can't," I said. "I have plans with friends."

"But I'm your mother and I'm visiting," she said. "We never see each other."

I shrugged. We ate, for a few minutes, in silence. Then:

"Chew your food," Anabel said.

"I am chewing. Calm down."

"Who is not calm? Respect your elders. Respect me."

"You're acting unhinged," I said.

I knew that my words—*you're acting unhinged*—were shots, fired. Anabel, I predicted, would detonate. Madness, I'd observed, terrified and disgusted her. Perhaps this was because she had experienced some form of it after my father died: depression, I believed, or PTSD. For a year or more, she spent nights crying into a wineglass. Her moods, then, teetered between cold silence and hot rage. In recent years, though, she had reinvented herself as unflappable and even-keeled. She spoke of other people's breakdowns, anxiety, and depression in hushed, haughty tones. One had to be strong, she said often, in the face of adversity. Allowing oneself to become morbid or hysterical helped no one. Disintegration was an indulgence. She was, she insisted, happy with her life because she had *chosen* to be happy with her life. She *chose* happiness every day. If I brought up the years surrounding my father's death, even to say how far we'd come, she'd change the subject. She seemed unwilling to entertain the possibility that she might experience any form of madness ever again.

I had never seen Anabel angrier than when I called her crazy—unhinged. I did this, from time to time, to win fights. The suggestion that her reinvented self was not entirely believable seemed more than she could bear. Her mask, I must say, was a good one. Only those who knew her best could see through it. Beneath the smooth, unlined skin, muscles twitched faintly, blood bulged in veins.

In the Chinese restaurant, I wanted to tear Anabel's mask off. I wanted to do it in public. I wanted her red-faced and exploding. I wanted to remind her I knew who she really was. She couldn't fool me. On the receiving end of her rage, I wanted to appear composed, and superior in my composure. It wasn't that I cared so much what the people in the restaurant thought of me or of her. It was that I knew a public display was not something she would recover easily from. She would play the scene over and over in her mind. The memory would return to agitate her when she least expected it. She would always remember my face—my undisturbed face. She would always remember the sharp looks of strangers, their shaking heads. My desire to tear Anabel's mask off was not, upon reflection, about what she said. Defensiveness is aroused easily between mothers and daughters, between stepmothers and daughters. Between Anabel and me, the defensiveness could very quickly turn destructive.

Instead of an explosion, though, Anabel's words hissed from between clenched teeth:

"Unhinged? How dare you. After all I have sacrificed for you," she said.

"What did you sacrifice?" I asked. "You only kept me around because it meant you'd get more of my father's money. You made it abundantly clear you didn't really want me or Yasmeen."

I knew that Anabel's reasons for becoming my guardian, and Yasmeen's, after our father died were more complicated than this. Wanting us and not wanting us were states that likely coexisted in her. They likely coexist in many parents—biological or not. But my intention in that moment was to wound her. This simplified story of her motivations would do damage. For what seemed like a long time, she squinted at me, mouth agape. Then her eyes became calm and cloudless, as though she perceived, in an instant, precisely what to say to win:

"You think your precious father was so perfect? He didn't die of cancer like you think. He was no angel. He died of AIDS. How do you think he got AIDS?"

The shape of my relationship with Anabel had always been jagged. After I moved to New York at eighteen, we drifted in and out of each other's life without explanation, without apologies. Before meeting for dinner at the Chinese restaurant, it had been over a year since we last spoke. She Facebook messaged me to say she would be in New York; to suggest we get together. Neither of us acknowledged the yearlong silence. In greeting, we kissed each other on both cheeks. We complimented each other's appearance: her braids, my earrings. There was no clear reason for the not speaking. Or, rather, there were a lifetime of reasons, a lifetime of unuttered resentments on both sides.

———

I met Anabel for the first time when I was five.

"This is Anabel," my father said simply, "we're getting married."

I don't remember if this first meeting took place at an airport or in the house in Rome where we would become a family. Yasmeen and I had recently joined our father in Rome after living with his sister—our aunt Harriet—in England for two and a half years. Anabel looked to me like a movie star: tall, thin, and otherworldly in her beauty, with high cheekbones, plush lips, and a large gap between her two front teeth. A pinky finger would fit nicely in that gap. I saw love in my father's eyes, saw it was not directed at me, seethed. Yasmeen's face, on the other hand, was open with hope. She jumped up, hugged Anabel. There was nothing my sister longed for more than a mother. Yasmeen called strangers in the grocery store *Mommy* when they bent to pinch her cheeks. She clung to our aunts, our father's female friends, and even our sour-faced German nanny. *Those poor little motherless girls*, people said.

Anabel patted Yasmeen's head. She looked at me expectantly. I wrapped my arms around my father. Anabel frowned.

I too longed for a mother, but I think I was already steeled to the reality that I would not have one, not in the same way all the other children I knew had one. But, my father was, I believed, mine. Mine and Yasmeen's. I did not want to share him with anyone else.

Of those first few months we lived together, before Anabel married my father, I have memories of her glaring at me when I climbed onto my father's lap while they sat together on the couch drinking gin and tonics. I remember knocking on my father and Anabel's bedroom door when I woke up scared during a thunderstorm. I remember her whispering that I should leave them alone when they were sleeping. I remember her shutting the door in my face. I remember bitterness broiling in my chest.

It is possible I misread Anabel, that I am misremembering, that my memories are tainted by that bitterness. Or perhaps Anabel was cold toward me because she sensed that I saw her as competition. Maybe she wanted to assert her authority as the woman of the house. I cannot be certain. I am quite certain, however, that as my father and Anabel's wedding day approached, my bratty behavior intensified.

On the day Yasmeen and I tried on our flower girl dresses, I was at my worst. The dresses were voluminous. We looked like little puffs of yellow cotton candy. Our headbands were adorned with giant bows. I was the kind of child who liked both rolling around in the mud and playing princess. I loved a bit of frill. But I was determined to hate that dress. It was itchy, I complained. Anabel ignored me.

"We really have to get them a relaxer," she said to my father. "They're growing dreadlocks."

She stuck her long, sharp nails into my coarse, tangled hair and yanked. It hurt a little. I exaggerated the pain—grimaced and cried out. Anabel smoothed her own freshly relaxed hair as though to make sure my nappy-ness wasn't contagious. My father did not come to my defense. I burst into tears.

"I don't want a relaxer," I wailed. "If you make me get one, I'll shave my head bald. And I won't wear these stupid frilly socks either. They make my shoes too tight."

I was not crying about my pinched toes or tangled hair. Anabel was taking from me what mattered most. The house and my father had been redecorated: Out with the old comfy couch; off with Baba's beard. I was not about to give Anabel everything she wanted, not without a fight.

Down the aisle, I walked without socks, without a relaxer. I had to walk down the aisle, but I did so with dignity.

Within a year, Anabel and I had established our territories in the house in Rome. Anabel ruled the formal living room with its uncomfortable flowered settees and Persian rugs. In there, she and my father drank cocktails and white wine, her long legs stretched out over his lap. She whispered her words, but her laughter was a soprano crescendo. I imitated her laugh in the mirror. My territory was my father's study. In there, we read books together in silence, him in his swivel chair, me lying on the rug. Or we wrote stories and read them aloud. He gave me editorial feedback. His stories, to me, were always perfect.

Each time we moved—from Rome to Addis Ababa, from Addis Ababa to Kampala, then back to Rome again—Anabel and I took over corresponding spaces in our new house. In our house in Addis, my father did not have a study. Instead, I owned the back porch. My father and I read and wrote to the songs of insects and birds.

Sometimes, when the UN agency sent my father on an extended mission to another country, Anabel and I settled into an uneasy peace. When he was gone, I forgot we were adversaries, that we were not supposed to love each other. She seemed to soften as well. Our conversations grew longer and less barbed. We laughed at each other's jokes.

When I was eleven, I got my first period, on the day my father was to return from a mission to Northern Uganda. The blood in my underwear and shorts terrified me. I had not known that the bleeding would be so heavy; had not known thát, unlike pee, it could not be held. The idea of uttering the necessary words about what was bleeding where to my father was horrifying, and he wasn't there anyway, so I told Anabel. We went for a drive to get thick sanitary pads and ice cream. In the car, she told me I was a woman now, a beautiful woman. There would be no shortage of men, she said, who would try to take, take, take from me.

"Remember," she said, "you can make them weak by not giving them what they want. Then you are the one with power."

I did not understand what Anabel was saying. I knew nothing, yet, about what men would want from me; did not know what a period was for. But she had called me a woman. She had called me beautiful. I wished we could always be like we were in that moment: two women in a car with the windows down, our tongues darting in and out of vanilla ice cream, talking about beauty and power to a Whitney Houston soundtrack.

But, later that evening, when my father returned with duty-free gifts—perfume for Anabel, Toblerone for me and Yasmeen, a toy train for Kwame—Anabel and I retreated to our rooms. I waited—I imagined we both waited—to see which door my father would open.

It was only after my father was diagnosed with cancer, after he was bedridden, that Anabel and I gave up our territories. We knew then that we might both lose him. We gave up our territories but not our resentments.

My father's death demolished me. It was perhaps because I had never properly grieved my mother's leaving that I approached mourning him with fierce intention. Grieving, I learned, was a process of story construction. I needed to construct a story so I could reconstruct my world. There were decisions to make about what to put in and what to leave out.

In my version of the story of my father's illness and death, my father and I were the protagonists: a hero father and a daughter who loved him more than anything. My siblings—Yasmeen and Kwame— were background players. This was self-centered, and I did not care. My father's illness, in my story, happened almost as much to me as it did to him. I watched him shrink. I smelled his stale, dying breath as I lay beside him telling him pointless stories about school, and films, and what I ate for lunch. I heard him cry out from pain or humiliation when his bowels failed and he woke up in a pool of his own feces.

My journal from that time is full of entries about his weight loss, hair loss, and chronic boils—the side effects of his aggressive course of chemotherapy. I noted the shapes of his protruding bones and the color of the pus that oozed from his boils when they burst.

Nowhere in those journals does Anabel appear, even though she was his primary nurse, even though his sickbed was also her bed, even though she was always there, cleaning vomit from the rugs and rubbing lotion on his cracked toes. Not once did I thank her for those things. I was already writing her out of the story, my story. I did not thank her, but I did blame her.

I remember the time my father asked for an apple and Anabel told him, voice full of venom, to get it himself. She knew he could no longer walk. She called a priest to say a prayer over him, something he would not have wanted, as he did not believe in prayer or God. When he tried to protest with the few words he still had, she raised her hand to silence him. I saw her actions not as the lashing out of a person in pain, but as proof I was the one who really loved him, she was the evil stepmother. My story, you see, required a villain.

"He didn't want a priest," I said. "He told me he didn't want any religion done to him. Those were his words."

"Oh, shut up," she said. "Just shut up."

I think she apologized later—for the *shut up*, not for the priest. But I am not certain about that.

After my father died, my mother told me, over the phone, that she would not come to Rome for the funeral. She would not come to claim Yasmeen and me. I vowed never to forgive her, never to speak to her again. Yasmeen, I think, was reluctant to lose another parent. She looked terrified when I told her our relationship with our mother was over for good. But my father had told her to trust me as her older sister and protector. He had told me never to betray her trust. Yasmeen let me make the decision.

"Stay with me," Anabel said when I told her about the call with my mother. "I promised your father I would take care of you and Yasmeen. And I need you. You're *my* daughters."

That day, Anabel and I wept together. We agreed to make a family of four: the two of us, Yasmeen, and Kwame. I will never forget that Anabel claimed me when my mother did not. But it was not long before we fell back into old patterns. We argued over my father's soul: if and where it lived and what it wanted. Anabel wanted to move on. A friend of my father's helped her get an entry-level position in the Rome office of the same UN agency where my father had worked. It was her first job. She had attained a bachelor's degree in accounting from an American university in Rome after she married my father, but she had not gone into the workforce. In her new job, she had a lot to learn and to get used to. She wanted to build a new life. I, on the other hand, refused to let go.

Anabel believed in heaven. I believed in memories. We fought over what my father left behind, both inanimate and intangible. She locked up his papers—notes, poems—so I could not read them. I squirreled away duffel bags of his socks and ties and hid them in the back of my closet. Yasmeen sided with me, though she was too weak to fight much. She smoked cigarettes and took laxatives. She weighed herself and counted calories. She counted crumbs before placing them on her tongue. My fury took up enough space for both of us.

"Get out of my face! I miss Baba!" I shouted at Anabel when she switched off the television and insisted I stop moping around.

"Go dig up his grave, then," Anabel said. "No wonder your mother didn't want you."

We didn't speak for a week after that fight. Then, one night, Anabel crawled into bed with me, heaving with un-cried tears. My father's ghost woke her up, she said, tried to lure her into a rosy light. I held Anabel's clammy hand beneath the covers and wondered why my father's ghost did not come to me too.

We lived in Rome for two more years after my father's death. Then we moved to Kampala, Uganda, where Anabel had been transferred. As was true of Rome, we had previously lived in Kampala with my father. He had been stationed there for two years. Memories of him were everywhere. When we arrived at the airport in Entebbe, it was my father's former driver Edward who picked us up. Daily, we drove past the house we lived in as a family of five. The international school Yasmeen, Kwame, and I attended had not changed at all. I played soccer on the same field where my father had once cheered me on as I won three blue ribbons at a sports day: the 100 meters, the 200 meters, a relay.

As a teenager, I had a lot of freedom in Kampala. I became close to a group of girls and the boys who followed them around. We went out at night—danced, smoked pot, got drunk, kissed in the corners of nightclubs. Anabel also stayed out late. She started dating. She only occasionally asked where I was going, what I was doing. Only very rarely—usually when she was in a bad mood—did she tell me I couldn't go out. On one such occasion, we argued. I called her insane. I was shocked to feel Anabel's hands at my shoulders, shoving me hard onto my bed. I looked up at her. She raised her hand, yelped, pummeled my head with punches. I curled into a ball, protecting my head with my hands. She did not hit me hard enough to hurt me physically. It was not my body she wanted to bruise. I did not hit back. There was a line, I knew, that must not be crossed. The beating ended abruptly when eight-year-old Kwame wandered into the room clutching his stuffed frog. At seeing his mother hitting his big sister, he burst into tears. He screamed until Anabel picked him up and carried him out of the room. That night, he slept at the foot of my bed. The sound of his soft asthmatic snores was both irritating and comforting. If it weren't for him, I thought, I would wake Yasmeen up and we would leave this house, move to Ghana or England with my father's family, move in with anyone but her.

The next morning, I came home to find an open Bible on my desk. Highlighted in yellow was Proverbs 29:15: *The rod and reproof give wisdom: but a child left to himself bringeth his mother to shame.* I could hear Anabel shuffling about in the hallway. I sat still, silent. For days after, Anabel and I refused to meet eyes. I stole money from her purse and bought three bottles of gin. When she had a colleague over for dinner, I got wasted. By dessert, I was slurring my words and laughing at the wrong things, laughing at Anabel. Her face was flushed but she said nothing. At a stalemate, we abandoned the battle. We never discussed it and Anabel never hit me again. The anger simmered. We were angry at death, at cancer, at the sky for still being blue, the rivers for not flooding, Kampala for not changing. But there was nothing we could do about those things. We had only each other to accuse.

At eighteen, I moved from Kampala to New York to attend Pace University. At first, Anabel helped with my tuition, but when the money my father left for my education had been spent, she stopped.

To finish school, I went into heavy debt, and worked two jobs— one at a restaurant and one at a nightclub. Even that wasn't enough for tuition, rent, bills, transportation, and food. Some weeks, the staff meal, offered at the restaurant where I worked, was my only meal. I could not afford both groceries and subway rides. I needed to ride the subway to work, so I chose hunger. Once or twice, I sent Anabel an email asking for money to eat or to have my electricity turned back on.

Sometimes she sent money, sometimes she did not respond. Between junior and senior years, I took time off school. A tuition bill had gone into collections, and I couldn't register for classes until it had been paid. Sometime during the period when I was not enrolled in school, Anabel came to New York for a conference. I was determined to go back to school and hoped she'd help me. At a restaurant where I was to meet her and a family friend for dinner, I was turning a corner to join them at the bar when I overheard Anabel say, in Swahili, that I had dropped out of school. She said I could not cut it—having to work and study at the same time. There was some truth to what she said. Being alone in New York, having to fend for myself, learning about money, struggling financially—all of that was a shock to my system. In many ways, my family's high-mobility, global lifestyle had made me resilient and self-sufficient. But it had, in other ways, made me spoiled. At a young age, I had experienced a great deal of loss. I had been made aware early of the existence of profound suffering in the world—extreme poverty, violence, disease. But, before I moved to New York, I had never done a load of laundry. My father and Anabel paid people to clean for us, cook for us, drive us around.

Being broke, I knew, was very different from being poor. Despite my overdrawn bank account, the advantages and privileges I had accrued through very little effort of my own—my private international school education, my multilingualism, my comfort with navigating institutions and bureaucracy—buoyed me. Those advantages and privileges opened doors. Still, I found it difficult to adjust to my new economic reality. I had always been a good student. In high school, with the exception of mathematics, I was able to get good grades without working too hard. Recently, I found it hard to keep up academically. Often, I didn't get home from my cocktail waitressing job until four in the morning. The stress of debt took a toll on my ability to focus. I had not failed any classes, but I got C's. I missed a lot of class. I didn't do the reading, turned in assignments late, turned in sloppy work.

The truth in Anabel's words about my failings stung. And she had not acknowledged how hard I was trying, how despite my failings, I was still determined to graduate. I was humiliated, but I did not show it. I hugged Anabel and the family friend. I ordered an expensive glass of wine, an expensive steak. Let her pay, I thought.

In the years after I graduated from university, Anabel came to New York several times—to drop Kwame off at college, for work, to shop. Always, we met for lunch, dinner, or drinks. Sometimes, we got mani-pedis, seated side by side, our toes in bubbling tubs. Our nails were trimmed neatly, filed into shape, and polished with glossy color. Perhaps we both wanted to believe the same could be true of the past. It could not. Beyond those meals, those manicures, she and I did not speak much anymore. Usually, Anabel would be the one to call. Usually, the calls would last just a few minutes. Our conversations were not intimate. We did not talk about what was happening in our lives, except in vague terms: I had been accepted to graduate school, she had taken her first yoga class. I would ask about her family. She would say everyone was fine. She would ask about my aunts in England—my father's sisters. I would say they were fine.

By the time of the dinner during which Anabel told me my father died of AIDS, it had been a decade since Anabel and I lived under the same roof. She had been transferred from Kampala to Islamabad. It was a dangerous post. To terrorist attacks, she had lost colleagues. I worried about her. I should have told her that. I never did.

When Anabel said my father died of AIDS, I slammed my hands on the table, rose from my chair.

"Liar," I said.

"You're acting like a spoiled child," Anabel said.

"Are you fucking kidding me?" My heart pounded, my head pounded.

"You always blame me for everything," Anabel said. "It's not my fault your father was out doing god knows what with god knows who and came home with AIDS."

"Liar," I said again and walked away from her, walked out of the restaurant.

Outside, I was stopped by a jolt in my brain, like a shot of electricity, followed by vibration and the quiet but unmistakable sound of an alarm. I held my head with both hands until I could walk again. I cried and screamed all the way home. I didn't care about the stares. If my father had died of AIDS, it meant that he had deceived me. It meant that I had not known him as well as I thought I had. Anabel had insinuated affairs. I could not, would not, believe her.

"Liar! Liar! Liar!" I shouted.

At home, I crawled under my bed and unearthed the dusty envelope that held a copy of my father's death certificate. As I read it, I held my breath. By the official ruling, I was reassured: *"Causa di morte: Cancro."* Cause of death: Cancer.

"Liar! Liar! Liar!" I shouted.

I shouted *liar* all night, like a mantra or a prayer. I shouted it to shift the doubt that had lodged in my throat.

For my father, over the years, I wrote several elegies. In them, he was canonized. I needed to believe in something big and pure and godlike. Because I could not bring myself to believe in a god I had never met, a god my father hadn't believed in, I chose to believe in my father. All his good deeds, I categorized and tabulated: the children he fed in refugee camps in Eritrea; the way he remembered so many of their names; how he always brought me cold Cokes in bed when I had a stomachache; how he paid his youngest sister's college tuition and his niece's private school fees; the way his laughter flooded whole rooms, whole houses.

There was nothing in my story, in the elegies, about my father having affairs.

Although I held on to the belief that Anabel was a liar, the vibrations in my brain did not stop. The alarm continued to sound. I believed the vibrations and alarm were caused by an instrument in my brain. My seismometer, I called it. I called it that because I had, since my mother arrived with an earthquake when I was seven, been obsessed with earthquakes and the ways we measure them; the ways we try to understand the size and scale of impending disaster. When I say I believed in my seismometer, I mean it was an irrefutable conviction.

I came to know my seismometer was there in the same way I knew I had a mole below the right corner of my bottom lip and a large black oval-shaped birthmark just left of my spine. As a child, I wanted to carve my mole and birthmark out of my skin. As an adult, I could have had them surgically removed. The surgery would have been minor, but by then they were too much a part of me. Once, a photographer photoshopped my mole out of a headshot. I hated the photograph. It didn't look like me. At first, I couldn't tell why. When I realized my mole was missing, I was furious. My seismometer was not just characteristic, though. It was basal. I didn't know if it was killing me, saving me, or both. Its removal, I believed, would be less excision and more amputation.

A few days after Anabel told me my father died of AIDS, I received a voicemail: "Hello, Nadia. This is your mama. Please call me back at this number. We need to talk. Please call me."

It was the first time I had heard my mother's voice in over a decade.

From her voice, my seismometer vibrated. I grabbed a jar of coins, raised it above my head, and dropped it, hard. It shattered. I picked up the shards, counted the change. One hundred and eighteen dollars and sixty-four cents. I counted change and glass to quiet my seismometer. I did not stop counting when blood sprang in red dots from the soft pads of my fingertips. The blood, on my tongue, tasted like copper pennies.

The voicemail from my mother had to be deleted, as did the record of her phone number, as did the cheerful messages Anabel left about meeting again before she returned to Pakistan. Anabel, as usual, was ready to move on. I could not. Not this time. I went back to bed for the rest of the day, and the day after that. Yet, even in sleep, the vibrations persisted.

Aches

Two weeks after Anabel told me my father died of AIDS, after my mother left me a voicemail, I came home to find a shoebox on my doormat. Inside: a pink toothbrush; a hairbrush; a photo of me and George in Central Park; my copy of *To Kill a Mockingbird*; a spiral notebook, its pages blank but for this in my handwriting on the first line: *Read Rousseau re. 'social contract.'* I had no idea when or why I wrote that.

George—the man I had convinced myself, despite much evidence to the contrary, was the love of my life—was moving to South Sudan the next day, without me. We had been together four years. He'd dropped my things off without ringing the doorbell for a last goodbye, without a note.

When George left me, I thought he was my leading man. Now I know he was a supporting actor. I mean no offense to him in saying this. He was—is—a lovely person. He hurt me by not loving me enough. Heartbreak of that sort happens all the time. I didn't love him enough either. It just took me a long time to see that.

When I met George, I was overflowing with want, need, heartbreak, and wrath. George's body was the one I chose to pour it into. From across a crowded bar, I chose George because I liked the way he laughed with such force that his head flopped back violently. I chose him because he wore a ratty baseball cap in a neighborhood gentrified by tailored suits and pocket squares. I chose him because he had lived in Kenya and Cambodia. I liked the way his eyelids lowered when he considered a question. He asked a lot of questions—of himself, of others, of the world—even when he knew he might never get answers. I also chose him because he was restless and because he could be so cruel with words they stung like bees. He spent Saturdays looking for jobs in war zones and natural disasters. He started leaving me on the day he told me he loved me, though it took him two years to do it. This caused me pain, but at least that pain didn't require me to self-examine. I focused on that pain rather than on the greater pains of my father's death and my mothers' rejection.

Finding the shoebox on my doormat made my seismometer's alarm sound so loud that the need to muffle it consumed me.

I picked up the box, charged back down the stairs, and threw it and all its contents into the garbage can on the street outside. The cook from the restaurant next door—the one that served a hybrid menu of bubble tea, noodles, chicken feet, tacos, and green tea ice cream—squatted outside, smoking. I wanted to grab his cigarette from his rough lips. I wanted to burn my flesh—any cigarette-sized section of flesh—with it. Then, for just a second, I wanted to burn his flesh instead. Perhaps I wanted to see physical pain in his eyes because I couldn't see my own pain, not really, not clearly. I was horrified by my thoughts, but my horror did not quiet them.

There was a door in my mind. It had, until then, been hidden from me. A sign hung over it: *The only solution is a permanent solution.* Once that door appears, you cannot help but imagine what is on the other side. You cannot help but consider ways to get there: *Jam a kitchen knife into the ripest blue vein in your wrist. Pills! Take all the pills! Step off the subway platform into the approaching Q train. Leap from the roof into the glittering city.*

I believed the door appeared because of George. But I know now that George was simply the last in a long line of people and places I tried and failed to belong to.

To my mother and to Anabel, I had never felt like I belonged indisputably. My ties to them had been broken, retied, and broken again many times over. And now I felt more disconnected from my father than I had since the year he died. Because of Anabel's claim that he had affairs, that he died of AIDS, I was losing control of my story of him. Even my grief could not be trusted. This was humiliating, unsettling. There were so many questions now. Belonging to my father was no longer uncomplicated. If what Anabel had said was true, why hadn't he trusted me enough to tell me? To whom else had he belonged?

If I could not find belonging in my story of my father, in my grief, where could I find it? If I belonged nowhere and to no one, then what was I? Who was I?

I cannot remember a time when I wasn't aware of the fact that I had multiple selves, or a divided self, and that I needed to behave differently with the different groups of people that made up my life. All people do this to some extent, but some must be more skillful at it than others.

I was quiet at my mostly white nursery school in the small English town of Hailsham, drawing as little attention to myself as possible. "My father says that black people are dirty," one boy said to me, "and if you touch me, I can kick you."

I only visited my mother in Massachusetts twice—once when I was four and once when I was eight. My memories of those visits are fuzzy, but I remember I spoke in a whisper so as not to disturb my stepfather. He was not pleased that Yasmeen and I—another man's children—were there. He shouted at us for running and screaming in the house even though my half sisters ran and screamed too.

During the visit when I was eight, I poked my head through an open window and called for my sisters to come out and play. My stepfather marched up to the window, furious. He tried to slam it shut but my hand was in the way. I still have the scar.

Toward the end of that visit, I was playing in my grandparents' backyard with my cousin Aaron, who is white—half-Armenian and half-Jewish. The neighbor poked his head over the hedge. He asked my mother how long it had taken for the adoption to go through. He and his wife were hoping to adopt a baby from Ethiopia too. Wasn't the famine there awful? My mother looked up from the novel she was reading and took a long, slow sip of her lemonade. She smiled brightly though her eyes looked fierce.

"How nice," she said. "I was lucky to have avoided all that paperwork. I just married an African man and gave birth to my own black babies. Ten long hours of labor, though."

The neighbor's mouth went slack, and he hurried away muttering something about a pot on the stove.

I can see now that it was the neighbor my mother mocked, but at the time all I heard was that I was her black baby. I wondered if my blackness was why I didn't live with her while my two half sisters did. They were biracial too—their father was Somali. But they were very light-skinned. People often took them to be white—Greek or Sicilian or fully Armenian. I had my mother's face, but because of the color of my skin, I didn't look to the world like I belonged to her.

On vacation in Ghana when I was seven and living in Rome, my grandmother woke me and got me dressed, quietly. She didn't want to rouse my father as he would have objected to an all-day church excursion. My sister and I went to church on occasion, when Anabel wanted to, but my father liked to be there. To prevent brainwashing, he said.

"There is nothing wrong with seeking truth or grace or light," he told me. "The problem with organized religion is the assertion that all questions have already been answered. I don't want you believing that. There is more to life, and to the universe, than what is in a single book."

My grandmother spent six hours at church every Sunday, with one break for lunch and one for afternoon tea with lots of milk and sugar. On the day she took me with her, we were met in the parking lot by a gaggle of women—my grandmother's friends. They pointed at me. "Where is she from?" one of them demanded. I thought about responding, but my grandmother often said children were not to speak to elders unless spoken to. I stared down at my shiny red shoes with buckles. Those shoes made me feel like Dorothy in *The Wizard of Oz*, that other little girl who kept finding herself in unfamiliar places, far-away lands.

"She's my granddaughter," my grandmother said. "Nadia, where are you from?" she asked, smirking.

"Ghana," I said, raising my eyes.

The women snorted and slapped one another's shoulders in amusement. They joked in Twi about me. Tears rose, but I willed them not to fall. The women probably thought I was spoiled, with my silly red shoes. I didn't want to be thought a crybaby too. It was clear, then, that self-selection into a group did not necessarily lead to acceptance.

Not only did being biracial mean that I looked out of place, but I also didn't always know how to behave within the norms of my chosen nationality: Ghanaian. My English was too posh-sounding, courtesy of my time in England. It earned me the nickname *Lady*. I wasn't proficient when eating fufu with my hands. I didn't sop up nearly enough soup with the sticky dough, so I had to finish up with a spoon. When I tried to run around outside barefoot like my second cousins who lived next door to my grandparents, my too-soft soles were scorched by the sunburnt earth. I hopped from foot to foot for hours until, defeated, I put my sandals back on.

Ghana, America, England, Italy, Ethiopia, Uganda—I could not lay claim to any of those places in an incontestable way. It has always been difficult for me to say the word *home* with any conviction. When I was a child, I often felt like an outsider among my own family. Between me and them were borders—geographic, spiritual, cultural, linguistic. And no sooner had we arrived in a place than we had to prepare to leave it.

My father used to say that no matter where lines were drawn, all human beings, all living things, are connected. We all belong everywhere on this small planet. We all belong to one another. I think he meant to comfort me from my accumulating rejections. But, in his words, I also heard that I was not supposed to ache for the people and places we left behind. Moving on was what we did. In some houses, we hadn't stayed long enough for our framed photographs to leave marks on the walls. Weeks later, in another country, we would hang those photographs again. But I did ache for the homes we left behind. I did ache when I said goodbye to the friends I'd made. I ached when I said goodbye to my grandparents, to my cousins, to my aunts, to my mother. I ached for lasting connection, for a place where rejection was not inevitable. No matter how many times I stood on bare floors, surrounded by blank walls, telling myself I belonged everywhere and to everyone, emptied houses never stopped feeling like ruin. Failing to fully belong in my father's family, and my mother's, never stopped feeling like disgrace.

For a time, I had imagined making a home with George. Only much later did I realize that the picture of that home in my mind had little to do with him. He was a stand-in. The home I imagined with him was a surrogate home. It would not have healed the aches. Still, I ached for it too.

THE BLUE CHAIR

New York, New York, Age 28

The Blue Chair

Two weeks or so after George left, I walked aimlessly around Manhattan for hours—from the corner of Mott and Bayard to 125th Street in Harlem. I stopped outside a little storefront church to listen to people believe in salvation. When they burst into song, I imagined, from where I stood in front of the closed white door, that they were dancing on their tiptoes. I imagined them stretching their arms high as though grasping at God. A man with pitted skin lingered by me. He had a neat little afro and wore red-and-black basketball shoes with holes in the toes. His eyes scanned me slowly up and down. I wrapped my scarf more tightly around my neck and listened, harder, to the song in the church: *I'm redeemed / From the darkness of the night / That so thickly enveloped my soul / In my heart there have gleamed / Rays of wonderful light.*

"Spare some change, sister," the man asked, "so I can get something hot to eat?" I gave him all the cash in my wallet: forty dollars. I was broke, as I had just paid my rent. The forty dollars was supposed to last me three days, until my next shift at the restaurant where I waited tables in a very skimpy black dress. It was difficult, over the bedlam in my head, to consider how to respond appropriately to a man who asked me for money after checking out my ass.

I had been seeing a psychiatrist for ten years, for anxiety and depression. Every other month, I went to her office to get the prescription for my medication renewed.

At my appointment in the month Anabel told me my father died of AIDS, my mother called, and George left, I wanted to tell her that my medication no longer seemed to work. Energy pulsed through every vein in my body. My toes tingled. My hands shook.

"Any luck finding a therapist?" my psychiatrist asked as she handed me a credit card slip to sign for my copay. She always had me pay before we talked.

"Still looking," I lied. So many times, I had taken her printed list of recommended therapists, but I had never actually called any of them. I didn't want anyone digging around in my mind. They might not know when to stop. They might go too far and break the mantle that protected the hot, molten core. My psychiatrist never cracked the surface. She only asked stock questions she read from a list on a clipboard. She asked if I heard voices; if I had thoughts of hurting myself or others; if I wanted to discuss any new side effects of the medication I was taking. I always answered no to those questions. Technically, I was always telling the truth until that appointment in January, one month before I turned twenty-nine. At that appointment, I half-lied about the voices. I heard voices, but they were all versions of my own voice or echoes of voices from my past. Those voices were not, I decided, the ones she was asking about. And I lied when I did not tell her about wanting to burn myself and the cook. I lied when I did not tell her about the door that had opened: *The only solution is a permanent solution.* My psychiatrist did not ask if there was a seismometer in my midbrain that warned of fissures that would widen into deep chasms and, eventually, into an all-consuming abyss. If she had asked about that, I might have answered honestly. It's difficult to say.

"I think I need a higher dose," I said. "I'm having trouble focusing."

"We can try upping you a bit," she said, "but medication alone might not be good enough."

While we are often led to believe that mental illness medications work by correcting underlying biological abnormalities, my psychiatrist told me that, unlike the treatments for most other kinds of diseases, they induce altered states. They do not cure mental disorders. They treat symptoms by covering them up with something else. Medication, she said, has its place in the treatment of mental illness, but we should think about it as a Band-Aid rather than a long-term crutch or cure, except in extreme cases.

"Okay," I said. I wondered what constituted an extreme case.

"You really should talk to someone," she insisted.

"Okay," I said again. Then I rushed out of her office, charged for the red exit sign, and stabbed the elevator button over and over again, until the doors opened.

———

The man in front of the church stared at the flimsy old bills in his hand. When he looked up at me, the yellow-and-brown marbles of his eyes were enormous. He opened his mouth, I thought to thank me. "I'm not usually attracted to black women," he said with a smirk, "but I'd marry you." I searched for something to say, but finding nothing, I walked north.

I walked because I had nowhere to go. It was Sunday afternoon. I didn't have graduate school classes to attend, nor did I have a shift at the restaurant. I couldn't bear the company of my friends. Their laughter was jarring. Their stories about first dates and breakups and bad bosses confused me now. The day was empty and I needed to keep moving. I needed to keep moving away from my dark desert of a room. Its window looked out on an abandoned courtyard littered with rotting cardboard boxes and broken beer bottles the frat boys who lived below me tossed out the window in nightly fits of intoxication and youth. My room was a desert because it was barren. True, it was filled with books, photographs, clothes, lotions, hair creams, perfumes, a bed with a firm mattress, blankets knitted by my grandmother, bad paintings, candles, old letters, and new shoes. But those things had lost their meaning. It was as though they belonged to someone else whose life I had been dropped into, whose life I wouldn't have minded torching until it was nothing but ashes.

———————

I had taken to sleeping on the floor—to the extent I could sleep, which was not much anymore. Lying in my bed only beckoned me into the dankest cellars of my memory or, even worse, into the delusions that were becoming more and more difficult to disintegrate, to reduce with the forces of reason and deep breathing into innocuous fragments. My delusions were not so much apparitions, but rather feelings of impending disaster paired with the certainty that I would be the one to cause it. My logic was built on long chains of images, like watching a slide show. Oversleeping an hour would lead to not finishing a paper in time, would lead to needing to call out of work, would lead to getting fired, would lead to not being able to pay for graduate school, would lead to dropping out, would lead to chronic unemployment, would lead to eviction, etc. Also, something was burning in my body. I bought a thermometer at the drugstore and took my temperature obsessively. The thermometer refused to find fever. Twice I broke out in a flaming full-body rash for which the allergist and then dermatologist I went to found no cause. All I could do, then, was lie in bed in front of a floor fan, rubbing little zip-lock bags of ice and smearing steroid cream over myself. I had also developed a persistent tremble between my shoulder blades, and my palms were always wet.

To understand the burning in my body and to distract myself from it, I read a lot about mental illness. In the diaries he kept from January to March of 1919, as he was going mad, Vaslav Nijinsky, one of the greatest male ballet dancers of the twentieth century, wrote, "The earth is the head of God. God is fire in the head. I am alive as long as I have a fire in my head. My pulse is an earthquake. I am an earthquake." *I know what he means*, I thought. But Nijinsky took the fire in his mind, his earthquake pulse, to mean that he was connected to God and therefore gloriously living. I took it to mean I was being burned alive.

———

After walking for eight hours, I turned away from the setting sun and walked east, then south—back to Chinatown.

As I walked, I checked my phone. My half brother Kwame had texted, asking for money. He was in college in New York City, alone for the first time. He had spent the allowance Anabel sent him on eating out with his girlfriend and drinking with friends. Could I send him enough to buy a rotisserie chicken and a two-liter of Coke? Just until Anabel could wire him more funds? He was my baby brother and I was supposed to take care of him. The fact that I had nothing to give him filled me with shame. The fact that I didn't want to talk to him filled me with shame. I didn't want to talk to him because I knew he would talk about Anabel. I didn't want to think about her, so I couldn't think about him. I shoved my phone back in my purse, left his text unanswered. My father, I thought, would have been disappointed in me.

Nearing home, I did not want to stop walking. I contemplated continuing downtown—through the Financial District, to the South Street Seaport.

There was a blue chair abandoned on the sidewalk, six blocks from my apartment. It called to me. A drop of rain splattered on my forehead. Above me the clouds were swollen, were the color of gunmetal. I stopped to examine the chair.

The blue chair's fabric was faded and frayed in places, but its seat was cushiony and I discovered it was a rocking chair. The rocking is what made me love it. There was a rocking chair in every house I had lived in with my father before he died. There was one in the attic of our house in Rome. A wicker one on our front porch in Addis Ababa, shaded by an acacia tree. When it rained, I liked to rock in that chair and listen to the *plunk plunk plunk* on our tin roof. There was an ebony one in the corner of our living room in Kampala. I used to sit on the floor as my father rocked. His bare feet slapped the floor and he told me stories about Anansi the spider. Ghanaians are raised on Anansi, part of an ancient oral storytelling tradition. My father would season the stories with the spice of his own experiences growing up in Ashantiland. Like Anansi's sons, he had bathed in the river that went *pon pon ponsa*. Like Anansi, he used to wake up from his afternoon nap to the smell of pepper stew. The Anansi stories were so powerful they had crossed the ocean and were told in Patois and English to the children of slaves, and their children and grandchildren, and on for generations, on the islands of the Caribbean. The stories mutated in the new world, but Anansi kept his name and remained, even to this day, a trickster. The Anansi stories are morality tales about truth and lies and good and evil. They are about how things came to be the way they are: how stars were born, how wisdom was spread all around, how people came to have stories.

"Baba, if wisdom was spread around the world," I asked when I was five or six years old, "how come some countries are rich and others are poor?"

"Because," my father said, "the world is not always fair. Wisdom does not guarantee wealth."

This answer disturbed me. I loved the Anansi stories because they gave order to things. They had clean, crisp, satisfying endings. Good magic always won over bad magic. Sinners were punished. Kindness was rewarded. Anansi got his comeuppance for his trickery. Fairness prevailed. In one story, Anansi's sons squabbled over whom should get to keep the glowing orb he found in the forest. Nyame, the sky god, got tired of listening to them and carried it back into the sky with him so all people could share in the light of what became the moon.

My father rocked slowly as he read to me. He rocked as he watched the evening news. He rocked as I sat in his lap and pointed at shooting stars and lightning outside the window. He rocked me to sleep, my head pressed into his chest, his book resting on my shoulder. We rocked together. His favorite color was blue.

The blue chair was not very heavy, but it was wide and therefore difficult to carry. I lugged it home—my back bent backward, my arms strained. The rain quickened. But I would not, could not, put the chair down. It was needed in my room. I pushed it up two flights of stairs and paused, panting, on the doormat. When I got it through the door, my roommate made me stand in the hallway while he checked it for bedbugs. There were bedbugs all over New York City that year—in nice hotels and movie theaters, restaurant booths and mattress shops. They had become immune to the chemicals that used to kill them. Two of my friends had them. My neat-freak coworker who ironed her T-shirts almost moved back to Connecticut when she found what she thought was a bedbug, but turned out to be a carpet beetle, on her bedspread. Bedbugs made people insane, setting all of their belongings on fire, scratching their skin raw and bloody.

"I didn't think you were the type to drag stuff in from the street," my roommate said. He seemed uncharacteristically irritated. "Weird."

I had to agree with him. I was not the type. I just really needed that blue chair.

The first time I rocked in the blue chair, it felt familiar. It felt like the kind of peace you find when floating in shallow water. It felt almost like sitting on my father's lap. It comforted me like all the rocking chairs that had come before it. I rocked and rocked for hours. As I rocked, everything else seemed farther away, almost inaccessible: my desert room, my roommate playing video games on the other side of the door, the street below. Nowhere except the blue chair mattered. I wanted to rock forever.

Day Zero

With a group of strangers on the Lower East Side, I drank heavily. I had failed to write a single sentence that made any sense about grassroots efforts to address urban poverty, so I went to the bar.

My graduate school thesis would have to wait. I couldn't think about grassroots efforts to address urban poverty because my mind was full of my father and my mothers. I wanted to throw my dying laptop to the ground. I wanted to push a button that would make everything stop. I wanted to hibernate in the blue chair, but I knew hibernation might turn permanent. The closest thing I could think of to hibernation was getting drunk. I ordered a Manhattan. The alcohol made me brave enough, or reckless enough, to allow my outsides to match my insides. Three cocktails in, I began to argue with a man named Jeremy about basketball, the current state of hip-hop, the influence of reality television. I didn't care about any of those things. My voice came back in a roar. I pushed my forearms hard into the sturdy wood of the bar and sat up straight. Our argument was foreplay and we both knew it.

Naked in Jeremy's bed, I wept. He asked what was wrong, and I couldn't tell him because I couldn't say *I think I'm going mad*, not when I didn't even know his last name or where he was from. He caught my tears on his index finger and told me I was beautiful. We were drunk so we passed out quickly. I didn't dream that night. I rarely had dreams anymore, and when I did, they were full of pallid ghosts.

My dream ghosts never spoke. They just watched me as I did normal things—made French press coffee and cleaned my room. Always in the dreams, I knew the ghosts were there but pretended I didn't. I also knew who they were, but when I woke up, I forgot.

In the morning, the darkness pushed down on my chest until I pushed hard against it. I pushed up against it until I was out of bed and on my feet. My underwear and bra were lost in the sheets, so I pulled my pants and sweater on without them. I didn't have time. I shoved my sockless feet into boots, grabbed my coat.

"What's the rush? I'd like to see you again sometime," Jeremy called out. I ignored him because I couldn't breathe, and oxygen was more important than politeness. There was a door and then another door and another, and then I was blinking in the cold, sharp sun. People around me walked quickly, and their breath formed little puffs of white. They were going places, their eyes full of resolve as people's eyes often are in below-freezing weather. I envied that look in their eyes. It meant they knew where to go to get out of the cold. There was, for them, a destination. For me, everywhere was a pass-through. Perhaps it was narcissistic to think that. Perhaps no one really knows where she's going.

My seismometer vibrated so that I felt my body might explode from the force of it. I was trembling and afraid I was going to create a public scene—by crying, by fainting, or even by dying right there during morning rush hour in Chelsea. I felt my neck redden with a rash. So I ran to the subway. I don't know where I got the strength to run, not having eaten in over twenty-four hours.

The Q train was a speeding purgatory. A duo of busking drummers came on and pounded thunderous rhythms, yelped and chanted. The thunder got inside me. I bent over and placed my head between my knees until the robotic voice announced my stop—*This is Canal Street*. Ecstatic for a moment, I leapt up and out of the train car. Then the doors closed behind me and I realized that nothing had been solved. The place I called home would not offer much more than the Canal Street platform. On the platform, people waited for the train.

At my apartment that was my home but also not, I too would wait.
I would wait, I decided, in the blue chair. For what, I did not know.

At home, I changed into an oversized sweatshirt and a pair of boxer
shorts George had left behind and collapsed into the blue chair. I
pulled a blanket around myself. *Here it comes*, I whispered. And a
voice in my head that may or may not have been mine said, *Finally*.

I did not know it then, but this was day zero. For seven days, I
did not get out of the blue chair except to sleep on the floor and piss
and shit and eat bran flakes, cans of tuna, hunks of dry baguette,
and slightly moldy cheddar cheese I forced down with lukewarm tap
water. Outside, the world carried on. My roommate puttered between
his room and the kitchen. A couple of times, I passed him on my
way to the toilet and we nodded hello. The delivery trucks unloaded
vegetables and paper towels in bulk. My graduate school deadlines
passed. My friends met for dinner without me. Snow fell and froze
on the street below. Shovels and salt got rid of it. I could not get out
of that chair until I had some answers to the unsolved questions of
my life.

To answer my unsolved questions, as I had done my whole life, I
turned to literature. I turned to the women I had long imagined as a
council of mothers: Toni Morrison, Audre Lorde, June Jordan, Zora
Neale Hurston, Toni Cade Bambara. They had advised me, consoled
me, sustained me, saved me before. I needed them now more than
ever. And, I turned to memoirs of madness.

In his memoir *Darkness Visible*, William Styron argues that depression, despite the cold, precise terms in which we currently discuss
it, is more than anything a disease of disorder and loss of control. He
writes that "our perhaps understandable modern need to dull the saw-
tooth edges of so many of the afflictions we are heir to has led us to
banish the harsh old-fashioned words: madhouse, asylum, insanity,
melancholia, lunatic, madness. But never let it be doubted that depression, in its extreme form, is madness."

Styron's symptoms were similar to mine—the loss of appetite and sleep, muddled associations, slowed responses, "fidgety restlessness," obsessions, sudden gut punches of fear, periods of physical paralysis and pain.

I found some relief in seeing my present state mirrored in the experiences of another. But this relief was, I knew, only a balm. To heal, I would need to look inward as well as outward. I would need to examine my memories. I would need to interrogate the stories I told myself—about myself, about my family, about the world. My unsolved questions were about my mothers and my father. They were about loss, longing, and fear; about my abandonment. They were about my upended, dislocated body and mind. They were about the geography and geology of my experience—about who I was and how I'd ended up in the blue chair. They were about finding my way out of it. But they were also about the borders and boundaries and fault lines on which we all live. They were about fractured surfaces and tectonic forces; about energies unleashed. This, I knew, was a reckoning. God of fire help me, I begged, or if you cannot help me, then show me how to set my world ablaze.

When I was seven, my mother showed up with an earthquake and red balloons. I remember her shaking hands and I remember the shaking earth. In me, private and seismic tremors cannot be separated.

TOPOGRAPHY

Topography:

1. the configuration of a surface, including its relief and the position of its natural and man-made features
2. the physical or natural features of an object or entity and their structural relationships

Note:

During an earthquake, shaking might increase or amplify due to topography. For example: The softer the soil, the stronger the shaking.

Navel

Once, when I was a little girl in a bubble bath, I asked my father why I had a belly button. He was sitting on the toilet lid reading while I splashed. He peered at me over the top of his book.

"So you know where your center is," he said.

"Why do I need to know where my center is?" I asked.

"So you don't lose your balance," he said. "Your center is where all the different parts of who you are come together. It used to connect you to your mother and to the first men and women in Africa—the first human beings." I cannot be certain this is true, but when I remember him saying this, I hear his voice catch on the word *mother*.

At the time, all I could say was *Oh*. But those words whisper in my ear often as I am making sandwiches or walking to the post office. Those words whispered in my ear when I read Toni Morrison's novel *Song of Solomon* for the first time when I was in college. In it, Pilate Dead was born without a navel. Her mother died before she was born. She found her own way out of the womb. Her missing navel symbolizes her independence, her self-possession.

In my journal, as I read *Song of Solomon*, I wrote about how the navel marks both connection and disconnection. It is corporeal evidence of maternal linkage, but it is also the place on our bodies from which we are separated from our mothers. I wrote that perhaps I held on to the memory of my father telling me about my navel because my father so rarely spoke of my mother without pressure from me. Maybe it was because I felt so disconnected from my mother that I did not dare lose a story about how I was once connected to her. And as for what my father said about Africa, as much as I wanted to belong to Africa or to any place for that matter, I knew that I didn't. Not really. Not completely. In countless ways and for countless reasons, I loved growing up in many countries, among many cultures. It made it impossible for me to believe in the concept of supremacy. It deepened my ability to hold multiple truths at once, to practice and nurture empathy. But it has also meant that I have no resting place. I have perpetually been a *them* rather than an *us*. I have struggled with how to place myself in my family histories.

The one family album I own is divided in three. The photographs in the first section are of my father's extended family in Ghana. There are photographs of my father and my aunts as children, of my grandparents as newlyweds. I don't recognize some of the people depicted. Perhaps we never met. Or, by the time we met, their freshly picked afros had grayed or been shorn, their striped bell-bottoms replaced with sensible khakis. But still, when I look at those photographs, I recognize the setting: the town where my father grew up, where I spent many school holidays.

In the second section, I am a toddler on my father's hip reaching for the wooden tobacco pipe clenched in his mouth. My sister Yasmeen and I, arms slung over each other's shoulders, flash half-toothless smiles at the camera against a backdrop of the Serengeti: flat-top trees, long yellow grass, clouds low in the sky and pregnant with tropical rain. There I am being carried on my father's shoulders toward the Eiffel Tower. Yasmeen is jumping across the finish line in a burlap sack at the British school in Rome while Anabel cheers from the sidelines. There's an eight-year-old me staring lovingly at baby Kwame cradled in my arms while Yasmeen pinches his chubby cheek.

This second section of the album is my favorite because Yasmeen and I look so much alike in the photos. We face each other, laugh at each other, hold hands, pull each other's ears, smack each other, sleep on each other's laps in the backseats of cars. We are bent mirror images. We shared clothes. We shared a story. In the photos, we are near-symmetrical. We all like to see ourselves, reflected.

My mother's cursive is smudged on the back of each image in the third section of the album. It informs me that Uncle Aram is at the Armenian picnic in Watertown; Grandma and Grandpa are playing golf in Florida; my two half sisters are dressed as a robot and a pirate for Halloween. These photographs were enclosed in letters written on pale blue or pink stationery that smelled vaguely of pears. Yasmeen received the same photographs in letters addressed to her. Sometimes we exchanged letters after reading our own. They were largely identical. They were mailed to us when we were in elementary school and our mother was mostly an abstraction. She was words on paper, a hummed lullaby on a long-distance phone call, a woman standing on her head and laughing in a home movie from a time before we were born.

On the days the letters arrived, I could feel my father watching us as we read them. The letters were intimate and cheerful. They told of trips to Walden Pond in the summer and sledding in Boston Common in the winter. They left me with an uncomfortable wistfulness. I would force my face into a silent expression and look up to meet my father's eyes. He would smile, perhaps relieved by my unaffectedness. Sometimes Yasmeen cried. I thought two crying daughters would be too much for him, so I trained myself to wait until I was alone, in my closet or in the bath. My father would wipe Yasmeen's face, hug us both, ask us if we wanted chocolate milk.

"Good girl," he'd whisper in my ear. I was *good* because I was restrained. My father, I believe, carried a lot of hurt from his relationship with my mother. He did not like to see the related pain radiating from his daughters' eyes.

Those letters taught me about longing. Reading them in front of my father taught me to hide it, often even from myself. I know now what a dangerous kind of denial that is. It leaves you ravenous. It makes your seismometer vibrate when the phone call you are shocked to discover you have been waiting for your whole life offers you precisely what you are terrified to want: *Hello, Nadia. This is your mama.*

My father's words about my navel provided a kind of simple hope. He seemed to promise that the solution to my perceived lack of center, to my lack of a clear home, to my disconnection from my mother was right there on my body. *Song of Solomon* spoke to the fear that was the flip side of that hope.

In *Song of Solomon,* Pilate Dead is rejected by potential lovers and mother figures because of her missing navel. She becomes a drifter. So she will remember where she has been, so no more of the past can be lost to her, she collects rocks. On her journeys, she carries a geography book, a sack of bones, an earring containing a piece of paper on which her illiterate father wrote her name, and a mysterious song. These things, to Pilate, are not unlike my photo album. They tie her to the past, to the father she loved and lost, to the mother she never knew. She spent most of her life not quite knowing what they meant. "I was cut off from people early," she says. It is only when her nephew reveals the full lyrics of her song, and with it her mother's true name, that she learns about her family's ancestral home of Shalimar, Virginia. It is only then that she learns the bones she carries are her father's, that she must bury them in Shalimar. This knowledge gives her roots. Though she dies soon after learning about her family's history, she dies free.

The idea of roots setting a person free is counterintuitive, but deracination from the past, from land, from family, from mothers, makes for an unstable present. We must have, or we will always search for, a place to bury our bones.

Photograph

There is only one photograph of my family in its original configuration—my father, my mother, Yasmeen, and me. In it, Yasmeen is being given her Ashanti name, Ama, in the traditional way: a finger dipped in sweet wine placed on her tongue, a finger dipped in whiskey placed on her lip, libation poured to the earth for the ancestors to drink so they will watch over her. This ceremony is meant to teach the newborn that life is both sweet and bitter, and that we are all part of something bigger than ourselves. In the photograph, my father's best friend Yaw is holding baby Yasmeen. He is her godfather. It is his whiskey-dipped finger in Yasmeen's mouth. My parents stand on either side of him. My father is wearing a kente cloth wrapped around his waist and draped over one bare shoulder. My mother is wearing a white-and-red embroidered Armenian dress. I am a one-year-old in a frilly dress and bare feet. I am clinging to my father's leg with one hand, reaching for my mother with the other. Probably, I was just learning to walk and was trying to maintain my balance. But I can't help but think of that clinging, that reaching, as an act of futile hope. Tiny hands refusing to let go. I don't often look closely at that photograph, yet I keep it on my dresser next to my anxiety medication and vitamin D.

In the photograph of Yasmeen's Ashanti naming ceremony, it is 1982. My parents are a representation of what is possible when love wins and freedom rings and the pendulum swings toward justice. The movements for equality, liberty, fairness, and self-rule of the sixties and seventies have ushered in a new sense of optimism. In this world, with a little enchantment and a lot of grit, a young black man from Kumasi, Ghana, can move to Cambridge, Massachusetts, and marry a young woman of Armenian descent whose grandparents escaped a genocide and arrived in America with little more than the clothes on their backs.

In this world, my mother can weave back together her grandparents' dreams that unraveled in Turkey. She won't work in factories like they did. She will write and paint. She will sing the lyrics of her grandparents' songs to music of her own invention. She will teach her daughters to sing too. She will show them that anything is possible. Perhaps dreams can be passed from mother to child through blood, or through whispering to womb, or through the sheer power of faith that can cross oceans and mountains and estrangements, because my mother's dreams have always been my dreams: to create beauty from ink and thin air.

In this world, my father can carry his father's dashed hopes of an academic life across continents. In his late forties, my grandfather got the university degree colonization had denied him. He studied liter-ature. My father got a PhD in his twenties. He dreamed he would return home with his knowledge and use it to help build the Africa the generation before him had fought so long and hard for. As a child, I watched him do this. As an adult, I believe it might have killed him—the heartbreak from all of the suffering he could not end. Yet his dream, like my mother's, was in me too. I was, in the year of the blue chair, working on a master's degree in urban planning and pol-icy. I spent my days analyzing data and writing essays about poverty. I worked for a nonprofit that served families whose children were at risk of being put into foster care. I wanted those children to have sturdy roots because I knew well the struggles of rootlessness. Mine was born of a father's dreaming, but also of abandonment. Once, a perfect little girl, maybe ten years old, with pom-pom pigtails, told me she wished she could go back to heaven and return as someone else. Her father was in jail. Her mother worked three jobs. I didn't ask who she wanted to be. I was too scared of the answer. So I just gave her a hug and my phone number. She never called.

On the internet, I looked up symptoms of brain cancer—the disease that killed my father (though he may also have had AIDS). I worried I would die young like him. He was just thirty-nine when he died. Sometimes, in my dreams, I saw him, sitting at his desk surrounded by reports of atrocities and tragedies and dying children, his forehead tense, a deep line between his eyes. Every morning, as I approached thirty, I checked my forehead to see how my own line had deepened.

At the time the photograph was taken, my parents are broke and happy. They are living in a small house in Dar es Salaam, Tanzania's Oyster Bay neighborhood. They moved there from Massachusetts after my father's dissertation about the future of food aid in Sub-Saharan Africa landed him a job with a UN agency. They are in love. Their future is rising on the horizon in blazing red and yellow. They look fearlessly toward it, confident in its beauty. Their two little black girls will be raised in the assured brightness of it. The earth beneath their daughters' feet will be lush and verdant and stable.

The photograph is blurry, as are my memories of the four of us together. My parents will divorce a year after it is taken. For years after that, they will only be in the same room for awkward handoffs in airports and train stations. They will avoid eye contact while my father delivers stiff updates about my allergies and Yasmeen's thumb-sucking. Then, gradually, my mother will fade from view. The visits and letters will stop. Once in a while, she will call out of the blue, her voice sounding far away and wet with sadness or regret or both. I resented that voice. I resented its emotions. I was the one being abandoned. That we were both being abandoned at the same time never occurred to me. My mother's second husband was a drinker and gambler. Unbeknownst to my mother, he had another family in New York. He had a daughter who was the same age as the elder of my two half sisters. He would ultimately leave my mother, broke and with three children—my two half sisters and my baby half brother—to raise on

her own. I could only think of my own pain then, but I know now
the agony of heartbreak. I know what it feels like to have your world
upended.

The space between the family in the photograph on my dresser
and what became of it is gaping and largely unknowable. My parents
rarely spoke of each other. They rarely acknowledged that the family
in the photograph ever existed. My father died before I was old enough
or brave enough to ask him all my questions about the end of our family. Once or twice, we stumbled onto the topic, but those conversations
were terse and awkward. I worried that he would take my curiosity
for ingratitude, that he would think the life he had given me was not
enough. My mother, when we were still speaking, would reveal only
scant details. I did not push her. Our relationship was too fragile. And,
always, below us, vibrations moved through solid rock.

When I was twelve, I snooped around in my father's things and
found a journal of poems about my mother. He described her face
in meticulous detail—the little mole above her lip, her giant hazel
eyes lined with kajal. It is from this journal that I know how my parents believed their love and the birth of their daughters to be a part
of something important—a movement fueled by borderless love. The
poems, or at least my interpretation of the poems, mourned not just a
lost love but also a certain measure of lost optimism about the current
condition. People on a street in Boston shouted *nigger* at my father and
told him to go back to Africa. People in Ghana, including members
of his family, bemoaned his decision to marry a white woman. They
whispered that he had turned his back on his culture in order to find
success in the West. *Any river loses its identity when entering the sea*,
they said.

Colonial Mentality

Kumasi, Ghana, Age 7

During a trip to Ghana when I was seven and living in Italy, my father took my sister and me to the stool house of the Oyoko clan— my grandfather's clan—on the outskirts of the Ashanti capital, Kumasi. The trip coincided with the Harmattan—the dry season during which a dusty wind blows from the Sahara Desert over West Africa.

We were in Ghana so that my father's family could get to know Anabel. The introduction was not going well. Anabel's mother had not been happy, at first, about her daughter marrying my father. She believed West Africans to be untrustworthy and aggressive. People from different parts of Africa believe lots of fatuous stereotypes about one another. Eventually, my father won Anabel's mother over, but, somehow, her comments had reached my grandmother. And now Anabel left banana peels and tea bags on side tables. She took long naps and did not come out of her room when elders came to pay their respects. She wore very short skirts and complained when there was not enough hot water for her bath.

"Does she think we are her maids?" my grandmother asked.

My grandmother and my father fought.

"She's my wife," my father said. "Please, Ma, please, don't do this to me."

My sister Yasmeen and I lay side by side on the bed in my father's childhood room, with the door cracked open. We did not have to speak our fears out loud. Family, for us, had always been a tenuous thing. If my father and Anabel fell apart, what would happen to us? Would we be sent away? For two and a half years—between our mother leaving and our father meeting Anabel—we had been sent to England to live with our father's eldest sister, our aunt Harriet. We loved Auntie Harriet, but we didn't want to be separated from our father again. And if our grandmother never grew to love Anabel, would we lose her like we had lost our mother? Would we only know her in letters and over the phone? On that trip to Ghana, Yasmeen and I slept with our grandmother in her bed. I could not remember ever sleeping in the bed with an adult before that. I loved how I could snuggle into her soft body and feel the warmth of her skin, the rising and falling of her breath.

As our grandmother and father fought in the living room, I moved closer to Yasmeen so that our arms touched. We listened to the raised voices. Anabel cried, my grandmother cried. Their cries were high-pitched and self-righteous.

"My only son," my grandmother said. "Don't you see what she is doing to us?"

It was the day after that fight that my father took Yasmeen and me to the stool house. As we drove there, I pressed my nose against the window, but the world outside was a haze of copper-colored dust. All week, it had been this way. We had been cooped up inside, hiding from the punishing air that made my nose bleed and my eyes feel like paper. My lips were so dry they were lined with scabs. During the Harmattan, the dry air can snap tree trunks. But my sister and I were not accustomed to being indoors for long periods. We felt like wild animals, caged. We bounced off our grandmother's furniture, broke things. My father decided that Harmattan or no Harmattan, we were going to see the black stools that were the thrones of our clan's leaders across history. At the stool house, they are preserved as a bond between the living, the dead, and those yet to be born.

The wooden stools are black because they are varnished with a mixture of soot and egg yolk. Each stool is believed to hold the spirit, or *sunsum*, of the leader to whom it belonged and to possess powers of protection for that leader's descendants. Family members pour

libation to the stools, offer them prayers. At the stool house, I drank a
warm, syrupy, orange Fanta, purchased from a nearby grocery shack.
The shopkeeper also tried to sell us a bar of English chocolate, PG
Tips tea bags, and tinned corned beef. My father said we were fine and
just wanted the soda. "But, these are imported goods," the shopkeeper
protested, no doubt rightfully taking us for people accustomed to such
things.

My father rarely allowed me to drink soda, so I wasn't thrilled
by the idea of having to share it with the spirits of my ancestors. I
was also unimpressed with the stools themselves. We had several that
looked just like them in our house in Rome. I sat on one in our hallway almost every morning when I buckled my shoes for school. This
hardly seemed worth the long, bumpy ride in the hot car driven by my
grandmother's favorite taxi driver, who chain-smoked cigarettes the
whole way. The smell of his Marlboros intensified his already strong,
sharp body odor. The odor was so strong it seemed to me to be a solid
thing—sitting on a cloud of exhaled smoke and dust.

"He must eat a lot of *kenkey*," my father said when I asked
him why the taxi driver smelled like that. This worried me because
kenkey—fermented maize—with *kontomire* and fish was one of my
favorite meals.

The caretaker who showed us into the stool house seemed very
excited to have visitors. He rocked back and forth on his heels and
pointed at this and that stool, excitedly naming the *Asantehenes* (kings)
to whom they belonged—from the very first Asantehene, Osei Tutu,
who ruled from 1701 to 1717, to Opoku Ware II, who ruled at the
time. These men—these kings—were my clansmen, yet they seemed
like characters from books. Indeed, I had read about Osei Tutu in a
book I found in my father's study. Osei Tutu commanded armies of
warriors and was carried about on a plank of gold and ebony, hoisted
on the shoulders of other men. He wore cloth woven with pure gold
thread. His arms were laden with heavy-looking solid gold bracelets.
Slaves were sacrificed and their blood used to cool the tempers of spirits who threatened his rule. I had a hard time imagining that such a

life had anything to do with mine. In Rome, my father drove an old
Fiat. I wore Benetton sweaters and corduroy skirts. I had seen *Roots*
and knew slavery was an atrocity.

The stools had arched seats. Their bases were carved with intricate
designs. Some of them were finished with gold; others had offerings of
mutton fat or yams placed before them. In the center of the room was
a large brass-and-copper bell. This bell, the caretaker told us, used to
be tied to the Golden Stool, which is kept in a secret place. People can
give offerings to the bell in its stead.

I was bored, so I pulled at my father's crisp, short-sleeved shirt to
get his attention. My sister Yasmeen plopped herself down on the floor
cross-legged and played Donkey Kong. I regretted my failure to claim
the Game Boy for myself in the car. I had been too busy considering
the taxi-driver's BO.

"How," I asked, "can our ancestors' spirits be in those stools when
the spirits of all Ashanti people are supposed to be in the Golden
Stool?"

We were still waiting to hear if we would be granted permission
from the Asantehene's office (which in my mind looked like Eddie
Murphy's palace in *Coming to America*) to see the Golden Stool, a
stool of solid gold that was said to have descended from the sky into
the lap of Osei Tutu. The Ashanti fought a war against the British
to protect that stool and save their collective souls. A British colonial
administrator had demanded to sit on it and had sent his men to find
it and bring it to him.

The Golden Stool sounded far more interesting than the
ordinary-looking stools in the stool house. My father laughed and said
maybe spirits could be in more than one place at a time. The caretaker
did not laugh. He narrowed his eyes and flared his nostrils at me, I
think irritated at being interrupted by a little girl. Once I had been appropriately silenced, he resumed his history lesson. Now he switched
from English to Twi, as though to make it clear just how unimportant
he thought me. He called my father *Nana*, a title that is added to the
names of people with royal lineage.

"Am I a princess?" I once asked my father.

"No," he said. "You are a descendant of royalty, but my father gave up his title."

"Oh," I said, disappointed. I was hoping that someday there would be a ceremony involving a jeweled crown being placed upon my head. My idea of such ceremonies was based on watching specials about the British royal family on television. I particularly liked the diamond tiara worn by Princes Diana on her wedding day.

I imagined Princess Diana's tiara on my head when I informed a group of older Italian girls who picked on me that I was royalty. They called me *sporca negra* and put twigs and pencils in my tightly coiled hair, laughed when they didn't fall out. They claimed that all Africans used to be slaves, so I should be theirs. One girl asked why I didn't have a bone through my nose and if I slept in a tree. Another chased me around with her belt and threatened to whip me for being bad. I demanded that my father call the principal, the girls' parents, my teacher, but he refused. Instead, he said, he would teach me about Ghana and about my family so their words would mean nothing to me, so I could stand up for myself.

"My grandfather, Nana Oheneba Peter Owusu Koko is the son of Nana Osei Assibey I, a chief and elder of the royal Oyoko clan," I told them.

As is the tradition, to become a chief, my great-grandfather had been nominated by the queen mother of the Ashanti within forty days of the death of his predecessor. She selected him from a pool of eligible men in the royal family. A council of elders approved his nomination. Then, for forty days, he was confined to a secret place to study the laws of the Ashanti Empire.

"He was both umbrella and tree," my father explained. "He offered his subjects shade and protection. He settled disputes, served on the Asantehene's council, performed religious ceremonies, enforced laws, and ensured peace and harmony between the community, the earth, and the ancestors."

The girls who picked on me were neither persuaded nor deterred by my recitation of this history. But my father was right on one count: their words no longer pierced my skin. When they approached me, I stuck my nose in the air imperiously and walked in the opposite direction. To their insults, I did not respond. I acted as though they did not exist.

My father continued to teach me about Ghanaian history after discovering that the entire continent of Africa was excluded from my world history textbook, except for Egypt. And the illustrations of ancient Egyptians in the book made them look decidedly European.

"Nonsense," my father said.

In the fifteenth century, the Akan people (the ethnic group to which the Ashanti, the Fante, the Guang, and the Anyi, among other tribes, belong) migrated north into forests they hoped to tame into farmland. This was no easy feat, and they came to deeply understand nature's power, to view the bush as a formidable adversary. To this day, Ashanti culture is centered around a spirit of collectivism. Without it, they know, they would not have survived, would not survive.

Rapidly, relationships between peoples linked loosely by language and clan deepened and formalized. In 1701, Ashantiland became a kingdom ruled by Osei Tutu. His high priest and chief advisor, Okomfo Anokye, in a nod to the ancient Akan tradition of stools representing clan leadership, either called for the Golden Stool to fall from the sky or, more likely, contracted an artisan to create it, as a symbol of the united Ashanti people and of the legitimacy of Tutu's rule. Future Asantehenes were to be selected from his descendants.

At the stool house, my boredom crept into the danger zone. Energy buzzed inside me and I danced from foot to foot, spun around in circles. My sister looked happy sitting on the floor, engrossed in her game of Donkey Kong, and I couldn't stand it anymore. I snatched the game out of her hand and she squealed. My father was listening intently to the caretaker's history lesson, but he turned and gave us the look we called *the bug-eyed stare*. We froze until he turned back around. Then Yasmeen shoved me, I shoved her back, she pinned me to the floor on my back, I flipped over and sat on her. We didn't dare confront our father about the fights between him and his mother, him and Anabel. The uncertainty gurgled and boiled in us. It erupted to the surface in the form of misplaced anger. Each of us shouted appeals to our father to punish the other. Our father picked us up—one wriggling daughter under each arm—and carried us outside. The caretaker made a clicking sound in the back of his throat to register his disgust.

"What is wrong with you two?" our father asked, setting our feet on the ground. A boy stared at us from where he squatted under a makeshift awning of banana tree branches. He had mangoes and avocados for sale, but there were no customers. People were too focused on getting where they were going, getting out of the dust. The taxi driver watched us too. He smirked. A cigarette dangled between his white-flecked lips. His face was ashy. My father made us coat our own faces with Vaseline and smother our entire bodies in shea butter every day during the Harmattan. "Just because it's the dry season doesn't mean you can walk around looking like you've never been in a bath," he'd said.

"It's so boring," I whined. "And Yasmeen won't share the video game."

"She didn't ask. She just snatched," Yasmeen protested.

"How can you say it's boring? You think your own history is boring?" my father asked.

"But the man is speaking in Twi," I said. "We don't even know what he's saying." I wanted to add that I was less worried about my family's history than I was about our future. I wanted my father to tell me we would not be separated again, no matter how harsh the winds. I couldn't bring myself to say any of that though. I couldn't find the words.

"You could have asked me," my father said. "Instead, you're both being bush."

When I misbehaved, my father, rather than telling me to stop being a brat or to stop acting up—things I heard my friends' parents say—told me to *stop being bush*, in other words uncivilized, wild, uncouth. Even then, the term made me uncomfortable. It reminded me of the taunts of the girls who picked on me. They claimed Africans were primitive people, that we were inferior. Was that idea not also implicit in my father's words? How was I to understand this from the man who always seemed so proud to be Ashanti, to be Ghanaian, to be African, to be black?

In Ghana, I learned that calling someone bush was a common insult. My grandfather said it of a neighbor who showed up at our house drunk and wanting to borrow money. A radio commentator leveled it against a politician who fell asleep during parliamentary proceedings and snored. Propriety was important to Ghanaians. A lot of stock was put in having good manners, in sticking to convention, in ceremony. And many of those manners, those conventions, those ceremonies had a decidedly British flavor. This seemed to be in direct conflict with the pride Ghanaians had in their own culture and precolonial history. I recall a song—my father's favorite—by the great Nigerian musician and activist Fela Kuti called "Colonial Mentality." Colonial mentality, as defined by Kuti, is the idea that people who have been colonized, marginalized, and enslaved feel themselves inferior to their colonizers based on the very fact of their colonization. *He be say you be colonial man*, Kuti sings in his beautifully rough voice, his Nigerian pidgin clear and defiant. *You don be slave man before / Them don release you now / But you never release yourself.*

My father stood firmly in his Ghanaian identity. He often wore Ghanaian-print shirts to work. When a colleague in Rome invited him to the American Club to watch the U.S. presidential election, my father declined.

"Will you be watching the Ghanaian election?" my father asked his colleague. "It is also taking place this year."

Above the mirror in my bedroom, my father hung a Ghanaian flag. He taught me about its meaning. The red, he said, is for the blood of the people who died in the struggle for independence. The gold is for the country's mineral wealth, the green for the forests. And the black star at the flag's center symbolizes black liberation.

"The black star shall rise," he said.

On our bookshelf Chinua Achebe, Wole Soyinka, Nurrudin Farah, Mariama Bâ, and Kofi Awoonor held the place of honor in the center of the top shelf. In our music collection Fela Kuti was joined by Miriam Makeba, Salif Keita, Youssou N'Dour, and E. T. Mensah and the Tempos Band. Yet I saw in my father's use of the word *bush* evidence that the colonial mentality existed even in him. This scared me, though I couldn't quite articulate why. Now I know it scared me because it spoke to a fault line in the African body—my body, my father's.

By the beginning of the nineteenth century, the Ashanti had defeated the powerful Denkyira and Fante states. They governed a territory as large as modern-day Ghana, from the Comoé River in the west to the Togo Mountains in the east.

At first, gold financed the Ashanti ascendancy. Osei Tutu claimed the kingdom's gold mines as royal property. The empire's currency was gold dust. For a time, I believed it was only gold that had made my ancestors rich and powerful. They traded that gold, I was told, for the weapons with which they won wars. I still have a gold bracelet my father bought for me during an outing to see the mines. It is carved with the *asase ye duru* symbol that signifies the Ashanti aphorism *The earth has weight*. My father chose that symbol for me because Asase Yaa was my favorite goddess—the earth goddess. She is a creator—the earth's mother—and she keeps everything alive. In Ashantiland, people don't farm on Thursdays because it is Asase Yaa day and she must have her rest. She is also the goddess who comes to carry the souls of people to the afterlife.

What my father left out until I asked the question was the story of how the Ashanti Empire was also financed by slavery. The enslavement of prisoners of war was very much a part of the Ashanti way of life. Today, many Ashanti people argue that until European influence, enslaved people in the Ashanti kingdom were not sentenced to bondage forever. They were allowed to marry. Their children were not born enslaved. They could lodge complaints of abuse and deprivation and request new masters. Social mobility was possible. Slaves could, after their period of enslavement, buy property. Some even rose to positions of authority. I have been told enslaved people often became part of their enslavers' families, even sometimes marrying into them. And it was believed that slaves followed their masters into the afterlife.

"But it is still wrong to make people slaves," I once insisted to my grandfather when he argued that slavery in Ghana was not what it was in Europe and America.

My grandfather and the uncles who had been listening to our conversation made the indulgent but dismissive face Ghanaians reserve for foreigners who claim to be experts on African affairs. It was a scrunching of nose, a tilting of head to the right.

"History is a story," my grandfather said, finally. "What is told depends on who writes it. They put this in, leave that out; decide where the emphasis goes." I was not satisfied by that answer. Perhaps noting my dissatisfaction, my grandfather added: "But, we are not acquitted. Our people sold human beings to the Europeans, to the Americans, to be treated like animals."

In the early 1800s, the Ashanti slave trade became an international market as the tribe's leaders hustled to meet growing demand from the British, French, and Dutch for captives. For human beings the Ashanti were paid in Western goods, including firearms.

We all know about the horrors that awaited the people whose lives were one side of that barter. And some of the Ashanti leaders who were doing the bartering were likely aware of them as well. Many people from the Ashanti upper class—the class to which my ancestors belonged—visited Europe in that era—for trade, for school. African elites traveled as passengers on slave ships that stopped first in the Americas. Given the Ashanti tradition of storytelling, I find it hard to believe that what was seen and heard on those voyages did not make it back to Ashantiland, did not spread. I think about this often, this culpability. In Ghana, slaving forts still stand. When I visited one—Elmina Castle—as an adult, African-American tourists wept in what were doors of no return for their ancestors. They wept, looking out onto the vastness of the ocean. Now there is a sign hung over the door of Cape Coast Castle—one of the doors of no return—that says, *the door of return*. The Ghanaian government has enacted programs—lifetime visas, relaxed citizenship applications—to invite descendants of enslaved Africans to go to Ghana, to think of it as their homeland. Yet these campaigns, at least to my ears, have focused largely on the present: *Come home, become part of the family again*. The story Ghanaians often tell of the past focuses on the wrongs of Europeans. It was the Europeans, the story goes, who tore the family apart. This is true but it is not the whole story. What would happen, I wonder, what kind of reunion would be possible, if there was a real reckoning with the role of Africans in the slave trade? If there was a conversation about the need to make amends, to right wrongs, to heal wounds? As I was leaving Elmina Castle among other tourists, a group of children ran up to us. I wondered what they knew about the castle, about slavery. They were delighted by the sight of us. All of us—African-American, white, me—the children called *obruni*. White foreigner.

As for the firearms, the Ashanti arsenal was eventually put to shame by that of the supplier. Between 1806 and 1900, the British and the Ashanti were at war. Both sides sought to control forts, and therefore trade, along the Gold Coast—the British name for the region. My father took great pride in the fact that it took almost a century for the colonial power to defeat the well-organized Ashanti kingdom. "The British had rockets and cannons," he said, "but they still couldn't stop the Ashanti warriors." But stop them they did in the end. The last battle—the one provoked by the idea of a British rear end on the Golden Stool—was a last-ditch effort to protect, if not Ashanti lands, then at least her dignity and the souls of her people. By then, the British had arrested Asantehene Prempeh I. He was forced to sign a treaty that made the Ashanti kingdom a British protectorate. He and other Ashanti leaders were exiled to the Seychelles.

The demand by the British colonial administrator to sit on the Golden Stool was viewed by the Ashanti as the worst kind of disrespect. I have always liked the story of what came next because its protagonist is a woman. Despite the fact that the Ashanti were, and still are in many ways, a matrilineal society—women inherit status and property directly from their mothers, husbands move into their wives' family compounds after marriage—the long history of war and conquest gives the story of the Ashanti a macho quality. Thank goddess, then, for Yaa Asantewaa, Queen Mother of the state of Edweso, who took command of the fight to protect the Golden Stool with these words: "If you, the chiefs of Ashanti, are going to behave like cowards and not fight, you should exchange your loincloths for my undergarments."

In the War of the Golden Stool, Yaa Asantewaa was not just an instigator, but also a negotiator and soldier. Some Ashanti men, perhaps smarting on behalf of their elders for the taunt about undergarments, have tried to rewrite history, claiming that Yaa Asantewaa was a man disguised as a woman. These are, no doubt, the same sort of men who told me, when I was a little girl visiting my grandparents, to stop playing like a boy when I scampered up trees faster than their sons and scored goals in soccer matches.

"Shut your mouth," my father told them. Then, in English: "My daughter could be the next Yaa Asantewaa!"

While Yaa Asantewaa was captured by the British during the War of the Golden Stool and died in exile in the Seychelles in 1921, the Ashanti were successful in protecting the Golden Stool. The British promised never to touch it. Three years after Asantewaa's death, Asantehene Prempeh I and the other Ashanti leaders in exile could return to the Gold Coast and were granted, as long as they protected British interests, day-to-day control over the Ashanti region. The British supervised from Accra—the capital of the Gold Coast, and now the capital of Ghana.

My great-grandfather was the chief who became responsible for the keys of the Manhyia Palace—the new official residence of the Asantehene, and the Ashanti government headquarters. He was a trusted advisor to the Asantehene. I am told he used to take his own plate and cutlery when he went to dinner at other people's houses. He didn't like to eat with his hands from shared dishes, as is the custom. "He ate fufu with a spoon," my father told me, laughing at the thought. There is a photograph of him, probably aged around forty-five. In it, he sits in a wooden chair with a high back. He wears a three-piece Western-style suit with a bow tie and white gloves. He looks stiff and serious. In the background are mahogany trees and a cloudless sky. My great-grandfather must have been very hot in that jacket and gloves in the tropical afternoon. He must have felt cooped up, as I was in my grand-parents' house during the Harmattan.

Indirect rule enabled the British to both cut the costs of governing and to render their power less visible. Ashanti and other tribal leaders' loyalties were split between the interests of their people, the interests of the colonial government, and their own self-interests. Titles and money were conferred based on loyalty to the British crown. Some leaders turned to corruption to gain more power.

While the precolonial Ashanti government was a monarchy, the Asantehene, like the chiefs who served him, was elected from a pool of eligible men from the Oyoko clan. A council of elders and chiefs provided checks and balances. During colonization, this system fell apart. Some of the elites also adopted what my father called *British airs*. They turned their noses up at the poor and uneducated and others they considered beneath them. Perhaps my great-grandfather was not alone in eating fufu with a spoon. Some men abandoned their *ntoma*—traditional robes—in favor of exclusively wearing Western clothing. Some spoke in British accents.

My grandfather, like his father, like my father, had an English-tinged accent. His Ghanaian name was Nana Oheneba Owusu Koko, but most people called him Peter or Mr. Owusu. He dropped the *Koko* from our surname because he didn't trust white people to get the pronunciation right. He didn't want our name to be turned into hot chocolate: cocoa. He knew his children and grandchildren would live and work in the white world.

My father's name at birth was Charles. He went to boarding school in Kumasi, not far from where his family lived. There, he got a very good British-modeled education. In college in America, he legally changed his name to Osei—his Ghanaian name. I didn't know he used to be called Charles until that trip to Ghana when I was seven. I found a photograph on my grandfather's desk of two little girls and a little boy. On the back of the photograph, in my grandfather's neat print, it said, *Harriet, Violet, and Charles in the garden.* I knew who Harriet and Violet were—my father's older sisters.

"Who's Charles?" I asked my father, carrying the photograph out to the porch, where he was drinking a beer and watching the sunset.

"Oh, that's me," he said, laughing, "before I decided to get rid of my colonial name."

"What does Osei mean?" I asked.

"It means noble," he said. "I was named after Osei Tutu."

"It is a peculiar sensation, this double-consciousness, this sense of always looking at one's self through the eyes of others, of measuring one's soul by the tape of a world that looks on in amused contempt and pity," wrote W. E. B. Du Bois. He was, of course, writing about the experience of African Americans—of people whose ancestors my ancestors sold into slavery. But, this double consciousness is true of Africans as well. It is related to colonial mentality. It is related to my father being both Charles and Osei. It is related to my great-grandfather eating fufu with a spoon. It is related to the pride of being Ashanti and the shame of being bush.

During colonization, Ghanaians had to abide by British rules by order of law. After independence, the reasons for continuing to abide by many of those same rules were more complicated. They were about the global economy and power structures. They were about the shame assigned to blackness. Internalized racism and oppression run deep. This can be seen in the fact that many African countries whose leaders fought long and hard for freedom from European rule adopted the European style of government after independence. It can be seen in the raw, red skin of some of my aunts and uncles who use bleaching cream to lighten their complexions. I remember thinking it hilarious when I turned on the television in Ghana to find the newscaster reporting on a trial. I have no idea what the case was about, but all the lawyers wore white wigs and red coats as they do in England. The long, curled wigs looked even more ridiculous, I thought, against black skin. My father found me rolling on the floor laughing. He took one look at the television and started laughing too, even though it was not a new sight for him. He was delighted by my reaction. "That's my girl," he said. "You know foolishness when you see it. The Ashanti had a very sophisticated legal system before the British arrived with their powdered wigs."

Ghana's first prime minister, Kwame Nkrumah, had intended to study law in London—to earn the right to wear one of those wigs. Instead, he became a political activist, participating in anticolonial protests and making friends with leading British Communists. Before arriving in London, Nkrumah had earned two master's degrees in the United States—from Lincoln University and the University of Pennsylvania. In America, he studied the writings of Karl Marx and Marcus Garvey. Eventually, he brought his activism, his philosophy, to the Gold Coast, where he had been lured back with a job as an organizer with the independence movement. That job did not last, however, as Nkrumah grew impatient with the pace of change. He launched his own party, demanding immediate self-government.

In January 1950, Nkrumah launched a nonviolent campaign of strikes, protests, and noncooperation with the British. He was arrested and sentenced to three years in prison. But the British understood they would lose the Gold Coast. The British government agreed to hold a general election to establish a new majority-African government with whom they would collaborate to create a constitution oriented toward eventual full self-rule. In the election, held in 1951, the party led by Nkrumah—the Convention People's Party (CPP)—won thirty-four out of thirty-eight seats. This while Nkrumah was still imprisoned. Despite misgivings, colonial leaders decided to release Nkrumah. They feared that unless they did so, the CPP would refuse to participate in the political process, would rile up their supporters, and all hell would break loose. In one day, Nkrumah went from prisoner to prime minister.

In 1954, Nkrumah and his party won another election. Nkrumah believed that, with his legitimacy reinforced, progress toward self-government could be accelerated. Then he picked a fight with Ashanti leaders over the price of cocoa. More than half of Ghana's cocoa crop was farmed in the Ashanti region, and many Ashanti people's livelihoods depended on it. Nkrumah announced he would be fixing the price of cocoa for four years at far below the price guaranteed under the colonial government. With support from the Asantehene and his chiefs, a new opposition party—the National Liberation Movement (NLM)—was founded. The NLM platform focused on defending the Ashanti economy and culture against Nkrumah's government, which they labeled as both corrupt and disrespectful of their traditions and institutions. Indeed, the board responsible for setting the fixed price of cocoa was engaging in corruption, much of it to benefit supporters of Nkrumah's party through contracts and jobs.

Nkrumah dismissed the NLM as the last gasp of old-fashioned tribalism. He saw his government as modern, as the future. There were violent clashes between NLM and CPP supporters. Startled by the division and what it might signify, the British called for another general election. This election too Nkrumah won, and with it the British announced a date for independence: March 6, 1957.

As the leader of the new free nation of Ghana, Nkrumah chose as his residence Christiansborg Castle, the slaving fort built by the Danish that had been the headquarters of British colonial rule. The castle, said to be haunted, was a strange place from which to launch a nation—in the halls of colonial power, among the ghosts of enslaved people.

Launch a nation, however, Nkrumah did. He quickly built roads, schools, hospitals, and a hydroelectric plant. But what was to be done about the elite class of tribal leaders who expected to continue enjoying the wealth and power they had been granted under colonial rule? What was to be done about the traditional roles of chiefs and kings that had preceded colonialism—the ceremonies, the traditions, the keeping of peace and harmony between the community, the earth, and the ancestors? What was to be done about the fact that some people who were now Ghanaian saw themselves as Ashanti, or Ga, Ewe, or Fante, first? The tribes had been united against a common enemy—the British. But what united them now? What did it mean to be Ghanaian?

The Ghanaian identity Nkrumah imagined was of a highly educated socialist people who held dear the belief that only when all people were free to live the lives they chose could any individual truly be free. And he wanted that spirit of collectivism to extend beyond Ghana to all of Africa. As other African nations won independence, he dreamed of and schemed toward creating a powerful alliance between free African nations, and economic and political cooperation between black people all over the world. He invited prominent African-American intellectuals like Malcolm X and Maya Angelou to visit and live in Ghana. He saw himself as the leader of the Pan-African movement. He saw himself as a powerful, rich man. He declared Ghana to be a single-party state with himself as president for life. He claimed the right to imprison opponents for up to five years without trial. His government became rife with corruption. Nkrumah set up a development corporation through which he took bribes from foreign businesspeople who sought contracts with his government. At the same time, he was taken advantage of by those same businesspeople, who convinced him to build factories, a dry dock, and a conference center for which the government paid enormously inflated prices. The national debt skyrocketed and the standard of living declined.

On February 24, 1966, while Nkrumah was visiting Beijing, the army and police seized power in a coup. Nkrumah sought asylum in Guinea, where he spent most of the rest of his life. He died of cancer in 1972.

It is difficult to speak in simple terms about Nkrumah's legacy. He was freedom fighter and dictator; father of the nation and pillager in chief. He decried tribalism and jailed those who disagreed with him. He hated colonialism and loved the Queen of England—a photograph of himself with the Queen at her estate in Balmoral was one of his prized possessions. Those same tensions that existed in Nkrumah still shape the lives of many Ghanaians. The old way and new ways coexist. People pour libation to their ancestors and proudly sing the national anthem. Members of my family were jailed for opposing Kwame Nkrumah, but both my grandfather and father saw Nkrumah as the father of modern Africa. My grandfather gave up his seat on a black stool. In doing so, he relinquished his claims on family land and property. Instead, he went to work as a sales manager for the United Africa Company, a British trading company that exported palm oil from Ghana to Europe. He also had his own freelance marketing business and several farming ventures. He wore Western suits to work, but after he retired, I rarely saw him in one. He preferred his ntoma and leather sandals. My brother, whose name should be Kofi because that is the name given to boys born on Friday as he was, was named Kwame, after Nkrumah. "So he will always be proud to be Ghanaian," my father said, "proud of his name that was the name of a great African man."

On our way home from the stool house, my sister and I sat in silence. I felt ashamed of my behavior. I hated it when my father was angry with me. Instead of looking out the window, I watched the back of his head as he chatted with the taxi driver. I was surprised when the car pulled to a stop at a place that was not my grandparents' house.

"Get out," my father said, turning back to look at my sister and me. His voice and face were soft. Outside, he held us both by the hand and walked us through the Harmattan haze until we stood at the grassy edge of a twinkling lake. The air was cool and wet. My nostrils did not smart from breathing. We were surrounded by palm trees and tall weeds. My father rolled up the legs of his pants and stepped out of his shoes. Without asking any questions, Yasmeen and I kicked off our flip-flops. Together we ran in, calf-deep.

"This lake, Lake Bosumtwi," my father said, "was created a million years ago when a meteoroid hit the earth with such force the explosion created a big crater that filled with rain. The Ashanti believe it is also the last place where the souls of dead people stop before Asase Yaa comes to take them into the afterlife."

I did not know that lakes could be created by meteoroids. This knowledge made the sludge between my toes, the cold water seem ancient, magical. I dove in, not caring that I would be sopping wet the whole ride home. Underwater, I opened my eyes and held my breath. When I came up gasping, my father grabbed me and tossed me back in. When I remember that day, I remember soaring through the air and landing with a splat. I remember myself unattached from everything and yet made of everything. I was the air and the water. I was made of living fragments. I was past, present, and future at once. I felt, more than ever before, and perhaps ever since, deliciously free.

Looking back, it is clear how desperate I was to feel that freedom. I had been held hostage by the Harmattan, by my fears of an unknown future. I wanted to move my breathing body through space—through air, through water, through grass and tall weeds.

The Ashanti conquered forests to build an empire, but they knew nature was from whence they came and to nature they would return. They would tame the land, but they would know when Asase Yaa needed her rest. Their most sacred duty was to ensure harmony and peace between the community, the earth, and the ancestors; to ensure justice. To the community, the Ashanti pledged loyalty. To the earth and the ancestors, they made sacrifices—to each their due. But harmony is a fragile thing, and so is justice. They bend and break easily. We bend and break them with greed, with violence, with lies and obscurations. The people sold into slavery are modern-day Ghanaians' ancestors too. Their backs and hearts broke under whip and weight. The incomplete story Ghana tells about slavery is a breach. Ashanti culture was breached by colonization. My family broke before and I knew it might break again. The earth broke from the force of a meteoroid, which sent shock waves in every direction.

History is a story, my grandfather said. I offer a friendly amendment: history is many stories. Those stories are written, spoken, and sung. They are carried in our bodies. They billow all around us like copper-colored dust that sometimes obscures everything. In those stories, we grasp at meaning. We search for ourselves, for our place, for direction. We search for a way forward: a woman warrior, a complicated man, an invitation home, a meteor, a lake, a child landing with a splat. Destruction and creation. Changes in light, terrain, and atmosphere. Delicate new freedom. Hope.

Blood Trauma

When I was five, I asked my father why my mother left me. His left eye twitched and he cleared his throat. My father did not lie to me, even when the truth hurt.

"She thought you were better off with me," he said. "She was not ready to be your mother."

"Why?" I asked again.

"There is no simple answer," he said. "Your mother grew up in a family that lost everything, and the trauma is in her blood. I think that's what made her leave."

After that, I stopped asking why. His words terrified me. I too had lost a lot: I had lost a mother. And if trauma was in my mother's blood, then it must also be in mine. Everyone said I looked just like her, except she was white and I was black. I inherited my mother's face and frame, my father's coiled hair and curled eyelashes. My skin color is my mother's olive and my father's ebony blended in equal parts, as though in a watercolor mixing tray.

It wasn't until years later—when I was ten or eleven—that my father told me precisely what it was that my mother's family had lost, why trauma was in her blood.

He told me that, in the years leading up to and during World War I, the Turkish government deported and massacred Armenians en masse. At the time, there were two million Armenians in the Ottoman Empire. By the early 1920s, when the violent campaign ended, it is estimated that 1.5 million Armenians had been killed. Most of those who survived did so by making dangerous treks on foot across the Middle East. They sought refuge in cities like Aleppo and Cairo, cities out of which refugees pour today. Many Armenians eventually found their way west to France and Argentina; Russia and Cuba; and to America. Despite the refusal of the current government of Turkey to use the word *genocide*, that is what it was. My mother's family members were among those who were killed and those who survived. My great-great-grandmother and my grandfather's two-year-old cousin were among the dead. The survivors' losses: their loved ones; their homes and earthly possessions; citizenship; hopes; dreams; security; Mount Ahir; pepper and potato plants; looms for weaving cotton; goat's milk ice cream; tea made from the root of purple orchids.

In 1915, my maternal grandfather's family was driven out of the town of Marash, in the southeastern part of the Ottoman Empire, when they refused to convert to Islam. They were Armenian Orthodox Christians. Other families were not given the option of religious conversion to avoid deportation, but the chief of police felt sorry for my great-grandmother because the family was without a patriarch. My great-grandfather had already immigrated to the United States under threat of imprisonment, or even the gallows, for the crime of treason. He had climbed a pole and replaced an Ottoman flag with an Armenian one. For nine years, after he escaped from the cell where he was being held pending trial, his whereabouts were unknown to his wife and children.

Three hours after the family—my family—left Marash, police rode up to the caravan of 650 refugees with whom they were traveling and rounded up all of the Armenian Catholics and Protestants. The Catholics and Protestants were, it was later discovered, all murdered, their bodies thrown in a giant pit to rot. It is unclear why the Orthodox Christians were spared.

I cannot remember the order of the ordeals my family faced on their way to America, but they included typhus, temporary blindness, several armed robberies, malaria, near-starvation, visa denials from multiple countries, and an earthquake. The story I remember most clearly, though, is that of my great-aunt Areka's abandonments.

Between the ages of four and seven, Areka—my grandfather's older sister—was three times abandoned in the Syrian Desert. She was left in the shade of a large rock, under a tree, and on a donkey. The donkey belonged to a man who named Areka as his price for a goatskin of water. Her mother decided to pay up.

Each of Areka's abandonments was reversed by my great-uncles Aram, Artin, and Gorun, who could not bear to leave their little sister behind and went back for her. In the case of the goatskin of water bargain, they found her in a village, where the man with the donkey had taken her to be his family's servant. She was sitting on a boulder, eating a piece of bread. When her new master refused to give her up, her brothers appealed to the tribal chief, who ordered her immediate return to her family. Areka wept bitterly as her brothers led her away. In the strange village, at least she'd been fed.

I have heard multiple versions of the story of Areka's abandonments. Once, my grandfather, who was not yet born at the time of the events (he was the only one of his siblings born in America), told me his mother was delirious from thirst when she left her daughter behind. Another time, he told me she did not believe any of them would make it out of the desert alive. At least, without Areka, no one would have to carry an extra burden to their death. Areka was too weak to walk on her own. My great-uncle Aram asserted, in a published collection of accounts of the Armenian Genocide, that Areka had become "unbearable with her pitiful crying for water." Crying children, he noted, were a liability. Quiet was crucial. The caravan often walked under the cover of darkness so they would not be attacked by the police or thugs. Aram recalled a vote to strangle a screaming baby to death for fear that she would get them all killed. Fortunately, the negotiation over who would do it took so long that the baby fell into a deep sleep and was saved.

When my maternal grandfather's family arrived at Ellis Island on April 15, 1924, the port of arrival manifest listed them as having "dark complexions." The Yugoslavian family listed above them was noted as having "fair complexions." But, in 1909, four Armenian immigrants had petitioned a Boston district court to become white. Previously, Armenians had often been racially classified as Asiatic Turks, or simply Asian. The judge ruled in the Armenians' favor, pointing to their Christianity as evidence that "the outlook of their civilization has been toward Europe." Being Christian in Turkey had gotten Armenians killed. In America, it bought them whiteness. This meant that, despite their "dark complexions," my family could be naturalized as full citizens of the United States with the rights to vote, hold office, and seek good jobs.

My maternal grandmother's family also came to America from Marash. They too were genocide survivors. They too had many losses, had trauma in their blood. My grandmother's mother was raised in an orphanage. Her parents had not made it out of the desert alive. She was brought to America at sixteen by my grandmother's father, who had gone to Armenia to find a wife. He wanted to marry a woman who was Armenian but didn't look it. He wanted his children to be blond, or at least to not have the prominent noses, low hairlines, and dark complexions that would mark them as different. He wanted a kind of whiteness that was in the skin as well as on paper. He wanted a pale wife because he wanted to hide his future children in paleness. He knew all too well the dangers of difference. He understood that race was a specious invention.

Arriving in Yerevan, my great-grandfather had gone straight to the orphanage, and among the many young, dark beauties with thick, glistening black hair, he spotted my great-grandmother: hair the color of a robin's breast, eyes the color of murky pond. *Her*, he said. And so it was. Not adopted, but claimed all the same. At first, she was relieved to have the answer to the question of her rapidly approaching future. She would have been forced to leave the orphanage in two years. But, upon arriving in America, she discovered that there was such a thing as choice—and she had been given none. For that, she punished her children, including my grandmother, until the day she died. She punished them for being yet another command, another binding rope.

I never met my grandmother's father. I wonder what he would have made of my parents' marriage, what he would make of me, of my blackness. My mother's family has never made much of it. It isn't discussed. When I visited them as a child, I watched my grandfather shake his fist at racist politicians on the evening news. *Those bastards*, he said.

My grandmother's father—my great-grandfather—understood the racial hierarchy, understood how race was used in America, in the same way religion was used in Turkey: to justify slavery, pillage, genocide. No immigrant group ever petitioned the courts to be classified as black. My grandparents don't call themselves white, and neither does my mother. They call themselves Armenian. But America does not agree. To America, they are white. That was precisely what my great-grandfather hoped for. Whatever they call themselves, whiteness has claimed them. Whiteness cloaks them and keeps them safe.

"She was always very distant," my grandmother told me of her mother. "She barely spoke. I was always afraid I would come home and find she had left us."

My mother has said similar things of my grandmother. If my mother had stayed, perhaps I would have said the same of her. There are different kinds of absence.

For most of my life, when people asked how I felt about having grown up without my mother, I would say I did not remember her leaving. I said my injuries were minor. This was not entirely true. I do have a shadow of a memory of her saying goodbye, of a kiss on my forehead, hair tickling my cheek, my eyes fluttering open, a warm feeling. Perhaps this memory is a dream or trick of the mind. As for injuries, pain is not always felt when and where it is inflicted. Grief is slow internal bleeding. And it turns out that my father was right, or almost right, about trauma being in the blood.

A study from New York's Mount Sinai Hospital found that genetic changes stemming from the trauma suffered by Holocaust survivors were capable of being passed on to their children. Our genes change all the time when chemical tags attach themselves to the DNA and turn genes on or off. The study found that some of these tags—found in the genes of those survivors—were also found in their children. The changes led to an increased incidence of stress disorders. This passing down of environmentally altered genes is called *epigenetic inheritance.*

My aunt Areka was abandoned by her mother three times. My mother abandoned me twice—the first time when I was two and the second time when I was thirteen and my father died. Even then, she did not claim me.

My abandonments were not the same as my aunt Areka's. There was never any threat of starvation, of typhoid, of death in the desert. But still: a pattern. The trauma had been diluted by time. But it was present, still discernible, in my blood.

Much of my twenties were spent in a thick fog of the mind. When the fog got too thick to see out of, I often turned to reading and writing, mostly about mental illness. I paid attention to studies of orphans and abandoned children.

In 1949, the pioneer of the attachment theory of psychology, John Bowlby, was commissioned to write a report for the World Health Organization about the mental health of homeless children in postwar Europe. He concluded that mothers and their children have evolved with a biological need to have loving relationships with each other. This relationship serves as a secure base from which the child explores the world. It also acts as a prototype for all other relationships. These findings seem obvious, but little empirical evidence had previously been gathered. The consequences of a disruption or deprivation of maternal nurturing can result in serious and irreversible mental health consequences ranging from despair and detachment to an inability to follow rules, form lasting relationships, or feel guilt.

When I read that study, I thought immediately of my father telling me about trauma being in my mother's blood. Add to that despair and detachment. Add to that an inability to follow rules, form lasting relationships, or feel guilt. Those are all things that are also true of me, in some measure. They are the qualities I most detest in myself. They are qualities that would make it difficult for me to be a mother.

When people ask if I want to have children, I say I am not yet ready to be a mother. I do not say that I do not know if I ever will be.

I pay close attention to news about refugees. I pay attention to the debates—in the halls of government, the courts, the media, at dinner tables. The stories often focus on the dream, achieved or deferred, of a new life in a new world. We ask what they deserve, what we owe them. We calculate the cost of their trauma, haggle over the bill. Little is said of what they've lost. Less is said of what they carry in their blood or what we must do to help them heal.

"She loves you in the ways she can," my father said of my mother. I tried not to think about the ways she couldn't, the ways she never would, except perhaps in that place between dream and daylight, in the split second between here and gone.

THE BLUE CHAIR

New York, New York, Age 28

Day One

Let's say you find yourself sitting in a blue chair for hours a day. As each day passes, you find it harder and harder to get out of the chair. In the chair, you rock back and forth and mutter to yourself. The chair feels like a coffin. But to be in a coffin is the better alternative, the other alternative being to be in your life.

Let's say, in addition to the muttering and the rocking, you also read a great deal about madness. You might have printed a stack of studies from a research database. You might also have gone to the library and borrowed several psychology and psychiatry textbooks, and multiple memoirs. You prefer the ones written by people as they were losing their minds, but redemption stories will do. There are, after all, far more published redemption stories. People like a happy ending. People want the cap back on the bottle, the gun unloaded, the foot stepping backward, away from the edge.

Reading about madness convinces you that you are, in fact, going mad. But it also makes you feel real, like what is happening to you is happening to you. Most of the time, you feel as though what is happening to you is happening in someone else's bad dream. In the dream, there is a chair, a blue chair that rocks when you rock it. Everything else—the rest of the world—rocks on its own and there is no way to make it stop.

Let's say that when you do leave the blue chair, you don't really leave the blue chair. For example, you look at the arm of the chair you

are sitting in and are surprised to find that it is made of wood instead
of upholstery, and it is brown instead of blue. You have no idea how
you got into this other chair. You also have no idea how a coffee got
into your hand. You do not remember ordering it or paying for it. You
do not remember sitting down in the brown wooden chair facing the
window that looks out on Canal Street. You do not remember getting
out of the blue chair, getting dressed, putting on your coat, walking
to the coffee shop. What is that called? That forgetting? What is it a
symptom of?

Let's also say you allowed your body to eat itself so the spaces between your bones look like valleys. The smell of food, even the smell
of plain, unbuttered toast, is so strong that vomit rises in your throat.
When you force the strong-smelling food into your mouth, it tastes
like cardboard. You are starving but you cannot possibly eat. The only
thing you can bear to consume is alcohol. In fact, you can more than
bear it—you need it. Alcohol is now water. You drink water only to
flush your system of old alcohol to make room for more alcohol. Alcohol still tastes the way it's supposed to. Whiskey is whiskey. Wine
is wine. Tequila is tequila. But chicken is cardboard. Broccoli is cardboard. Chocolate truffles, pizza, hamburgers: cardboard, cardboard,
cardboard. If that happened to you, what would you google?

What if you discover that your life has been reduced to a series
of rote actions? You go to your graduate school classes, to work at a
restaurant on West 4th Street, to bars with friends, but the purpose has
grown vague. This does not make you numb, as one might expect. It
makes you furious. You might punch the door of your bedroom. Your
fist might swell with hot blood, but you will barely have made a mark
on the outside world. Perhaps, then, you will try screaming, but that
only makes your voice hoarse. No one can hear you. Well, they might
hear you, but they will hear only the sound. The sound doesn't carry
the weight of meaning.

What if you are already taking two pills a day—Lexapro and
Xanax, for instance—and they are having no effect? What if they cannot stop what is coming, what has already come?

Inside of you is an earthquake. And it is also outside of you. You are not sure if you are the epicenter. With the earthquake comes flood and fire. Perhaps, from disaster, all will be born again: a new origin story. Or perhaps all will be destroyed. The two little white pills that are supposed to stop earthquake, stop flood and fire, are the size of half of your pinky fingernail. Imagine that.

What if you are so terrified of your own thoughts that you ripped the pages of your journal into tiny pieces? When the pieces still felt too big, did you rip them up even more, picking up each piece individually and tearing it in half with the tips of your fingers? When you threw the even tinier pieces into the garbage can in your room, could you still hear them talking to you? Did you have to fish the pieces out of the garbage can—every last one? (Did you make sure you got every last one?) Did you put the pieces into a sandwich bag? Did you dispose of that sandwich bag in a garbage can down the street so the words on the pieces could be drowned out by banana peels and half-drunk sodas? If you did that, does it mean that you are mad? If so, is there a name for that kind of madness? Is there a cure?

Let's say that from where you rock in your blue chair a car horn sounds like a knife. Children's laughter sounds like bullets. Who are you supposed to call in such a case? What are you supposed to tell them when they pick up, if they pick up?

When you go outside and you are confronted with a world still in progress, despite the earthquake and the flood and fire, perhaps a gauzy film covers your eyes. Air to your lungs becomes so inadequate you feel you might faint. What if you faint? When a group of tourists in *I Heart New York* T-shirts appears through the gauze of your eyes, haloed in yellow light, what will you say to them? Will you tell them you just forgot to eat that day, or will you tell them to get down on the ground with you, to get on their backs, to feel how the earth moves, how it spasms? Will you ask if they can hear it? The banging! The voices! The terrible voices! And trumpets! An announcement!

After you decide it's probably best to tell the tourists you are fine, you might return to the blue chair, where you are the one doing the rocking. Once there, perhaps you say out loud to no one and every-one you know that, under the surface of the earth, time is being blown apart. Or maybe it is coming together. Or just coming: expansion and contraction. Climax, but not rapture. The end is not a beginning, only endless ending. Let's say all of this feels true but you also know it's mad.

What if, one day, you sit in the blue chair and you are not sure you will ever get up again? What then?

Will you scrawl the same sentence on every single line in a jour-nal, as you were forced to do when you were a naughty child? Will that sentence be both punishment and reward?

That sentence: *Let madness come. Let madness come. Let madness come.*

Day Two

Blue Chair. It is my second day in the blue chair, and I am still rocking. I am rocking and staring at the streaks on the wall from when the ceiling leaked. I am thinking about how a leak is matter escaping through an opening. I am thinking about water leaking, oil leaking, blood leaking, spirit leaking. I am thinking about madness, about how madness is an opening from which the spirit leaks.

Demons. I am in Ghana visiting my grandparents. It must be the vacation there when I was seven because I am old enough to remember and young enough to play double Dutch in the street. A girl trips over the ropes and falls hard, face in the dirt. She sits up and examines her knees and elbows. She pokes a finger into the pool of blood on her knee and licks it. Blood also trickles out of her nose. She does not notice. She shouts in Twi at the girls who were turning the ropes. They shout back at her. I cannot understand what they are saying.

The girl who fell runs home, crying. She doesn't look back.

"What's wrong with her?" I ask the others in English.

"Maybe she's crazy like her mother," a boy tells me. He lives in England and, like me, is here on holiday, visiting grandparents. I am jealous because he speaks Twi, so he blends in more easily.

"Her mother was sent to a witch doctor because she was talking nonsense. She talked to imaginary people and she cursed at strangers in the street."

"What did the witch doctor do to her?" I ask. "Did she get better?"

"I heard he covered her in paint and cut lines in her face with a razor. But it didn't work, so now she has to be chained to a tree."

I know that traditional healers often cut people's faces with razors in order to pour medicines directly into the bloodstream. That is how Auntie Harriet was cured of dengue fever when she was a little girl. I like to run my fingers over the gashes in her cheeks, feel their ruggedness where the skin grew back uneven.

Later that night, I ask my father if crazy people are ever chained to trees.

"Some people believe that people who hear voices in their heads have demons inside them," he says. "Unfortunately, sometimes people are chained to trees. Their families don't know how to help them. Maybe their families are afraid of them."

For days after that, every time I hear a voice behind me or from outside the window, I spin around or run to see who it is. I want to be certain the voices are not coming out of the mouths of demons inside me.

Naked. A cocktail party thrown by one of my father's colleagues at the UN in his garden in Addis Ababa. I am nine, I think. I have been allowed to stay up late with the grown-ups because my father is having a good time. Somewhere in the big white house with leather couches and cowhide rugs, my sister is asleep with the hosts' children. Adults dance to soukous music and drink from long-stemmed glasses. A beautiful woman I know—a friend of my father's and Anabel's who once braided purple flowers into my hair—strips off all her clothes. She keeps her purse and high heels on. Across the lawn, she runs, screeching. I sit, my feet dangling in a heated pool. Steam rises. As the woman runs, she tosses money from her purse into the air. Her brown skin glistens in the moonlight reflecting off the water. She stops a short distance from the rest of the party, facing us. She arches her back and throws her head and arms behind her. Her nipples, large and dark, point upward. A man—her husband—rushes to her, spreads his arms wide to shield her from our eyes.

"How embarrassing," says a woman behind me in the tone of a whisper, but loud enough for all to hear. "That poor, poor man."

"She'll have to go back to the loony bin now," whispers another woman. Both women, I can tell without looking at them, are stifling laughter.

"Control your wife," shouts a Nigerian man, a friend of my father's, to the naked woman's husband. "There is a child here. You should be ashamed of yourselves."

My father remembers that I am sitting here in my favorite dress with pink roses on it. He swoops over and picks me up.

"Time to go home," he says.

"Why was she naked?" I ask into his ear, my arms wrapped tight around his neck.

"Something's not right in her head," he says.

Devil. Dar es Salaam. I am eleven. Another school holiday. I am eavesdropping on Anabel and her mother, who do not know I am not really reading *A Wrinkle in Time*. I have finished it already, but I hide behind its cover. They are speaking Swahili, so I don't understand everything, but I have lived in East Africa long enough, picked up enough Swahili, to understand that a woman from their village has gone mad. She broke into her own husband's pharmacy and tipped over all the shelves. Her family had a meeting after which she was sent away to a hospital in America.

"There is no cure for madness," Anabel's mother says, shaking her head. "It is the devil inside her. We can only pray that Jesus saves her."

Seismometer. I am sitting on a bench outside a hospital in Rome with my father. We watch ducks float around a pond. I am thirteen. The leaves on the trees are still green, but they rustle as the evening breeze is more forceful now. Cold weather is coming. We wear woolly sweaters. My father, who is bald from chemotherapy, has on a tweed ascot cap.

I struggle to find things to say that aren't about his sickness and my fear, so I don't say much.

"You have to be strong," he says, putting his hand on top of mine. "No matter what happens. You are the oldest, and you have to keep your mind strong. You have to take care of your brother and sister.

When things get hard, you have to work harder. Work hard for them and for yourself. If you do that, you will always be okay."

I squeeze his hand to promise him I will, without acknowledging aloud what the promising means. It means that, soon, he will die.

"The air feels good, doesn't it?" he asks.

"Yes," I lie, stiffening so that he cannot feel me shiver against his arm. That shiver will never leave my body. Sometimes it will feel like it might overwhelm me, explode out of me and leave me empty. Eventually, that shiver will become madness. It will become the madness from which my seismometer will warn me to seek asylum in a blue chair.

Scream. I am sixteen. I am volunteering at a hospital in Kampala. I am a high-school junior at the international school, and I must complete sixty hours of community service in order to graduate.

The hospital is short on beds, so some patients have to share. I struggle not to cover my nose from the smell of too many sick, sweaty bodies in such close quarters. I play cards with two women. They are just girls really, not much older than me. They are dying of AIDS. They tell me their names are Lovely and Beauty. Those names cannot possibly be real, so I assume they used to be prostitutes. I know about prostitutes—we call them *malayas*, Ugandan slang. I often drink shots with them at the bars in Kabalagala. When I drink with them, I laugh too loud. Boys from school, and even older men, stare at me. It makes me feel powerful.

I can tell that Lovely and Beauty used to live up to their chosen names, but now they are gaunt, and the luster of their skin has faded. Lovely's eyes flicker to the corners of the room and settle, shocked for just a moment, as though she can see something, or someone, there. Beauty's eyes are mute. We finish our game, and because I am a little disturbed by Lovely and Beauty and the ghosts in the corners, I decide to go cuddle the babies in the children's unit, but I make a wrong turn. I find myself in a ward full of patients who are screaming. The screams echo. The sound has girth. I freeze. One woman sits in the middle of the floor in a puddle of her own piss.

A nurse in a white dress and little cap rushes over to me. "What are you doing here?"

"Nothing," I say.

"These people are insane," she says. "You have no business here."

"I know," I say, but I feel unsure. A scream of my own tries to leak out. I turn around and walk away, coughing into my tightly balled fist.

FAULTS

Fault:

A long crack in the surface of the earth. Earthquakes usually occur along fault lines.

Note:

Some faults are visible at the surface, but others lie deep within the crust.

The Heat of Dar es Salaam

Dar es Salaam, Tanzania, Ages 0 to 3 and 16

On the day I was born, the air was a supple stew—heavy with over-ripe fruit and armpits, ocean salt, and slow-roasted goat meat. Of course, I don't remember that day, but I was born in the Tanzanian city of Dar es Salaam—just Dar to the locals—and the viscosity of the air is the first thing visitors note. It is what they remember most. More than the satin-white sand and the warm-bath water of Kunduchi beach, the children who scuttle up coconut palms to fetch the hard shells to crack, sweet flesh to eat, cold milk to drink. More than the sticky dough of the greasy fried *mandazis* sold by women walking car to car with colorful *kangas* wrapped tight around their breasts, Swahili wisdoms printed at the hems—*Fadhila za punda ni mateke* ("The donkey expresses gratitude by kicking") and *Mgeni siku mbili, siku ya tatu mpe jembe* ("Treat your guest as a guest for two days; on the third day give him a hoe"). More than the *dala dala* motorcycles and the *boda boda* minibuses: Dar's overcrowded, under-regulated version of public transport. *It's so hot there*, tourists say once they have been deposited back in a more temperate climate by KLM or Delta. They drag the backs of their hands across their foreheads, the mere thought of Dar raising body temperatures, slowing movement.

My parents did not belong to Dar es Salaam. They had temporary visas and diplomatic plates on their cars. My Ghanaian father had just been hired by a UN agency after finishing his PhD in the U.S. My Armenian-American mother was thrilled to get out of Massachusetts, where she had lived her whole life. I was their firstborn child, their Tanzanian baby. When I was born, they decided I looked like the locals. Many Swahili people are an ethnic mix of black, Arab, and Indian.

In Arabic, Dar es Salaam means "the residence of peace." And, indeed, when compared with other major East African metropolises— Nairobi, Kampala, Bujumbura, Kigali—it is a peaceful city. Those other cities have all seen varying degrees and various brands of horrific violence: genocide, coups, civil war, rampant armed robberies, terrorism. Tanzania has often been pointed to as a shining example of what is possible when leaders adhere to the constitution, when division and extremism are rejected. Ask any Tanzanian how she feels about her country and she will tell you about the poverty, about how survival is a struggle for far too many. She will tell you that it is hard to be a woman there, that too few parents send their girls to school, that too many girls are forced to marry young. She will tell you about how people must wrestle a salary from the earth, the ocean, or the tourists because other jobs are scarce. But she will also tell you, with a clear sense of pride, about peace. Then, if you are speaking to a resident of Dar, she might make a joke about the weather: Who has the energy to fight in this heat? If you are a foreigner and you laugh at her joke, if you agree with her about the weather, she might slap you on the back and say, *But* hakuna matata, *right, my sister?*

Disney spread the phrase *hakuna matata* to the world. Its inclusion in that catchy song from *The Lion King* was likely inspired by a different song written by a popular Kenyan hostel band, meaning a band that made a living playing for *wazungu* tourists. The word *wazungu* (and its singular form *mzungu*) is derived from the Swahili word for "wander." *Wazungu* can be applied to anyone who wanders but is most typically used to refer to white people, with the unspoken implication that white people are perpetual wanderers; that their privileges allow them to always be moving toward something, even when they don't know what that something is.

Perhaps someone from Disney heard the original *hakuna matata* song at a safari lodge or a beach resort. The song sounds nothing like the one from the cartoon, but it repeats the jolly refrain, meaning "no worries," over and over again, interspersed with other basic Swahili phrase book fodder: *jambo bwana* ("hello, sir"), *habari gani?* ("how are things?"), *nzuri sana* ("very well"). There are several recorded versions of the song by several different bands. It is ubiquitous in all establishments where *wazungu* can be found sipping local beer and eating giant kebabs of zebra, antelope, and alligator. People in Tanzania, from my observation, however, are more likely to say *hamna shida* than *hakuna matata* when speaking to one another. On the surface, it means the same thing. The hostel band might have chosen the less colloquial *hakuna matata* for its number of syllables, its rhythm. But, it's clear from the way people shrug and smile when they say *hamna shida* that the sentiment is not quite the naive happiness expressed in the Disney cartoon. It is not quite the naive happiness locals express to *wazungu* with *hakuna matata* and a slap on the back. It's not about "no worries for the rest of your days," but rather about carrying on despite those worries. It's about acknowledging there are things in this world beyond your control. Things like the economy, the weather, and mothers.

I too remember the heat of Dar es Salaam. I remember it as a permanent imprint in my nerves, flesh, and blood vessels. "Are you feeling all right? Your skin is so warm," men have said to me when we've shared a bed. I am a hot-blooded animal, I tell them. My circadian rhythm seeks the warmth of the sun. Humidity is my preferred climate. Even in the summer, I shun air-conditioning and sleep under a billowy duvet. I live in New York. As soon as the first snowflake lands on my head, icy water tickling my scalp, I prepare for inertia. My bed becomes an island where I read by red wine and candlelight instead of going to holiday parties. I pile on scarves and sweaters and thick socks. In the event I must venture out, I keep a running list of restaurants, coffee shops, and bars that have fireplaces or overactive radiators. In the cool and cold months, I mourn the mugginess of summer, resent the need to resort to artificial heat. It dries out my hair and makes my eyes and heart itch, messing with my vision and motivation. The winter fills my mind with dark sounds—grating, repetitive, angry. It appears that all the worst days of my life have been in winter, though this might be a sensory error caused by weather bias. We color in the outlines of our memories with our beliefs.

In one of my earliest memories I am, I think, aged three, running naked, crying, and covered in baby powder; being chased by my Somali nanny, who laughed and clicked her tongue, calling to me in a guttural language I did not understand. I don't know why she spoke to me in Somali. She spoke perfect English, I am told. Maybe she was cursing, or maybe the words wet on her lips in such a moment were the words she would have used with her own children. She wanted to dress me; I wanted my pores to breathe.

I remember, from that same time period, a little Indian boy who was my friend—perhaps the son of one of my father's colleagues at the UN. Ratul or Rahul? We sat in the back of a white Pajero, swimsuits on, arms squelched into inflated orange armbands. We were on our way to one of the beach hotel pools. Our tiny bodies sprang into the air as the car flew over the rocky dirt roads. Every time we landed, we dislodged dirt from the old polyester seats. Sparkling dust filled the car: magic out of filth. We never wore seat belts. Country music played on the radio. My father's driver, Francis, sang improbably along in his Swahili accent. Tanzanians love country music. I think they like the gritty sagacity, the stories from an America that is more familiar to them, more like home, than the skyscrapers of New York or the glitz of Los Angeles: the American landscape that is bucolic and coarse and full of God-fearing people who corral bovine beasts on open plains and tell stories around campfires.

Tanzanians believe in God. They believe in the Muslim version introduced by merchants from Oman and Persia who came to East Africa in the seventh and eighth centuries to buy and sell ivory, cloves, and slaves. They believe in the Christian versions brought by German Lutheran and British Anglican missionaries and colonial authorities. Growing up, after my father married Anabel, whenever we were in Dar over Christmas or summer holidays, we would attend the Lutheran church on Kivukoni Road with her family. Rather than staring at the portrait of the fair-skinned, blond-haired Jesus behind the pulpit, I focused on the blank walls that were so clean and white I could paint the ocean on them with my mind. Instead of singing along with the choir, I closed my eyes and listened hard for the sound of waves coming into the harbor that was so tortuously close. Dar is where I first fell in love with the ocean. I wasn't sure about the existence of a higher power, but I believed in floating, in clear blue above me and clear blue beneath me. I believed in the silence I could find only when I was lying, weightless, in salt water. In salt water, there is nothing looming over me but sky, nothing that might collapse.

Tanzanians believe in the Hindu gods brought by the large Indian population who first came to East Africa to build railroads for the British. And they believe in the versions of god that came before the *wazungu*—the versions that even my very Lutheran stepgrandmother turns to when the capital G god does not seem to be listening. She has paid traditional healers to commune with those gods in order to "save" a grandson (my stepcousin) from his homosexuality, to cure a daughter's (my stepmother's older sister's) cancer. On the latter, her prayers and libations were answered, on the former they were not. Only in recent years have I heard Tanzanians discuss homosexuality. Many deny that it exists in Africa or at all; claim that it is a matter of choice, that it is a sin against God. Gay male sex in Tanzania, to this day, carries a thirty-year jail sentence. That law has been on the books since colonial times. LGBTQ activists who seek to change discriminatory laws, to fight bigotry, are routinely harassed, attacked, and detained. Members of the LGBTQ community in Tanzania would likely not, if asked how they feel about their country, tell you about peace. They might not, because they fear for their lives, say anything at all. If they did talk, they might say that religion, that gods, are used to fuel hatred against them.

Here on earth, Tanzanians believe in hard work; in long days swinging machetes in banana fields, picking corn, and digging up beetroots from dirt. They believe in Dolly Parton. And, long before

Francis learned the lyrics to "Jolene" and songs sung by George Strait, Willie Nelson, and Johnny Cash, he believed in cowboys. He knew the tribal dances of the Maasai: Tanzanian cowboys and cowgirls. When they dance, they leap into the air, their tall, thin bodies reaching, straight as arrows, for the clouds. The men grow their hair long, braiding it down their backs, reddening it with mud to match the deep red cloth they drape over their shiny skin. The women shave their heads. They wear layers and layers of butterfly-colored beads around their necks. The Maasai are some of the most beautiful people in the world, but their beauty belies their toughness. They have maintained their way of life for centuries, coming in and out of the modern world as they see fit. They fight tooth and nail when their way of life is challenged to make way for tourism. Their god, they claim, gave them all the cattle in the world. They used to raid other tribes to take back cattle they believed was rightfully theirs. That happens less now. They have enough battles—with the government who threaten every few years to evict them from their land and with the warming planet that threatens the grass they need for grazing. But cows are still their currency, their primary food source, the center of their lives.

At sixteen, I stood outside a traditional Maasai cow-dung-and-mud hut. I wore long, ripped denim shorts, a Wu-Tang T-shirt, and Converse sneakers. In my JanSport backpack was a large plastic bottle of Evian water, some Italian salami and Camembert cheese wrapped in tinfoil. I also carried a disposable camera, a *Seventeen* magazine, and a paperback copy of Nelson Mandela's autobiography *Long Walk to Freedom*. The cheese and salami were for my family's lunch. The magazine and book were for avoiding conversation with my family during that lunch.

We lived in Uganda at the time, which Anabel loved because it put her so close to home, made it so we could be in Tanzania several times a year. We were on vacation in the Serengeti National Park, and our safari package included a Maasai guide and a cultural tour of a Maasai village. The *wazungu* took photos of the hut. They took photos of the children, some of whom wore traditional dress, but most of whom wore concert T-shirts and frilly pink dresses that had probably found their way to this cow-dung-and-mud village from a Goodwill donation box somewhere in Iowa or Vermont. They took photos of themselves standing next to Maasai warriors holding spears. They took photos of Maasai women plunging a sharpened spearhead attached to a gourd into a cow's jugular artery and letting out enough blood to fill the gourd but not enough to kill. The Maasai women took turns drinking from the gourd, smiling as they passed it to their children, revealing their stained red teeth. I was as fascinated by the Maasai as the *wazungu* were. Their way of life was only slightly less foreign to me than it was to the safari suit–wearing Swedes and the Americans with fanny packs around their midsections. My Africa was not this Africa. I had taken one photo, but I put my disposable camera away because I felt suddenly embarrassed.

Years later, I was walking to a bar in Bedford-Stuyvesant, Brooklyn, when I noticed a white man wearing a backpack. An elaborate-looking camera dangled from his neck, and he held a subway map in his hand. He was talking to three older black women who sat on lawn chairs on the sidewalk in front of a low-income housing development. The women had on house slippers and sipped what I assumed to be beer from brown paper bags. They had gotten together to watch the world go by under the fluorescent lights of the building's entrance, to gossip about their neighbors. As I got closer, something made me slow down, unplug my earphones. The man was asking to take the women's photograph.

"Get the hell outta here," said one of the women.

"White boys," said another, shaking her head as the man hurried past me, toward the A train.

I too hurried away. I felt the same smarting on the back of my neck as I felt that day in the Serengeti. It was the photographs, I realized, that disturbed me most. Human beings taking photos of other human beings as though it were the same thing as photographing the sleeping lions and bathing hippos. *There they are in their natural habitat*, they— we—might as well have said.

"Thank you," I said to our Maasai guide as we climbed back into our Jeep.

"*Hakuna matata*," he said, waving goodbye.

———————

Tanzania gained its independence from Great Britain in 1961 under the leadership of Julius Nyerere. His obituary in the *New York Times* in 1999 noted that he had ascended to power without a single shot being fired. It remembered that he introduced free and universal public education and brought the nation's extremely low literacy rate to 83 percent; that he united a land of nine million people with one hundred twenty tribes, who previously had no common language, under the lingua franca of Swahili. Rather than replacing other languages, Nyerere hoped Swahili would give Tanzanians a way to speak across difference in a tongue other than the one imposed by colonization. Swahili was an appropriate choice because it had started as a fisherman's language, believed to have been a hodgepodge of several tribal tongues, spoken on the coasts of Tanzania and Kenya. It was spread, by means of trade, to what are now Rwanda, the Democratic Republic of Congo, Zambia, Mozambique, Malawi, and Burundi. As it spread, it absorbed words from Arabic and English and Hindi.

Nyerere is remembered in Tanzania, and around the world, as a humble man who was committed to egalitarianism, human dignity, government for and by all, and peace. He chose as a title, rather than the *President for Life* moniker preferred by many African heads of state, the Swahili word for "teacher"—*Mwalimu*. However, not all his policies aimed at national unity and shared prosperity were as uncontroversial as his choice of Swahili for an official language. The best-known of these policies, Ujamaa, was, in its philosophy, a blend of traditional African collectivism, the ideal of Christian brotherhood, and the socialism he had studied while at graduate school in Scotland. Nyerere translated the word *ujamaa* into English as "familyhood."

Ujamaa encouraged Tanzanians to relocate to newly created villages in rural areas. In those villages, people were to reject materialism and the accumulation of personal wealth—values that Nyerere argued were part of the damaging legacy of colonialism that threatened to create division and widen inequality. Residents of the Ujamaa villages were, instead, to practice cooperative living. Communities would live close together, farm together, make decisions together, and administer services together. In his book *Freedom and Development*, Nyerere wrote, "We can try to cut ourselves from our fellows on the basis of education . . . we can try to carve out for ourselves an unfair share of the wealth of society. But the cost to us, as well as to our fellow citizens will be very high. It will be high not only in terms of our own satisfactions, but also in terms of our own security and well-being."

Egalitarianism, to Nyerere, was not just a question of morality. It was the foundation upon which nations should be built. On that, he was willing to walk the walk, never taking more than an eight-thousand-dollar-a-year salary as president and being driven about in an old beat-up car. And he wanted, more than anything, for the new Tanzania to be self-reliant. *A poor country cannot run itself if it relies on foreign help* was a slogan he had painted on public buildings. I remember reading it out loud when I was a little girl and determined to read everything out loud—showing off for my father. I had to squint to make out the faded letters on old brick in the brash sunlight.

"Very true," my father said, tapping me on the head with his newspaper. My father said Nyerere had tried to create an African system that was not understood solely in relation to Western philosophies and systems. "We in Africa have no more need of being converted to socialism than we have of being 'taught' democracy," wrote Nyerere. "Both are rooted in our past."

At first, relocation to Ujamaa villages was voluntary. But too few people volunteered. Farmers were reluctant to give up their ancestral lands. City-dwellers were not thrilled by the prospect of rural living. So Nyerere's government offered incentives: schools, water infrastructure, money. The number of Ujamaa villages increased, but for the most part, they were not run in the egalitarian, collectivist way Nyerere had hoped. He grew impatient, announcing that, within three years, resettlement for all rural Tanzanians would be compulsory. He went on the radio to reprimand his people for not holding up their end of the bargain. They had, he said, been given free education and health care and still they were lazy and ungrateful. Some local officials took Nyerere's words as a signal to move from tactics of persuasion to intimidation. Homes of people who refused to move were burned. Their crops were destroyed. There were stories of people being driven from their land and forced to live in the bush, to make of the bush an Ujamaa village. Some of the villages had been built on unfertile soil. Food production across the country fell dramatically. This was compounded by drought and plummeting global agricultural prices. In 1975, the Tanzanian economy, in what was Nyerere's worst nightmare, had to be saved by grants and loans from foreign governments and the World Bank.

In 1981—the year I was born—Nyerere gave a speech to mark twenty years since independence. In it, he admitted that Tanzania was poorer then than it had been in 1972. The country was still amid a food emergency. That food emergency is what led to my father being stationed in Tanzania by the UN agency for which he worked; that led to my being born in Dar es Salaam.

———

At a hotel pool in Dar es Salaam when I was three, my little friend Ratul or Rahul and I spent the day swimming in the kiddie pool under the supervision of my Somali nanny. Eventually, Ratul or Rahul's mother showed up with clean, dry clothes and a comb. She summoned him out of the water, stripped him down so I could see his bare bottom that was so much paler than his umber-colored skin. After combing his hair carefully, she patted him on the head. She thanked my Somali nanny for watching him, made small talk with her about the heat (what else?). As my friend and his mother left, they waved to me. I waved back and kept splashing. I refused to get out when my nanny said it was time to go home. She was not my mother. She hadn't even brought a comb. My mother lived beyond the horizon, in America, with a new husband and a new daughter who had taken the place of my father, my sister, and me.

Years later, when I was eight and living in Rome, I visited my mother in Massachusetts. She told me she would love to retire in Dar es Salaam. She too loved the ocean. She loved to swim into its depths. Dar was the place, she said, where she felt most at peace. This was surprising to me as Tanzania was the place where she had left me, where my parents' marriage fell apart. It was also surprising because she had, just moments earlier, complained about the heat there. She had told me the story of my birth. Her labor, she said, was long, and too hot. She almost lost two teeth—her hormones went haywire and weakened them. The doctors at the (*scary*, she said) hospital did not do anything to stop her from grinding her jaw. Still, she said, my birth was one of the best things that ever happened to her. Despite the fine dark hair that covered my upper back and forehead until I was a month old, she thought I was the most beautiful creature she had ever seen. For a year, she carried me around in the style of Tanzanian mothers, in a *kanga* swaddled tightly to her breasts. My sweat seeped through her thin cotton dresses. My breath warmed her neck. The unformed soft spot on my skull pulsed against the soft place under her chin. When I was a year old, when she was pregnant with my sister, she tried to phase out the *kanga*, to put me down. I would scream and throw my legs up into a perfect split so I would not be forced to stand on my own two feet. I applied such a tight lock to her neck that she struggled to breathe. Once, I almost split her earlobe in two when I yanked her hoop earring. The look on my face, my mother said, was one of pure terror, as though she were trying to lower me not onto a soft green lawn, but into boiling water.

———

Despite the failure of Ujamaa, despite the fact that Tanzania remains a poor nation today, still very much reliant on foreign aid, Nyerere's legacy is one of peace. It is, as he hoped, one of the values Tanzanians hold most dear. It is a value I feel whenever a Tanzanian says *hamna shida*. It is a value whose shadow side I feel when I talk to my Tanzanian stepcousins about the homophobia and gender discrimination in the country we all love. When people are oppressed, peace is tenuous, is unjust. It is maintained through the rejection of progress, through denial.

I was born in a hot city with many gods who don't always answer prayers. The Maasai did not get to own all the cattle in the world. Some of them must make a living giving cultural tours. My stepgrandmother learned to accept her grandson's homosexuality. To find peace, he forgave her for trying to "cure" him of it. My mother and I never floated side by side in the turquoise warm-bath ocean. In the end, I could not stop her from lowering me onto the lawn when I craved the comfort of her *kanga*. I could not stop her from leaving. I do not pray, but I hope Tanzanians will choose a more just peace, that LGBTQ people will be included in the egalitarianism and familyhood that were at the center of Nyerere's vision. Some things are out of the gods' control. And some matters require more from us than hope or prayer. They require us to see and support one another. They require us to defend one another. We must all, in the end, make peace with that.

The Other Side of the Wall

Addis Ababa, Ethiopia, Ages 8 to 10

We watched from a safe distance. The civil war and the poverty it wrought had brought us here, but we were only observers. In the morning, the guards, armed with rifles and machetes, opened the gates to let out our fleet of chauffeured white SUVs bearing diplomatic plates and the logos of UN agencies, international NGOs, and embassies. From behind tinted windows, we watched the other Ethiopia go by. It was built of mud and cardboard. Concrete buildings crumbled. We passed through it on our way to ballet lessons and the Hilton pool.

Behind the walls and barbed wire of the compound, we lived in cozy cottages with manicured gardens of roses and chrysanthemums. We had seesaws, tire swings, and paddling pools. Our parents entertained one another with cocktail parties and barbeques under the stars. Our families were from India and Bangladesh, England and America, China and Japan, Sweden and Denmark, Kenya and South Africa. Some of our families were multinational and interracial. We ate one another's food, listened to one another's music, celebrated one another's religious and cultural holidays. We were the kind of community people wrote hopeful songs about.

After school, all twenty-one of us children would gather on the large green lawn at the compound's center. We'd ride bicycles and fly kites until our private tutors and house girls summoned us indoors for homework and dinner. Later, our parents would come home with family-sized bags of potato chips from America and chocolate from

Switzerland, purchased at the UN commissary. They would ask us about our days spent at the international school, where we did not learn about the history that was being made around us. We learned to speak French and made erupting volcanoes out of papier-mâché. Our parents would read us bedtime stories and tuck us into mosquito-netted beds, leaving us to sleep peacefully under whirring ceiling fans while they whispered to each other about impending coup d'états, rebel armies, and food shortages upcountry.

On the other side of the walls, shantytowns sprawled as far as the eye could see. People with amputated legs dragged their bodies along dirt roads, balancing themselves on one hand to stretch the other up to stalled cars for pittances. Donkeys carried sacks of grain to barren markets. Raw sewage flowed like creeks between corrugated tin shacks. There were days after school when we would sit in our tree houses, built for us by the compound's gardeners, and look down into that other Ethiopia.

Sometimes, we called out to the children in the shantytown who played with balls made of plastic bags and tin can cars on sticks. They fashioned those toys themselves with scrap from Addis Ababa's giant landfill, which was patrolled by vultures, and by stray dogs our parents warned us never to touch. To keep from gagging, we held our noses when we drove by the landfill. The shantytown children climbed up its rancid hills of waste, scavenged for plastic, metal, clothing, and food their families might repurpose or sell. We waved to them and they waved back. We were fascinated by their lives.

Once, bored of our tree house perch, a small group of us contemplated going into the other Ethiopia to find adventure. Because it was forbidden, even talking about it made us tipsy with fear and excitement. After hours of plotting, and assessing the repercussions of our parents finding out, we voted to fly the coop. In just a few breathless minutes, we threw a rope over the wall and shimmied down one by one. We played soccer with the children from the other Ethiopia, weaving around their makeshift homes and kicking up dirt. The house girls, discovering that their charges had escaped, deployed the guards from the gate to apprehend us and bring us safely back behind the walls. We were easy to find. A multicultural group of children in brightly colored T-shirts and shiny white sneakers, Swatch watches on our wrists, did not blend easily into the backdrop of extreme poverty. Our parents scolded us for our recklessness.

"You could have been abducted," they said. "You could have been . . . hurt. It's not safe out there." Their pauses were full of dangers we did not yet understand.

Sometimes, on Friday afternoons, the children of the women our families called "house girls" came to visit. The house girls lived in the servants' quarters that were attached to the back of each cottage. There would be knocks at the compound gate, and the guards would ask the children's names and the names of their mothers, who in turn would come to our doors to seek our parents' permission to allow their children in. Our parents would say, *Of course*. They would give the house girls the evening off.

Most of the house girls' children disappeared into the servants' quarters, and we wouldn't see them again until Sunday when it was time for them to leave. Sesai was different. He was the son of the house girl who worked for my family—Mulu. Sesai would walk through the gate swinging his long arms and whistling. He would gravitate toward us and ask us about our game. If we were running races around the lawn, he would sprint past us, pumping his fists. He would jump into our games of double Dutch and skip faster and higher than any of us. Mulu would stand in front of the servants' quarters, laughing and waiting for him to run over to her for his dinner of injera and stew.

We loved it when he came to visit. He didn't come often because he worked as a gardener at the home of a wealthy Ethiopian family. He spoke English quite well and he liked to ask each of us where we were born. When we named the country or countries, he would nod his head with a serious look on his face and say, *Ah, yes*. He had a big gummy smile, and when he laughed, he opened his mouth wide and his whole body shook, but no sound came out. He taught us to do backflips and to walk on our hands. Sesai was thirteen.

One weekend, some of us were playing cards in one of the cottages when we heard what sounded like rain falling on the tin roof. The weather had been sweltering, so we threw down our cards and ran outside to feel the cool drops of water on our skin. The sky was blue, and the sun blazed. One of the guards ran over, shouting at us to go back indoors. He went around to every cottage to give all who were home a warning. The pattering on the roof was not rain. It was the sound of falling bullets.

Bands of rebel soldiers had been arriving in the city by the truckload. They waved their weapons from truck beds. When we were driven to school, we pressed our noses to the windows and stared at them. They did not look like the guards at the compound gates, nor did they look like the uniformed, government soldiers we saw everywhere we went. They looked wild and desperate. Their hair was matted into dreadlocks, their skin ashy with dust. Some of them were children.

The week after the bullet rain, school was closed due to a security alert. On the eighth day of our unexpected break from study, we were playing tetherball on the lawn when Sesai walked through the gate. We shouted his name and started to run to him, but he did not look at us. He did not ask us about our countries of origin. He just walked straight into the servants' quarters behind my family's house.

We waited for Sesai to come back out. When he didn't, disappointed, we went inside, into my family's cottage, to watch cartoons. My aunts in England recorded children's programs on VHS tapes and sent them to us in the mail because there was nothing to watch on Ethiopian television except for the news in Amharic. We piled onto the couches or sat cross-legged on the floor. Someone went to get us chocolate chip cookies and Kool-Aid from the kitchen. We sat there for hours. The sun set and darkness fell. My father came home from work and patted some of the other children on the head, asked after their parents, kissed Yasmeen, Kwame, and me on the tops of our heads. Soon, it would be time for our friends to go home for evening baths and meals. Anabel, in the kitchen, was talking to the woman who cooked our food, Hannah, about dinner.

Mulu and Sesai burst into the room where we were watching television. Mulu, whose voice rarely rose above a whisper, was shouting, trying to get my father and Anabel's attention.

My father came out of his bedroom with a newspaper in his hand. Anabel emerged with a cup of tea. They looked irritated or confused, but Mulu's obvious terror jerked the lines of their foreheads apart so their faces were wide and alert.

"What is it? What is happening?" my father asked.

"The soldiers!" Mulu searched for more words but could not find them. Pointing in the direction of the gate, she opened and closed her mouth like a fish out of water.

Sesai stepped in front of his mother. "They have come for me," he said.

Both the rebel and government armies had been forcibly conscripting soldiers. They did not care how young they were. We never learned why two soldiers had demanded to be let into the compound that day. Perhaps they were looking for potential recruits like Sesai whom we might have been harboring. Or perhaps they were angered by the sight of our pristine enclave, our oasis in the desert of their bloody battle.

The soldiers strode confidently into our cottage. They carried weapons. They barely acknowledged us children as we sat trembling on the floor, holding one another and crying. On the television, Wile E. Coyote blew himself into bits. My father tried to be brave.

"I am calling the United Nations," he said, waving the telephone around as though it was a match for guns. The soldiers sneered.

Sesai had been standing when the soldiers threw open the door, but as they tore through the house, he nestled among us on the couch.

Mulu distanced herself from where we sat. She leaned against the door to the kitchen.

After what seemed like a flash and an eternity at the same time, the soldiers left. As they made their way around the compound, I could hear my friends' parents' shrieks and protests. Sesai stayed seated with us on the couch. We stared at the television, no one speaking, until the guards came in to tell us that our brief occupation was over.

All of us, children and parents, rushed out onto the lawn to discuss what had happened. The house girls came outside too. They told our parents about how their sons, nephews, neighbors' children had been taken. Some wept. They stretched their arms up in the air. They asked God or the moon to grant them mercy. Mulu cried while she held Sesai's head to her chest. He was safe because the soldiers had thought he was one of us.

Not long after the soldiers came looking for Sesai, most of our parents were told by their employers that nonessential personnel and their families were to evacuate Addis as soon as possible. We were to board planes destined for Kenya.

Anabel, Yasmeen, Kwame, and I went first to Nairobi and then to Dar es Salaam to stay with Anabel's parents. From the plane's window, we watched Ethiopia fade from view until all we could see was sky and clouds. My father, for a month, stayed behind. Not long after our departure, rebel soldiers raided the compound. They stomped on the roses. They threw porcelain plates and glass vases to the ground. They threatened my father's life, and the lives of the other fathers and mothers who had remained. They told them to get in their cars and leave—to leave the compound, to leave Ethiopia, to go back where they came from.

"This is our country, not yours," they said.

I don't know how long the soldiers were in the compound. My father moved temporarily into the Hilton Hotel. When he was told it was safe to go back to our house, he walked into our living room to find that someone had taken a shit on the floor.

I never returned to Ethiopia. After my father joined us in Dar es

Salaam, he received a phone call from headquarters telling him he had been promoted, that we would be moving to Uganda. A moving company would pack our things. My father told me the violent and oppressive government of Mengistu Haile Mariam had been toppled, the country had been split in two: Ethiopia, Eritrea.

I'm no longer in touch with the children who were my neighbors in the compound. Some of them, I see on the internet. We are adults. We have children and master's degrees. We create global monetary policy and write for newspapers. We go on safari vacations in Africa. We wonder what happened to Sesai, but we don't wonder enough to find out. We see him trembling in our nightmares. We tell this story, the parts of it we know, anyway, to friends and lovers.

African Girls

My father told Yasmeen and me he was sending us to a Catholic boarding school in England because he had been transferred from Uganda back to Rome. All the moving around, he believed, was disrupting our education. He had gone to boarding school in Kumasi at the age of nine. Boarding school, he said, would grant us stability. It would teach us to be independent. It would provide more educational rigor and discipline than the American school in Rome. When we had lived in Rome previously, we attended the British school. I did not think to question why that was no longer an option.

My father called the American school in Rome "Foolishness International." When we went there for a tour, the principal let us peek into the classrooms while lessons were in session. Later that day, my father told Anabel the children seemed to spend all day painting, watching films, and expressing their opinions. How could they have opinions when they didn't know anything yet? Nobody knew anything until they were at least eighteen. First you should learn facts; then you could form opinions. Anabel laughed.

"That is not how they think in America," she said. "Everyone is entitled to an opinion, even children. Facts or no facts."

"Very true," my father said.

Years later, I learned that the real reason, or at least a big part of the reason, why Yasmeen and I were sent to St. Mary's was because my father knew he was sick, and he wanted to spare us from seeing him suffer. At the time, Anabel eventually told me, he was still hopeful that treatment would work. As it was, Yasmeen and I would be at St. Mary's for less than a year. We would be summoned back to Rome as my father began to face the reality that he might not get better. If he was going to die, he wanted to spend whatever time he had left with his wife and all his children. When Yasmeen and I returned to Rome, we were enrolled in the American school.

When I first arrived at St. Mary's in the middle of the term, I noticed almost immediately upon entering my dormitory that there was only one other black girl. She was tall and had a broad, square-shaped body with muscular arms and legs. Her skin was dewy and dark. The dormitory mother, Sister Miller, introduced me to her before she introduced me to any of the other girls.

"Agatha," Sister Miller said, motioning for her to come over to us, "this is Nadia. She is from Ghana." She said it like "Gay-Na." "Is that near Kenya?"

"Not really," said Agatha. "Nice to meet you."

I had told Sister Miller I was Ghanaian because that is what my father taught me to say when asked where I was from. Once, I overheard him tell a friend my American passport was just a practicality. It would enable me to go to college in the States without any trouble. And it would easily open doors for me that had taken him many years to jimmy open. He sounded angry about all of this. He said the word *American* as though it were an insult.

A few days after I overheard my father call my American passport a practicality, a woman on the metro in Rome asked me if I was Indian. She looked back and forth between my father and me with a furrowed forehead. People often asked me questions like that. The woman's tone suggested she couldn't figure me out and she didn't like it. "My daughter is black," my father snapped. The woman hurried away. "Don't ever be confused about that," he said to me, as though being confused were a choice, as though blackness were a simple thing.

At St. Mary's, Agatha sat on her bed watching as Auntie Harriet, my father's sister who lived in England, helped me unpack my things. All the other girls lounged on the sofa and armchairs at the front end of the long, narrow dormitory. They were painting one another's toenails bright pink and eating a large tin of Quality Street chocolates. They were all white or Asian. The girls had not looked up when Auntie Harriet and I walked in with Sister Miller, who asked me if I had brought a hot water bottle to sleep with. It could be rather cold at night in this part of England. It didn't get cold where we were from, did it?

I was often the only, or one of very few, black students at the schools I attended. When I was six and attending the British school in Rome, a boy refused to hold my hand during a game of ring around the rosie because his mother said God left black people in the oven too long. That meant we were mistakes. The teacher corrected him: *Colored people are just like us.* I was not supposed to correct teachers, so I didn't say anything about her use of the word *colored*. Everyone in my class called me burnt toast behind my back for months. Then a popular girl started passing me notes to tell me I was hideous. Once, I grew hot and shoved her hard. She skinned her knee and I was pleased. She looked ugly when she cried. For a full year, until she moved away, I was excluded from parties and recess games. My best friend stopped talking to me. From experiences like that, I learned to observe carefully.

I am not proud of this, but when I met Agatha and noted that we were to be the only two black girls in the dorm, I was relieved she was dark-skinned. I was relieved she had a wider nose, coarser hair, and fuller lips than me. I was relieved because this meant I would not be at the bottom of the racial pecking order. To be clear, I did not believe that this pecking order was just or right. My father was dark-skinned, as were many of the people I loved and respected the most. But it did not matter what I believed. The rules had been written long before I arrived at St. Mary's, long before Agatha and I were born. I knew the rules well because they had shaped my life, and because I was obsessed with reading historical texts and literature about people like me: black people, in-between people, people who complicated the rules.

In America, I knew, mulatto slaves, as they were then called, were viewed by white people as more intelligent than their darker-skinned kin and were thus assigned indoor domestic work instead of strenuous outdoor, manual labor. Some were taught to read and write, and in some cases were even freed before it was required by law. This preferential treatment was designed to stratify the black community and to establish whiteness as the ideal to be aspired to, even among black people. And it was also designed to assuage slave owner's guilt, as their mulatto slaves were often their own children through rape.

After the American Civil War, these divisions persisted, as some lighter-skinned former slaves internalized and guarded their privilege. They often distanced themselves from darker black people, forming separate churches, schools, and clubs. And the transition into freedom was easier for light-skinned black people because of the stereotypes white people held about blackness. White slave owners claimed dark-skinned slaves, particularly men, were more violent and more likely to steal. They claimed dark-skinned slaves were animal-like, incapable of controlling sexual urges. Given these lies, it is not surprising that, after slavery, darker-skinned black people found it more difficult to find paid work.

The same forces that led to the privileging of lighter-skinned black people in America were also exerted in Africa during colonialism. In *Black Skin, White Masks*, Frantz Fanon writes, "The colonized is elevated above his jungle status in proportion to his adoption of the mother country's cultural standards." This truth was evident in Rwanda, for example, where first German and then Belgian colonists favored the Tutsi tribe over the Hutu tribe based on the Hamitic hypothesis.

This hypothesis, believed by many Western scholars at the time, held that there were two races present in Africa: the Hamitic race and the Negroid race. The Hamitic race was thought to be a superior race of people who originated in northern Africa. British historian C. G.

Seligman went so far as to claim that all significant discoveries and advancements in African history, including those of the Ancient Egyptians, were achieved by Hamites. He argued that Hamites migrated into central Africa, bringing more sophisticated customs, languages, and technologies with them. Hamites were believed by Westerners to be more closely related to white people. Tutsis were believed to be descendants of Hamitic people because they had more "European" features. Hutus were believed to be fully Negroid. Tutsis were therefore allowed better educations and jobs. Ethnic identity cards were introduced to ensure tribal division. Many have argued that this division was at the root of the Rwandan genocide of 1994, during which members of the Hutu majority murdered as many as eight hundred thousand Tutsi people.

———————

After pointing to the wardrobe and telling me I should put my things in it, Sister Miller disappeared into her small private room in a corner of the dormitory. We heard the theme song for *Coronation Street* through the open door. Agatha sat on the chair next to the bed that was to be mine. She listened to Auntie Harriet and me as we chatted about how I should make sure to wear two pairs of socks if it snowed and how much money I would get each week for chocolates and sweets at the tuck shop. Agatha nodded at everything we said as though she were somehow a part of our arrangements.

Auntie Harriet tied her shoulder-length box braids back with a hair band that had been around her wrist. She took my things out of my small suitcase and placed them neatly in the drawers. My new green-and-red school uniforms were hung in the closet, and a teddy bear was placed on my pillow, even though I was twelve. Then, Auntie Harriet hugged me and told me she would come back to get me in two weeks. She would bring a hot water bottle. I was to spend every other weekend with her in London.

"Nice to meet you, Agatha," she said. "I hear Kenya is a very nice place."

"Yes," said Agatha, nodding more vigorously.

In the dining hall that night, I learned that all of the girls in my dormitory—the Year Nine girls—were to sit together at every meal. Agatha told me this as we stood in line to be served our shepherd's pie and side of peas. She had not left my side. She showed me where the toilets and the showers were. She explained the schedule—what time the bells for breakfast, assembly, church, and classes would ring. I had already gotten this information in writing from Sister Miller that morning, but I let her tell me anyway. As she talked, I watched the other girls. I wondered why Agatha was not with them. They seemed to be enjoying themselves, looking at teen magazines and gushing over boy band members. If there was something wrong with Agatha, I didn't want to inadvertently become associated with whatever it was.

Agatha set her plate down at the very end of the table, leaving a space on the bench between herself and a pretty blond girl with rosy cheeks. The blond girl looked like the girls in the school's brochure, the ones running around in a field of geese. I sat across from her rather than across from Agatha. I could feel Agatha staring at me, but one of the boarding mistresses said grace, so I was able to close my eyes to avoid looking at her. A twinge of guilt tightened my heart, and I resented it. It was not as though I'd sat so far away from her, I told myself.

"I'm Nadia. What's your name?" I asked the blond girl as the room filled once again with loud conversation. She perked up at my question.

"Are you American?" she asked.

"Yes," I said, sensing immediately that this was the right answer. My father was the one who had exiled me to this school. I couldn't be expected to follow his rules about nationalities now. I was alone and had to fend for myself. If my American accent was an asset, why should I not use it to my advantage?

"I'm Claire," she said. "Everybody, Nadia's American."

It quickly became clear that Claire was the most important of the Year Nine girls. The other girls watched her while they talked. When her upturned nose wrinkled, they stammered, reversed what they were saying. It also quickly became clear that Claire did not like Agatha. Claire doled out her attention evenly, giggling at jokes and smiling at each girl as she asked her a question or approved of an opinion. But she never so much as glanced at Agatha, who ate her meal in silence.

After dinner, we were allowed to watch a film in the common room. Claire selected *The Wizard of Oz* from the sparse collection on a small bookcase against the wall. There were not many films the nuns deemed appropriate for young ladies. Nobody else even attempted to weigh in on the decision. As I settled into a beanbag chair and Claire turned off the lights, Agatha walked by the common room in her pajamas, a book in her hand.

"Thank God she's not coming in here," said Claire. "She smells so horrible. Didn't you notice, Nadia? It's really awful, isn't it?"

All the girls turned to look at me.

"Oh, yes," I lied. "It's so bad. I've been holding my breath all day." In reality, Agatha smelled like my family. She smelled like home: cocoa butter, Luster's pink hair lotion.

Everyone laughed and Claire pressed play.

The next day, when my father called, I could barely bring myself to speak to him, I was so ashamed.

In George Schuyler's 1931 novel *Black No More*, Dr. Junius Crookman develops a process that makes black people white.

"My sociology teacher had once said," Dr. Crookman tells reporters during a press conference, "that there were but three ways for the Negro to solve his problem in America. . . . To either get out, get white, or get along." When I read that book in my twenties, I immediately thought of my time at boarding school. There was no way for me to get out of St. Mary's, though I begged my father. Becoming white was not an option. So I had to find a way to get along. This would, I knew, require Claire's approval.

In my first week at St. Mary's, I carefully considered every move I made. I got to know each of the Year Nine girls and to understand her place in the social order. Claire's full name was Lady Claire

Suggitt-Jones. Her father was a member of the House of Lords. Her mother was a beautiful socialite who was frequently in the pages of *Hello!* magazine at polo tournaments and ribbon cuttings. Most of the other English girls were of a similar ilk—either titled or moneyed. My family could only afford the school fees because they were paid by my father's employer. Claire's sidekick, Victoria Ivanenko, was the most beautiful girl in our year, more beautiful even than Claire, but without any discernible personality of her own. Her father was a Russian millionaire. Her parents were divorced, and her mother was now dating a pop star. The three Asian girls were from Hong Kong. They occasionally wandered off together, speaking Cantonese. Of them, Patricia was the leader because she had a wicked sense of humor that even Claire, who prided herself on being quick to jab a precise joke into the fleshy part of other people's stories, had to admire. Around Claire, Patricia was quieter, more prudent with her dry wit. She too played by the rules.

I began to develop my role in the group. Because I was believed to be American, I was expected to behave like the teenagers in the American television shows the girls watched a great deal of when they went home to their parents: *My So-Called Life*; *Beverly Hills 90210*. Luckily, I had watched the same shows. I was supposed to roll my eyes frequently at the stuffiness of life at St. Mary's. This was not difficult to do as St. Mary's was stuffy. I was also supposed to have some experience with boys and other forbidden things like cigarettes and alcohol. I didn't have experience with any of those things, but it wasn't difficult to pretend otherwise. Because I had often found myself without friends in the past, I had spent a lot of time alone with nothing but books and my imagination to keep me company.

Always, Agatha watched me. As I walked to the tuck shop with Claire and Victoria she followed close. Her eyes seared my back. Once, I entertained the girls by arguing with Sister Miller, who wanted to tear the pages about dating and menstruation from our magazines. *Puritanical suppression of ideas*, I called it. Agatha listened, but did not laugh when everyone else laughed. Since her bed was across from mine, sometimes she walked over to talk to me before lights-out. I didn't ignore her, but I didn't encourage her either. I answered her questions in as few words as possible.

"The food here is not nice, is it? Do you miss eating food from home?"

"Not really," I said, even though every time I went to Auntie Harriet's for the weekend, all I wanted was fufu and peanut soup.

"Is there a place in London where you go to do your hair? I need to get my braids redone."

"My aunt does it," I said. In truth, Auntie Harriet took me to a place in Wembley. I felt bad for lying about that because Agatha's hair had started to look bad. There was a lot of unbraided growth. The extensions in the front of her head hung on to her short baby hairs for dear life. But I didn't want to risk losing my status by inviting her to come to the salon with me.

A month after I started school at St. Mary's, I began to find Agatha's braided extensions everywhere. I found one in the shower and one in the entrance to the laundry room. One of the Belgian nuns who washed our clothes (I never learned why the nuns were assigned jobs based on nationality—the Belgians did laundry, the Irish worked in the kitchen) handed it to me thinking it might be mine. Given that potential confusion, I made sure to dispose of every braid I found, wrapping them in toilet paper and throwing them into the garbage. Meanwhile, Agatha's hair looked more and more desperate. She tried to cover it up with headbands and ribbons, but they weren't much help. Unlike me, she had no family in England. I was the only African girl she knew.

One day, during PE, it was warm enough to play field hockey outside instead of playing handball in the gymnasium. We all changed into the very short green skirts and matching bloomers we wore for sports activities. We ran three laps around the field to warm up. Claire and Victoria jogged right in front of me.

"Look at her go," Claire said, pointing at Agatha. "She looks like a gorilla. Like a giant ugly gorilla."

I picked up speed and passed them. It would be easier for me to pretend not to have heard her. I ran faster than I had ever run in my life.

That night, at dinnertime, Victoria found one of Agatha's braids in the bread basket as we stood in line for roast beef and potatoes. She shrieked so everyone turned to see what was happening. Claire picked up the braid with a napkin.

"Oh my days," she said. "It's Agatha's filthy weave. It probably has insects in it. I've completely gone off my food." She said this in a loud voice for all to hear. She dropped the braid on the floor dramatically.

The hall roared with laughter. Even Sister Harris, who adored Agatha, laughed.

"Nadia," Claire squealed, "are your braids going to fall out like Agatha's?"

"No," I said trying to sound light, "mine are not fake like hers." This was, at the moment, true, but I had worn extensions in the past. I decided, right then, to put a photograph of my mother on the wall behind my bed. She had olive skin and straight, silky hair. Never mind that I barely knew her.

Behind me, I heard a tray slam onto the counter. I turned to see Agatha walk, calm but stiff, out of the dining hall.

After that, Agatha stopped trying to talk to me before lights-out. She stopped watching me.

One of my favorite novels is Toni Morrison's *The Bluest Eye*. It was one of the books I had brought to St. Mary's with me. I did not read it while I was there, though, I think because I could see myself in it, and what I saw wasn't pretty. In the novel, Pecola longs, painfully, for blue eyes. She idolizes Shirley Temple and detests her dark skin that even her own mother deems ugly. She is tormented at school. Whiteness, she believes, is the key to being loved. She obsessively eats candies, the wrappers of which are printed with a photo of a blond-haired, blue-eyed girl named Mary Jane. She hopes the candy will transform her eyes to blue. She also appeals to God. But her eyes only turn blue in her mind, through madness, after she is raped by her father, gives birth to his child, and is shunned by her community. She decides everyone is jealous of her blue eyes. Perhaps her fixation on blue eyes as opposed to white skin speaks to a deep-seated knowledge that it is the world that needs to change, not her. Because she cannot change the world, she chooses to see it differently, through different eyes.

I too chose not to see the world as it was. I chose not to see the horrible way Agatha was treated. The narrator in *The Bluest Eye* tells us this of how people felt about Pecola: "Her simplicity decorated us, her guilt sanctified us, her pain made us glow with health." I cannot claim that I did not relish the fact that I was accepted by Claire while Agatha was not. I cannot claim that under Claire's blue-eyed gaze, I did not, despite my guilt, glow with health.

On Friday, Auntie Harriet came to take me to London. Agatha was seated on her bed reading a book. She had headphones on. She almost always had headphones on in the dormitory now.

"Ay!" said Auntie Harriet, catching a glimpse of the state of affairs on Agatha's head. "We should take her with us to Wembley. Does she have no one to braid her hair?"

I could not think of a reason that would make sense to Auntie Harriet as to why Agatha should not come with us. So Auntie Harriet spoke to Sister Miller and then to Agatha, who looked up at me, surprised. Agatha called her parents in Nairobi to ask for permission.

As we walked out of the dormitory, Claire stared at us open-mouthed. There would be questions, questions I would have to answer. My answers, I knew, would be lies.

"Thank you," Agatha said to me quietly in the car. A fat tear swelled from my eye. Agatha had nothing to thank me for. I would be nice to her while we were in London, but things would not change when we were at school. Not if I could help it. She observed me, smiling a sad little smile. Then she turned to look out the window. It was gray and raining. It was always either gray or raining or both.

"Whatever these English people did to deserve this weather," Agatha said, "must have been bad, very bad."

MAINSHOCKS

Rome, Italy, Ages 13 to 14

Earthquake:

a series of vibrations induced in the earth's crust by the abrupt rupture and rebound of rocks in which elastic strain has been slowly accumulating

Note:

"An earthquake like this," Charles Darwin wrote after experiencing a massive earthquake in Chile, "at once destroys the oldest associations; the world, the very emblem of all that is solid, moves beneath our feet like a crust over a fluid; one second of time conveys to the mind a strange idea of insecurity, which hours of reflection would never create."

Minor Aggressions

My father's cancer spread and the delicate harmony in our house de-
teriorated. When he was in the hospital, Anabel and I fought about
everything. Minor aggressions that previously would have ended with
both of us sulking and perhaps not speaking for a few days now ended
in the hurling of vicious insults and heavy objects. We both hurled the
insults; she hurled the objects. To be fair, I wanted her to. I pushed
her until her eyes became wild. I wanted someone else to lose control
so I didn't have to.

One such argument resulted in a lamp flying past my head and
hitting the wall behind me. Its pieces sprayed onto the floor. Anabel
screamed at me to get out, rushing at me fingers first as though she
wanted to claw at my skin.

Running into the hall, I heard the lock click behind me.

I didn't know where to go or what to do. I couldn't go to the hospital to see my father because visiting hours were long over and because
I found it difficult to be there at all anymore. Often, he did not recognize me. I couldn't face the pain he was in. If I asked a friend to let
me stay the night, their parents would have questions. The questions
would embarrass me. So I just wandered about our building—around
the courtyard, up and down the stairs.

It was after midnight when the middle-aged bachelor who lived
on our floor, Antonio, came out of his apartment to put his garbage in

the chute. I was slumped down on the floor in the hall, back against the wall, legs crossed. I was tired. I could hear my sister's voice still pleading with Anabel to let me back in. Anabel said nothing.

"Are you locked out?" Antonio asked me in Italian.

I nodded. He invited me in. I had only been inside his apartment once, to help the elderly woman who used to live there turn on the taps to run herself a bath. That was over a year earlier. A few months later, she either fell or threw herself out of the window and died. The super told me when I was reading in the courtyard. He described the scene in detail—the way her body was mangled, what her skull looked like protruding out of her flesh.

Antonio lived alone, but his apartment still looked like it belonged to an old woman—all lace curtains and little bowls of hard candy. He offered me a glass of white wine, which I thirstily accept. I wondered if he knew how old I was—thirteen. He surely knew about my war with Anabel—the reason for my temporary displacement. The walls were thin. He spoke decent English.

He told me I could sleep in the spare room. I curled up in all my clothes on the very edge of the bed. I didn't get under the covers. The blanket smelled like mothballs and flowers. That was how the old woman smelled on the day I ran her bath.

In the middle of the night, the door creaked open. I pretended to sleep, but the air gained weight as Antonio stood over me. The hum of the apartment grew louder. There was also a humming between my ears. I felt Antonio's hand slide up my shirt and cup my breast lightly.

"No bra," he murmured. I kept my eyes closed and held my breath. He paused a moment before leaving, shutting the door behind him. I counted backward until I fell asleep.

In the morning, I snuck out before Antonio woke. Down the hall, our door had been unlocked. Anabel was at the kitchen table eating a croissant with jam. She stared past me as I walked in.

"Acting out will get you nowhere," she said, still not looking at me. "I will not have it."

I opened my mouth to say something about fear and grief and pain and loss. I considered telling her about Antonio. I wanted her to share my shame.

"Not one word," she warned me. "Don't you dare start."

I said nothing. Something about me, I knew, was no longer true, something about what my body was for. Or, rather, what some men would expect and demand from my body in return for opening a door, for letting me in. It was not the first time those demands had been made. It was the first time I had agreed to them. I had agreed with my silence. Since I had agreed, I told myself I had wanted it.

I spent many more nights in Antonio's spare room. Eventually, I opened my eyes when he snuck in and stood over me. Eventually, he climbed into bed with me. I let him hold me and press himself against me. Sometimes, when he thought I was asleep, he touched himself and his breath quickened. After he finished, he snored, his hand warm on my heart.

Sentinel

My father was in the hospital. The ambulance had come to take him away on a Saturday. The arrival of an ambulance was so much a part of our lives that no one had woken me up to tell me. I stumbled down the stairs for breakfast as usual, half-blind without my glasses, wearing my fuzzy slippers and pajamas.

I was startled by an unfamiliar voice: "*Buongiorno, signorina.*"

I squinted to make out two men carrying a stretcher, the thin body of my worn-out father lying on it.

"Baba?" I asked.

"Good morning," he said.

I couldn't be sure if he said it in reply to my question or if it was a reflex of deeply ingrained politeness. I couldn't tell if he knew that I was me and I didn't want him to go. The tumor in his brain had taken most of his memory.

"We're going to the hospital," said Anabel, emerging from the coat closet. "He had a difficult night," she added as she pulled on her hat.

Every night had been difficult—every night since the doctor told us that the cancer was too aggressive, his body too weak. Sometimes he was himself, just smaller and tired. Other times all he did was stare blankly at the wall, talking to himself quietly in Twi, his native language that none of us, wife or children, could understand.

A month after my father was carried away on a stretcher, a call came in the wee hours of the morning, before the light. My father was not doing well. He was having seizures. We should come right away. In the car, Anabel, Yasmeen, Kwame, and I sat in silence. In those days, between Anabel and me there was silence or fury, and not much in between.

At the hospital, my father was in a coma. We sat with him awhile, listening to his exhales. I went to touch his hand, but Anabel said, "Don't. Let him rest." I was about to argue that he was not resting, he was in a *coma*, but her lip quivered, and her eyes filled with tears. She looked so very young. She must have been only around thirty at the time. I suddenly felt sorry for her, and I put my hand on her shoulder. She looked up at me, surprised.

When we got home, Anabel made us a dinner of spaghetti Bolognese. It had been months since we all sat together at the dinner table, months since she had cooked. We were scavengers, cobbling together meals from old boxes of cereal and heels of bread with butter. We would nod at one another on the way back to our bedrooms with bowls of grapes and sawed-off hunks of salami on pretty flowered plates. Only Kwame had regular feedings. He was placed at the table at seven a.m. and five thirty p.m., in the booster seat he was outgrowing. He ate scrambled eggs and microwaved fish fingers.

Later that night, Yasmeen and I were awake in the darkness of our shared bedroom. We would not sleep because we had to stand sentinel over our father's life. If we did not sleep, we would not wake up without him. This did not make sense, but we did not care.

"What will happen to us?" Yasmeen asked, sitting up in bed.

I did not know the answer, so I got out of bed and sat next to her. She put her head on my shoulder. She was so very frail. Instead of drinking to excess, as I had started to do after I learned of my father's illness, and fighting with Anabel constantly as I did, she had taken to starving herself. I didn't ask her questions about it, just as I didn't ask Anabel questions about the pounding and bellowing sounds that came from her room at night, just as they didn't ask me where I had been when I came home after sunrise. We each had our private grief.

Yasmeen and I stayed up all night, sitting together like that. I don't think we said anything else. What else was there to say? The near empty fridge buzzed. The elevator went up and down. One of the neighbors coughed, hacked, coughed. Kwame stumbled, crying from a bad dream, into Anabel's room. Anabel sang to him. Yasmeen and I blinked and rubbed our eyes and willed the phone not to ring.

For a week, through nights and days, Yasmeen and I struggled to stay awake. We stood sentinel over our father, over our family, over the life we knew we were losing.

My father did not come out of the coma. He died on a Thursday morning. Anabel was with him. Yasmeen, Kwame, and I were at school. At the exact time he died, I was on my way from English to biology. To this day, despite my lack of religion, I believe I felt him leave the earth. I missed a breath, shuddered, stood still for a moment in astonishment, whispered goodbye. Then, I went to one class and another. I heard nothing of what the teachers said, spoke to no one, took no notes. I waited. Two hours later, over the intercom, my name was called.

The Wailing

Downstairs, on the first floor of our duplex apartment, it was hot and smelled like sweat, flowery perfume, and food—pepper soup, fish in palm nut oil, coconut rice. Upstairs, in the guest bathroom, where I hid, the fluorescent lighting added to the calming cold sterility. In here, nothing had changed.

I stole away by pretending I had a headache. Slowly, I walked up the stairs, leaving the ladies to continue their observance. They sat shoulder to shoulder, crammed into our small living room. Four of the eldest, most important ladies were squeezed onto the couch; two large-bottomed ladies perched daintily at the edge of each of the two armchairs; the younger women squatted on the floor or sat on stools dragged in from the kitchen. Mrs. Karamagi, the loudest wailer, sat in my brother's little red plastic chair, her hips spilling over the sides, her knees up by either ear as though to shield them from the sound of her own piercing cries.

The day Baba died, I was summoned to the principal's office. My sister was already there, staring at the floor. A friend's mother had come to pick us up and drive us the hour from school on Via Cassia to our house on Via Laurentina. She offered no explanation, except that Anabel needed us to come home. We knew. Only when we stopped the car did she acknowledge why we were at home at lunchtime on a school day, telling us we would get through it, no matter how impossible it might seem now. She didn't say what "it" was. She didn't have to. We stepped out of the car, through the front door, and right into the wailing, already in session.

Every morning for the past three days, the wailers had arrived as the sun came up—a straight line of women snaking its way from the other side of the park. They wore colorful head wraps on which they balanced their trays of samosas, rice, and stew. I watched them from my bedroom window, marveling at this very common African scene playing out in this unlikeliest of settings: Rome in January. Men on their way for morning espresso stopped in their tracks to observe the exotic procession. Teenagers slowed their Vespas as they rode through the park, helmeted heads swiveling dangerously to get a better look.

The rules of civility required that the whole household be at the door to greet the ladies, to take the trays, to accept the ginger biscuits and condolences. But as soon as I could, I escaped to the quiet coolness of the guest bathroom.

I hated the questions, the concerned looks. Most of all, I hated the wailing. I knew the wailing was customary, that they were doing it out of kindness and tradition. Most of the ladies had barely known my father. In many African cultures, including the Ashanti tribe of Ghana, to which my father belonged, and the Chagga tribe of Tanzania, to which my stepmother belonged, it is believed that, after death, one is rewarded for living a good life by being made an ancestor. If a person is not properly mourned, it may be taken as a sign that he did not do enough to gain the love and respect of those around him. In this case, the dead person may become a ghost who will likely torment the living. There is no greater insult than to have your death ignored.

I wouldn't have minded being haunted by my father's ghost. And the theatricality of the mourning ceremony horrified me. I couldn't grieve, because other people's flamboyant, feigned grief was all around me every second of the day. Only when dusk descended did our guests wipe their faces with flowered handkerchiefs and, their voices hoarse, say goodbye until the next day. By then I was too angry and frustrated to cry.

Once, he had been everywhere in the apartment, whether he was actually home or not. Even before the cancer, before he was constantly in and out of the hospital, he traveled a lot for work. When I missed him, I walked around poking through his things, rediscovering private jokes and familiar rituals. Every corner I turned, I could hear his voice, his gleeful laugh.

An old copy of the *Economist*, lying open on his desk in the study: *Nadia, come and read this article out loud to me. Let's hear what's happening in the world!*

Eggs and Nutella next to each other in the fridge: *Crêpes! Crêpes pour tout le monde aujourd'hui!*

Paul Simon's "Graceland" in the CD player. *Did you hear that line, Nadia? Did you hear it? He is a poet, Paul Simon, a true poet.*

Soon his voice, the faint but steady whisper, was drowned out by the voices of the United Nations African Wives Association. To make matters worse, they had been cleaning nonstop. They picked up every yellowing edition of the *Corriere della Sera* and the *Herald Tribune*; packed the legal pads covered in his scribbles into boxes; polished every surface, wiped away every remaining fingerprint. I was desperate to know I could still find him if I needed him, but with them here, I couldn't poke through his things without attracting attention. And with attention came more well-intentioned, but exasperating, cooing and coddling: Had I eaten? Was I all right? Did I want tea with milk?

On the fourth day after he died, the women did not make their procession across the park. It was the day of the funeral at the American Episcopal Church on Via Nazionale. The house felt strangely still. I had grown accustomed to the crowds, to slipping away from them. I dressed slowly: new black dress; black tights; soft black leather shoes I had only worn once. I preferred my Doc Martens, but Anabel said absolutely not. As I stepped into the drizzly day, it occurred to me that I had barely been outside all week.

The church was full. The ladies, wearing fancier versions of their procession dresses, were dispersed among the crowd. They sat with their husbands—my father's colleagues at the United Nations. Family and friends had flown in from Ghana, Tanzania, England, Germany, the United States, and Canada. I caught myself looking for my mother, hoping in spite of myself that she had changed her mind.

My mother was my only living parent now—I needed her. Two days after my father died, I called her on the phone, my hands shaking. I didn't know what I feared until she told me she couldn't come for the funeral. Arizona was too far from Rome, she said. She said she had responsibilities to another husband, and other children. The last thing I remember her saying was that, down the line, Yasmeen and I could come to Arizona so that we could talk. She did want to talk to us about our future, but she wanted to do it on her terms and on her turf.

Down the line was not now. Now was when I needed her. Talking about our future was not a promise, was not a claiming. My mother's use of the term *my turf* is what my mind focuses on whenever I reflect on that conversation. *My turf* suggests a contest between equals, suggests opposing sides, suggests a winner and a loser. But I wasn't her equal. I was her thirteen-year-old daughter. Her thirteen-year-old daughter whose life had just been blown apart. I wanted her to choose me. I wanted her to be my mother. I wanted her to tell me, unequivocally, that she wanted me. I needed her to tell me what to do. She didn't do any of those things.

My mother left before I was old enough to grasp what the leaving meant. I had never been forced to face the rejection. Now here it was. I cut her off in the middle of her reasons and vowed I would never speak to her again. I hung up and sat in the ebony chair by the phone, panting.

Closing my eyes, I held my breath until my heart no longer raced. I counted my losses and waited for the cold ice of them to melt into tears, but they hardened even more. They frosted and stuck to one another, heavy in my chest. The heaviness made me keep that vow to my mother for over a decade, despite her attempts to reconcile. It made me slow to love people and quick to leave them, to hurt them before they could hurt me.

At the church, my sister and I took our seats in the front row, filing in after Anabel, who cradled Kwame in her arms. He had worn himself out from screaming bloody murder all the way to the church. He was six and didn't understand why we couldn't stop at McDonald's.

The priest gave a sermon, the details of which I do not recall. I was too busy thinking this wasn't at all what Baba would have wanted. He was an atheist and attended church only when Anabel insisted, or when we were in Ghana and my grandmother threatened him. The last time he and I had been in church together was for his friend's baby's baptism. The baby had projectile vomited over his mother's shoulder before he could be handed to the priest to receive his blessing. Baba had clapped his hands once, a giant smile on his face, before he realized what he was doing. He quickly corrected himself before anyone noticed his enjoyment, but he whispered in my ear: "That baby's an independent thinker."

I imagined his ashes blowing in the breeze on his beloved beach in Accra. Instead, they would be placed in concrete at a nearby cemetery. Anabel said we couldn't afford to make the journey to Ghana. I suspected she didn't want to go there because she was engaged in a bitter fight with Baba's family. They had never gotten along. The night before the funeral, Anabel had accused Baba's sister, my aunt Violet, of stealing a framed photograph of Baba from the coffee table. When Baba's father arrived from Ghana without a winter coat, Anabel refused to let him wear one of Baba's. She didn't want *them* taking anything out of the house.

Everyone argued over things they would later throw away. Baba's family wanted us to live with our aunts in England. Anabel argued that, in his last coherent days, Baba had asked her to finish raising us. I was surprised that Anabel wanted us to stay with her. Our relationship had always been a roller coaster. When Baba got sick, we hit a steep dip and plummeted at high speed. Now we were barely speaking, though when we did speak, there was a quality to her voice and a look in her eyes that spoke to a longing I recognized—a longing for nothing else to change. We didn't know how to live without him.

But, if we maintained the world exactly the way he built it, perhaps we could survive.

I had inherited Baba's atheism. Instead of God, Baba was my guiding force. I was afraid I would never believe in anything again. I was afraid until Mrs. Karamagi began to sing.

Father Michael was introducing my father's best friend, who was to deliver the eulogy, when the doors burst open. There stood Mrs. Karamagi. She paused in the doorway as everyone turned to see the source of the interruption. Regarding her audience seriously, she spontaneously began to sing a Swahili hymn, arms reaching for the sky. The only word I could make out was *Mungu*—God. Her shrill voice filled the room. It sounded like a feral cat that had been splashed with cold water. People shifted in their seats, unsure of how they were to react to this impromptu performance. Just as she hit a note so high I was certain the stained-glass windows would shatter, I caught my sister's eye. She smiled, I snorted, and we began to laugh, stifling our giggles in our hands, disguising them as weeping.

Necks craned in our direction. The ladies were eyeballing their fake-crying competition. I pretended to wipe away tears and was surprised to find real ones on my cheeks. Perhaps they were tears of sadness, perhaps of release. I didn't know what would become of me when I walked out of that church. This ceremony marked the end of my life as I had always known it. But in that moment, all that mattered was Mrs. Karamagi's horribly off-key song. My father would have loved it. I heard his laughter one last time.

Homesick

After my father's funeral, my mother did not call. She wrote one letter. Both my name and Yasmeen's were on the envelope. Anabel left it on the kitchen table for us to find. I threw it—unopened—into the trash. I don't think I told Yasmeen about it.

What could my mother possibly have to say? I did not want to know. I still don't. What could be contained in that letter other than another act of jettison? I was not interested in apologies. There was no offer that would make up for what she had declined to offer. She hadn't offered to claim me. She hadn't offered a home.

I was so tired. My thoughts were full of blunt force. They left bruises. They left cracks. I remember thinking I would never again be loved in the absolute way in which a parent loves a child. I remember counting the lives I would have gladly sacrificed to spare my father's life. That list was long. I named names. My mother's name was on that list. I remember thinking how horrible I was for making that list. How horrible I was, how horrible I was, how horrible I was. I spent hours obsessing over my shortcomings. *No wonder your mother didn't want you*, Anabel had once said. In silences, I heard her say it again and again. One night, I jerked awake, hopeful. The man snoring upstairs sounded like my father snoring. Upon realizing it was not my father snoring, that it was not even his ghost, I felt illogical hatred for the man upstairs. I added him to the sacrifice list. He was a nice man. He always said good morning and held the door open for me. He had two daughters.

I would have slept all day had it not been a struggle to fall asleep, to stay asleep. Instead, I went back to school just two days after the funeral. At school, I could hide in routine. With scissors, I cut bullet-like holes in all my jeans. All day, I drank from a water bottle of gin I kept in my backpack. In class, I took careful notes and answered questions correctly. At lunch, I rehearsed for the school play and gossiped with my girlfriends. Sometimes, the gossip on my tongue was bitter. I was cruel, crueler than I had been before my father died. I targeted girls whose families seemed happy. Girls who seemed light and optimistic. Vapid, I called them, and desperate to be liked. It was jealousy. My girlfriends laughed at my new meanness. I declined invitations to sleepovers and birthday parties. I didn't want to hear the casual laughter, to see the intimacy of other families. I practiced laughing in the mirror. Laughter no longer came naturally.

At school, I maintained good grades. To teachers and classmates, I assume I seemed largely unchanged, except for the bullet jeans, except for the bitter tongue. No one asked me about grief. No one smelled the gin. I chewed pink bubble gum.

At night, I stayed up shaking. Alone, my heart raced. My breath gathered speed. I could not slow it. My breath felt like smoke rising from fire, like sickness, like rage. My rage was silent. It was secret. I shook with it. I sat on the windowsill where I could feel the outdoor air and watch the moon be still. I remember many nights of rain. My father wasn't coming back. My mother wasn't coming.

My family would soon pack our old life into crates, move someplace smaller. Anabel was looking for a new apartment. There was no place I wanted to be except in my father's study, with him, before the tumor. Without him, I felt homeless. I had thanked my aunts for the offer of a home with them in London. I told them I wanted to stay where I was, with Anabel. When Anabel and I fought, the thought of Auntie Harriet's familiar apartment did entice me. She would make me jollof rice and fried chicken. Her voice was warm. It calmed me, slowed my breath. I could share a room with my cousin Laura, who had shelves full of *Sweet Valley High* books. We'd lie in bed listening to R&B: Shai and Mary J. Blige. My father's cousin had also invited me and Yasmeen to move in with him in Canada. "Your father was like my brother," he said. "You are like my daughters." Having only met him twice, the second time at my father's funeral, I was touched by his kindness. But I couldn't be certain I wouldn't be a burden to my father's family. Nobody was wealthy. My father's cousin was a truck driver and had a wife and three children. Auntie Harriet often worked double shifts as a nurse. Yasmeen and I would be two more open mouths. At least Anabel received my father's pension and life insurance. And I was used to feeling like a burden to her. Besides, I was too tired to start anew. I was too tired for exigencies.

Leaving Rome would mean a fuss. It would require the making of a case, the articulation of motive. It would require an indictment. People would have questions: my father's friends and colleagues, Anabel's family. I would have to tell them about how Anabel and I fought; about how afraid I was of her anger.

I didn't want to tell anyone about my anger; about how I poured gin onto the fire of it in the day and breathed out the smoke of it at night. Then I poured more gin onto the fire. I sweated. I shook. I rattled around the apartment in my nightgown until Anabel came out of her bedroom and asked me to be quiet. I sneered at her, swatted at her with my eyes until she snapped. I didn't want to confess any of this to anyone. I didn't want to betray what was left of my family.

If I left Anabel, it would be, I knew, the end of us as mother and daughter. She would never forgive me. Despite our anger, our fights, we reached for each other in the dark. Once, when I had plans to sleep over at a friend's house, Yasmeen called me and asked me to come home.

"Anabel is crying," she said. "She keeps saying she wants her Nadia." *Her Nadia.* I went to her. We sat on the couch, side by side, in silence, in the dark. I touched her sleeve and she turned to face me and nodded, just nodded, eyes full.

Sometimes, when Anabel went out with her friends, I waited up until I heard her key in the door. She was mine too.

And what about Kwame? Yasmeen would go with me wherever I

went, but not him. He was unquestionably Anabel's child. But he was also my baby brother and I loved him. When we walked to the school bus together every morning, he would take my hand in his little hand. He'd look up at me with those big wet eyes of his. On the bus, he was a terror. He got in fights with other kids, and I'd have to yank him out of his seat and hold him in my lap while he kicked his legs and screamed. He pinched and bit. He was angry too. But his hand in mine was so small and soft. I felt responsible for him and for Yasmeen. I wanted to keep us together. It was what my father had wanted, I knew. So I chose to stay where I was. I chose ongoingness.

We soon moved to a new apartment that was just ten minutes away from where we lived when my father was alive. Sometimes I'd walk over to the old place and sit on a big rock at the edge of the park across the street and stare into the darkened windows.

For a month, the apartment was empty. I could imagine myself back inside. I imagined turning on the lights in the living room. There was my father in the rocking chair, scotch on the side table next to him. His eyes were closed. On the CD player, Miles Davis blew his horn: *Autumn Leaves*. My father's fingers tapped the bass line on the chair's arm. Anabel lay on the daybed by the window with Kwame on her belly. They slept sound, easy. Yasmeen and I played checkers on the rug.

I always sat on that rock long enough so that my face and feet began to sting from the cold. Then, one day, a light did turn on inside. A woman stood in the living room window. Behind her were piled-high cardboard boxes. She was moving in. She would make a new home. I didn't stay to see if there were others with her: a husband, children. It would be impossible, I knew, to find my family there again. That apartment had been my home only because it had contained us: my father, Anabel, Yasmeen, Kwame, and me. In that apartment, we were whole. We were five. When we left, we were four. Homesick, I walked slowly across the park. My temporary footprints trailed behind me in the mud.

FAULTS

Fault:

any division or rift that is perceived as inevitably leading to con-
frontation

Note:

The rocks on either side of a geological fault move past each
other, causing friction, but they do not pull apart.

Failures of Language

I do not have my great-grandfather's worn but carefully pressed cotton handkerchief. My father's family aren't much for holding on to material things. I do not have my maternal great-grandmother's red hair or my paternal grandfather's coffee bean skin. *What an unusual combination*, people often say when I describe my parentage: Ghanaian, Armenian. And more than once: *How did that even happen?*

I speak three and a half languages that do not belong to me, that do not run through my veins: English, Italian, and French, decent Swahili. When my relatives and country-people maneuver between English and their home languages—Twi, Armenian, and Turkish—I grip the ropes of the English words as firmly as my jittery hands will allow and loop them into knots. I watch for cocked eyebrows and pursed lips to translate the rest. The warm, round, percussion of Twi and the orderly harmony of Turkish (which, spoken by my family, is diluted with a splash of archaic Armenian and a heavy pour of Boston accent) are familiar but impenetrable. I can spot members of my two disparate tribes in a crowd, but I cannot address them except in basic greeting and pleasantry: *Good morning. How are you? Welcome.*

In Twi, I can also say *even the elephant can swat flies with its short tail* and *any river loses its identity when entering the sea*. My father, when his intention was to remind or chastise, was fond of proverbs and folktales. The heroes of those tales were animals of the forests, spirits, and gods. I know them by name.

My Ghanaian relatives are at times tickled by my inability to speak Twi. At other times, they are affronted. "How can you not speak your own language?" they ask, not acknowledging that my learning it would have required them to teach me. Once, when I was in the market with an auntie—I cannot remember which one—a woman asked why no one had taught me to speak my father tongue.

"Nobody wants to hear her speaking Twi in an American accent," the auntie replied. Since she replied in English, I can only assume she meant for me to understand.

In Twi, I cannot say *love me, accept me, I need you, please don't die*.

In Turkish, I know the words for eggplant, yogurt, and savory pastries. The stories of my mother's family are very much concerned with food: what was served, whose dish was tastiest, and (delicious gossip) who messed up the baklava. As a child, when I visited them in Massachusetts, we talked about eggplant, *losh kebab*, and pilaf with little chopped up noodles in it. We planned for dinner as we washed lunch dishes. We ate to remember those who escaped genocide and nearly starved in the desert, to honor what they made possible for us. My grandmother taught me to roll rice and lamb into grape leaves. My mother read to me from *One Thousand and One Nights*. Ali Baba said, "open sesame," and discovered a stolen treasure. A genie emerged from a lamp to do Aladdin's bidding. Scheherazade told tales to a king to delay her own execution. "Another one," I said to my mother after each story. "Tell me another one."

I do not know the Turkish word for *stay*. I cannot say *Mama, come back*.

In Armenian—the language largely lost to my mother's family generations ago at the hands of the Ottoman Empire—the only word I know is the word for underwear: *vardig*. This knowledge I cannot explain.

When I encounter strangers from my tribes, they are startled by my attempts to communicate. They do not recognize me as one of their own. They laugh, charmed and perhaps a little disturbed by the discrepancy between appearance and sound. When I explain myself, they think me a curious hybrid. They speak to me, always, in English.

Fault Zone Voice

As far as I know, only one home movie exists of me as a child. To my ears, the voice in it, but for the accent, is clearly mine—the pitch, the tone, the timbre, the too-long pauses between thoughts. Yet when I was in my mid-twenties and I showed the video to my then-boyfriend George, he exclaimed, "I can't believe that's you." His eyebrows rose into sharp mountain peaks. He couldn't get past the fact that the voice coming out of the mouth of the six-year-old version of me—the bony, bespectacled girl wearing the green pinafore and red kneesocks of my school uniform—was British.

For four years, from age twenty-four to twenty-eight, I believed George was the love of my life. I believed we'd make a home. In some ways, our home would be my first since my father died. I heard the possibility of a home in George's voice: ease, warmth, belonging, permanence.

My British voice was quite posh but with the North West London tick of saying *yeah* with an implied question mark after nearly every sentence: "Auntie Harriet's not here, yeah? She's on night shifts." "My dad's in Bangladesh, yeah? He'll pick me up in August."

George only knew my current, standard American voice—the one that has more than once been described as sounding like an evening news anchor's; a white American evening news anchor's.

George is American, white, and from a wealthy, largely homogeneous neighborhood of Long Island, New York. His accent is flat, his voice stable. He liked categories and frameworks. He liked order and linearity. Cause led to effect. Action led to reaction. When we argued, he often called my claims and conclusions groundless, illogical, and contradictory. That my ground was different—was less constant, was wilder—than his ground was not something he was willing or equipped to consider. He understood the world through analytic deduction. I leaned more heavily on a more corporeal form of knowing. But citing my feelings in an argument was met with immediate dismissal. "That's an emotional argument," George would say. Emotional arguments, in his mind, were unhelpful and even manipulative. Once, near tears, I said I suspected I was having a hard time finding a job at least in part because hiring managers, even those who worked for nonprofits with social justice missions, were more comfortable hiring white people. He demanded to know what was said that made me feel that way. I said everyone sounded so enthusiastic about me on the phone, but their eyes darted about, and their heads dropped when I arrived for in-person interviews, hair braided, skin brown. From my voice on the phone, I believed they had assumed I was white. Everyone thinks my first name belongs to them: Italians, Russians, Persians, Indians. My surname is confusing to Americans. It has been mistaken for Scandinavian, Romanian, Japanese.

"Evidence!" George said. "What's the evidence? It seems to me that someone working for that kind of nonprofit would want to hire a person of color." My voice, that day, he said, sounded girlish and whiny. Not like me.

"Stop talking like that," George said. "It's not going to help you get a job."

Contradiction, to me, spoke to the existence of context and complexity, and beyond that, to the reality that, no matter how much we know, there is much that cannot be known. The universe, the earth, our bodies, are ever changing. What is real in us might not be real, might not be who we are, tomorrow. We might be one person in our houses and another person at our neighbor's house down the road. For some of us, this is also true of our voices. But, to George, contradiction in an argument, discontinuity in a voice, signaled laziness, dishonesty. It was grounds to assume moral failure.

Zadie Smith, who is biracial and British, and from North West London, opens her essay "Speaking in Tongues" with this greeting: "Hello. This voice I speak with these days, this English voice with its rounded vowels and consonants in more or less the right place—this is not the voice of my childhood. I picked it up in college, along with the unabridged *Clarissa* and a taste for port." She goes on to argue that, in Western culture, "we feel that our voices are who we are, and that to have more than one, or to use different versions of a voice for different occasions, represents, at best, a Janus-faced duplicity, and at worst, the loss of our very souls." It is no wonder, then, that people like her, people like me, are often portrayed in books and films, from *Pygmalion* to *To Kill a Mockingbird* to Fannie Hurst's *Imitation of Life,* as unlucky or deceitful.

I hadn't told George that I had used a few other accents—voices— before settling into my current one. I hadn't wanted to tell him my voice is a fault zone, that it is really multiple voices that grate against one another. I didn't think he'd like that about me. It would, I believed, lead him to wonder if my voice—the voice that told him I loved him—was to be trusted.

———

After my mother left, my father tried for a time to take care of Yasmeen and me on his own. But he had to travel a great deal and didn't want to leave us with nannies. So when I was three and Yasmeen was two, we were sent to live with our aunt Harriet in Hailsham, England. We lived in Hailsham for two and a half years, until my father and Anabel got engaged.

Of my time in Hailsham, I remember that I was one of very few black children at the independent school (what is called a private school in America) in town. And for some reason unknown to me— perhaps an administrative glitch, uncorrected—I was the only girl in my class. I remember that we called our next-door neighbors Auntie

Lily and Uncle Ernie. They were a kind retired white couple with fluffy gray hair and a beautiful garden of pink and yellow roses. They babysat for my cousin Laura, Yasmeen, and me when Auntie Harriet worked night shifts. Auntie Lily read to us and Uncle Ernie taught us to tend to the roses. The man who owned a local Chinese restaurant also babysat for us sometimes. We called him Uncle Chang. Chang was his last name. I cannot remember his first. He let us eat all the noodles and dumplings we wanted. He sounded British, not Chinese. He was both. Once, I asked him if he spoke Chinese. He did, he said, and offered to teach me. I said yes, but I was only being polite. Speaking Chinese would make me stand out. I already knew it was best, in some places and with some people, to conceal rather than to cultivate my vocal complications. I remember that everyone at school liked the boy with Pakistani parents whose name was Neil. He didn't have a Pakistani accent. I remember some of his friends making fun of the Indian man who owned the sweet shop near school. He wore a turban and turned his v's into w's.

Race matters in England. So too does class. So too does voice. My race was what it was. It could not be changed. Class was not something I intellectually understood yet. But I understood there were "right" voices and "wrong" voices. I understood this had something to do with the value of whiteness and also of houses. People who lived in the biggest houses were said to be posh, and their voices were to be respected and minded.

I remember wondering why Yasmeen and I were the only children we knew who didn't live with our parents. We came home to Auntie Lily and Uncle Ernie or to Uncle Chang. I loved Auntie Harriet. I sometimes called her Mummy. But I wanted to be like everybody else. Living with her instead of with my father and mother made me different.

I remember imitating the voice of my best friend Jenny. We were in the same after-school ballet program, and although we were in different classrooms at school, we were in the same year, so we found each other in the playground at morning break and in the cafeteria at lunch. She had long, curly blondish hair and rosy red cheeks. Mornings, she was often dropped off by both her parents. They would each hold one of her hands and swing her forward and backward as she squealed with delight. I saw the way they looked at Jenny. I saw the way other adults looked at Jenny: like she was something precious. "She's a proper English rose," one teacher said. I wanted to be loved like Jenny. I understood enough about England to know I would never be a proper English rose. White English people could say they were English, but black and brown people called themselves British, even if they were born and raised in England, even if their parents and their parents' parents were born and raised in England. I asked Auntie Harriet why that was. She said, "Because black people aren't English," which wasn't an answer, but the finality in her voice told me it was all I was going to get. But if I couldn't be a rose, perhaps I could be some other type of equally charming flower. Jenny had a bit of a lisp and bad year-round allergies. She sounded like her nose was blocked. I tried on the lisp and the blocked nose, but when my father came to visit, he told Auntie Harriet she should take me to a doctor to see why I was lisping. "Maybe something's going on with her teeth," he said. I didn't like doctors. I dropped the lisp stat.

When I was five, we moved in with my father and Anabel in Rome. By the time I was seven, I spoke fluent Italian. By age nine, I was also conversant in French (language immersion classes twice a week after school) and able to get the gist of eavesdropped family gossip in Swahili (Tanzanian stepmother). As we moved from Europe to Africa and back again, my accent zigzagged between British and the hard-to-codify accent of children who attend international schools. The yeah/question mark was copied from my cousins (the children of my father's three sisters who all eventually planted roots in London). I spent many Christmas and summer holidays with them in Kingsbury, a working-class neighborhood in North West London that is predominantly West African, Caribbean, and East Asian. It is a neighborhood populated by people with fault zone voices. The people I knew in Kingsbury, my family included, switched back and forth between *proper* English at work and something more cockney-leaning among friends. They spoke a few words of Urdu to the halal butcher and nodded *All right?* to the Liverpudlian man who owned the fish and chip shop; Nigerian pidgin was for the cabdriver and Jamaican slang for the Rastafarian family who lived next door.

In Kingsbury, it was not the color of my skin that made me stand out, but my experiences that were outside of the realm of financial possibility for most of my neighbors. The UN agency paid my father a modest middle-class salary, but there were many perks. My international school tuition was covered. When we were in Africa, we had a driver and live-in maids and gardeners who cleaned our house, cooked our meals, and kept our lawns green and growing year-round. We took vacations in Switzerland and France. I had been on safari, and to Disney World, twice. At first, I mentioned these things casually to the children I ran around with in the playground of the council housing estate where my aunts and cousins lived. I did not realize there was anything unusual about my experiences. As I talked, I noticed that my friends' eyes widened with confusion or squinted with suspicion. Once, I complained extravagantly that someone had taken a piss in the elevator, and my friend Ernest told me to get over myself. He asked if I thought I was better than him. I did not think I thought that, but I was abashed by the question. My solution was not to examine my entitlement and insensitivity but rather to hide from scrutiny. When I met new playmates, I neglected to mention I was visiting for the summer, that I lived in Italy. I told white lies. I claimed my cousin Laura's school as my own. I started saying *innit* instead of *isn't it*. I started saying *yeah/question mark*.

———

After George saw the home movie of me speaking in a British accent, he quizzed me: "What accent did you have when you said your first words?" (Vaguely African of indeterminate origins, I am told—likely a blend of my father's and my Somali nanny's.) "How long did you have a British accent?" (Ten years, give or take.) "What kind of accent did your father have?" (Upper-class Ghanaian, so British-influenced, but peppered with American colloquialisms and inflections from his time in college and graduate school in the U.S.) "Your mother?" (She started out with a thick Boston one, but later adopted a voice that pulls from her Armenian ancestry and her time spent married to my father and then to a man from Somalia. I have, hypocritically, made fun of her fault zone accent, calling it affected.) "Did you change your accent on purpose?" (It wasn't a fully conscious decision, but it wasn't completely without effort either.) "When it changed, did it change who you are in some fundamental way?" (Almost certainly, yes. Our voices, I think, are not just the vehicle through which we express ourselves, but also affect how we process and translate the world, how our dreams are made.) "Did changing accents ever feel confusing?" (Not really. Only because of other people's reactions. Many people of color I know code switch.)

Code-switching is dancing between vocal styles and rhythms. This dance is part celebration—of the richness, intricacies, and blurry borders of our cultures. For example, there are more than two hundred and fifty languages and dialects spoken in Ghana. Many people speak multiple. They might speak Twi with their parents, Ga with their friends, and English at school. They might speak English with an English accent to a white tourist and pidgin with their lover. And this dance is also part survival mechanism. Just as there is pressure in our largely white-colonized and white-dominated world, with white rules, to look whiter, there is also pressure to sound whiter. Adopting a "white" voice and "white" language is often required to access schools, jobs, and services. I have heard brilliant black colleagues with black voices be described by white higher-ups as *unpolished*. White people, to avoid accusation of bias, often speak in code. People of color must learn those codes. We can translate them: "By unpolished, do you mean black?" But we do so at our own risk. Whiteness can rebuke, revoke, exile, largely with little consequence to the white people wielding its power. And its power need not be named. "She was just too angry. Bad for the culture. Unproductive," they will say as they close your personnel file and post a job description to replace you, making sure to note that diverse candidates are welcome to apply. We can name whiteness and call it out, and face the consequences, or we can sit on our hands, bite our tongues, watch our grammar and enunciation. Sometimes white people are so blinded by whiteness they do not even know, or can't imagine they do not know, what pain they inflict by exerting it.

People of color know that not all of the safety and spoils of whiteness are available to us. Yet we can speak in the voice of whiteness if we so choose. Some of us know no other voice. It was born in us. It is the voice colonization left us. Some of us adopt it later—in childhood or early adulthood—and lose our other voices. Some of us never allow whiteness into our throats. Some of us code-switch. I am a code-switcher.

After George learned of my British voice, he would occasionally ask me to speak in it, and sometimes (for laughs or to see if it would get me special attention at a nice restaurant) I did. He would laugh, but later, when we were alone in bed, he seemed to withdraw from me.

I can still access my English voice. In fact, I am sheepish to admit that I used it when I first moved to America, long after it was no longer my default. I felt lonely. I was lost, in the spiritual sense, but also, often, in the literal sense. I found that new classmates and strangers I asked for directions were more open to me if my voice sounded like I was from somewhere else. My English voice is not, however, the voice I dream in. In my dreams, I speak only in an American accent.

I have made my home, for all my adult life, in New York. Now, when I am in Kingsbury or Dar es Salaam, I am a visitor. I can speak like the locals, but I often choose not to. I stick to American English. I have been shamed for code-switching: by an old roommate who said it was the same as lying, by a colleague who called it appropriation. People relish the opportunity to catch you in a stutter or mispronunciation. I have, on occasion—when I was wavering between British and American, or when I was tired and something in my brain reverted and caused me to place a heavy emphasis on my t's—been accused of *faking* an accent. And I have lost count of the number of times that people, black and white, have told me I *sound white*. To some African Americans, this makes me suspect. Telling them I am Ghanaian only further confuses the matter. *Isn't that in Africa? You don't look or sound African.* This, of course, is not true. There are many Africans who look and sound like me. Sometimes I explain this. Sometimes I let it go lest I sound defensive. I don't want people to think I mind being mistaken for African American. I don't. There are, however, many African immigrants in America who, to climb the social ladder, resist being categorized, by white people, with African Americans. Some even go so far as to claim superiority. This is not surprising. In America, the racial hierarchy has white at the top and black on the bottom. *We're not that kind of black*, I have heard a member of my own family—an uncle—argue when a white person leveled a racist insult against him. Given this, it is also not surprising that there exists some animosity between the African immigrant and African-American communities. And I have been told by white people that I am *articulate* or *well-spoken*. They often follow this up with something to the effect of *I don't see you as black*. This, to me, makes them suspect. It makes them dangerous. They mean it as a compliment. It is an invitation with bloody strings attached.

Someday, a fault zone voice might be seen as a wonder. Code-switching might be seen as an act of empathy, might be universally seen as joyous, as divisions made into love. Someday my voice might be free. But today is not that day.

"I love you," I said to George in my American voice. He said he loved me too. But, he never really heard me, not all of me.

Queen

1. Dar es Salaam, Tanzania, Age 8 Months

A lovely young woman gets off a plane in Dar es Salaam. She is my mother. Her thick dark hair is pulled back in a loose bun. Tendrils frame her face. Her olive skin is paler than it was when she left. She is coming home from home. Meaning that Dar is her home now, but she has been to visit her parents in Massachusetts, where she was born and raised. She wanted them to meet her baby daughter.

My mother has a giant suitcase full of new clothes for herself and my father and mostly for her baby, her baby girl whose very name— Nadia—means "delicate," "tender." That baby is me.

My mother also has a box of books: novels for reading under the mango tree in the garden and under an umbrella on Oyster Beach. Nadia is tethered to her chest with a *kanga*. *Japo kidogo chatosha kwa wapendanao*, it says on the hem: "A little is enough for those in love." And she is—oh she is—so very in love with her firstborn, her husband, this magical place. She feels she is in a dream. Perhaps it is only the heat, or perhaps it is that everyone is smiling at her. She hardly notices how hard it is to lug her suitcase, box, and baby off the plane, onto the tarmac, and through the double doors; into the chaos of arrivals. She shines despite the weight.

My mother sets down the suitcase and the box and untethers her baby. A porter drops a white man's suitcase and runs to assist her.

"That," he says, "is a beautiful baby." And he picks up my mother's suitcase and the box. He awaits her orders. Even the white man who has lost his porter nods in agreement.

"Just over there," the woman says, spotting her husband—my father—in the crowd. In his hands are a red balloon and a piece of cardboard that says *karibu*: "welcome."

"Half-caste babies," says the porter, noting the woman's husband's black skin, "are always the most beautiful. Your baby's name should be Malaika. It means 'angel.'"

2. Addis Ababa, Ethiopia, Age 9

Picture a little black girl: Four braids held together with shea butter and bobbled elastic bands. Skin massaged with baby lotion. Blue glasses with a blue string attached in case she tries to take them off. She is wearing a pink leotard and a pink tutu. On her feet are dirty white tennis shoes with red stripes. Her father, walking just two steps in front of her, is carrying her ballet bag. In it are soft pink slippers and a Care Bear canteen of black currant syrup diluted with water. The little black girl you are picturing is me.

The little black girl is skipping. She is happy. She feels safe. The tanks parked by the side of the road are not her concern, nor are the uniformed soldiers walking in pairs. They swing their weapons. She skips to ballet lessons at the United Nations.

Suddenly the ground opens beneath her. She falls into darkness, a dark hole, a deep dark hole. She lands crouched. The ground is damp and squidgy under her hands and feet. She screams. Where is she? She screams for her father. She has disappeared into a place where she cannot be seen. Even in her favorite pink leotard and pink tutu, she cannot be seen. Her father calls her name. *Nadia? Nadia? Nadia?* His voice is desperate.

Something is lowered into the deep dark hole. It pokes her scalp, between her braids. She reaches up and grips it and is lifted out into the hazy afternoon. She looks up into the eyes of a soldier. He smiles and his teeth are rotten. Her feet dangle above the ground. She is holding onto the stock of a rifle. Her father grabs her.

"You disappeared," he says, breathless. "You disappeared."

The little girl starts to cry.

"Don't cry," says the soldier. "You are beautiful." He reaches out and touches her face.

Her father grabs her hand, yanks her hard, away.

"Thank you, sir," he says, but he doesn't sound like he means it.

The little girl does not stop crying. She does not care that the soldier finds her beautiful. She knows now that she can be made invisible.

3. Rome, Italy, Age 12

In a park, in mud, behind green bushes, there is a white man holding a red Swiss Army knife to a twelve-year-old black girl's throat. The black girl is me. She wears a tracksuit and soccer cleats. From where she lies, she can see the roof of the apartment building where she lives.

"Don't scream. You whore, you dirty black whore," the white man says in Italian to the black girl.

Knife still in hand, the man grips the girl's wrists and rubs his hardness against her. He pulls down her pants and shoves his dirty fingers into her cotton panties, shoves his fingers inside her.

The thunder in the distance is like a too-late warning. The sky spits. The man licks the girl's neck.

"Mmmm, you taste like chocolate," the man says as he sits up straddling her. He unzips his pants.

"Look at it," he says. "Look at my cock. My big white cock. Tell me you love it." He touches the point of the knife to the fleshy part under the girl's chin.

"I love it," the girl says. She can hear, close by, the sound of children's laughter. The sound moves toward them. A woman's voice calls out, says, "Wait, my loves, wait."

The man twists his neck to see if he can be seen by the woman.

The girl senses his fear, his weakness. She gathers all the fight she has, propels herself up to seated. Her face is so close to his face that his breath enters her nostrils. She grabs his throat and squeezes. He grabs her throat and squeezes. A little white girl screams. Her mother screams her name. The white man releases the black girl's throat. He stands, runs, trips, runs, curses, runs.

The black girl jumps up, runs home as fast as she can.

"Where have you been?" her stepmother asks. "We have been frantic. Your father is sick. You cannot worry him like this."

"I'm sorry," the girl says.

In the bathroom, she takes off her clothes and stares at her body in the mirror. She tries to see herself, but she can only see her body through the eyes of the white man in the park. Her body, through his eyes, disgusts her.

The girl wonders if she has ever really seen her body through her own eyes. She cannot remember. She can remember what she has been told: angel, beautiful, dirty black whore.

"Me," she says to her body in the mirror every day for years. "Mine," she says, and "I." She repeats *me, mine, I* until, finally, she catches a glimpse of her body that seems unfiltered. She learns, gradually, to shift her focus, to find her true reflection. Seeing herself in this way requires intention. It is not always possible.

4. Kampala, Uganda, Age 16

The women at Al's Bar wore very tight, very short dresses. They had long blond or red weaves. Their faces were smooth and shiny with foundation that was at least two shades lighter than their skin. Thick lips were painted red and pink. Restless eyes were heavy with liner and caked-on mascara. Some of the women, I could tell, were very beautiful beneath their masks. They slithered and wiggled between the middle-aged white men who chased swigs of Tusker's beer with shots of tequila. The men bought shots for the women and made a big show of demonstrating how to pour salt on the webs between their thumbs and forefingers. They licked the salt, downed the shots, bit down on lime slices, grabbed the women's asses, pumped their fists in the air.

Rob looked delighted by the scene. He had only been in Uganda for three weeks. He was an American Marine, here to guard the embassy. I met him at the Sheraton Hotel. I was at the pool with a group of girls from the international school where I was a junior. We had grown tired of swimming and were lying around in the sun in our bikinis. We ordered rum and Cokes and pizzas from the waiters who wore crisp white shirts and stiff khaki shorts. They called us *Madam*. They did not ask if we were old enough to drink. At sixteen, we were not. Our wallets were crammed with our parents' money. That money was too good for the waiters to pass up, even if it meant dealing with a bunch of bratty teenagers. We smoked weed on the terraces of restaurants. We got wasted and threw up in flower pots in hotel gardens.

Rob, when I met him, was eating lunch by the pool with fellow Marines. He stared at me all afternoon. He had light brown eyes that made him look like he was laughing even when he wasn't. He was twenty-six and from Georgia. When he asked my age, I told the truth. He didn't seem to care. He called me Dorothy, told me I looked like Dorothy Dandridge. I didn't know who she was, but he assured me she was beautiful. He was into old films and exotic women, he said. I told him this was Africa and he was the exotic one. He invited me to the Marine House to watch *Island in the Sun*. They had a projector. When I arrived, the other guys made themselves scarce.

Rob spread out a blanket on the floor of the living room. We took turns swigging from a bottle of waragi—the cheap Ugandan liquor that tastes how nail polish remover smells. We didn't watch much of the movie. His mouth tasted like raw onions when we kissed. He had chopped some to put in the ground meat he ate for dinner with white bread. I lied and said I had already eaten. While Rob ate, his dog barked.

On the living room floor, Rob tried to put his hands up my shirt, down my pants, but I gripped his wrists tight. At midnight, I writhed out from under him. He was snoring and it was past my curfew.

The next night, Rob invited me to come over again, but I wanted to go out. All my friends from school would be at Al's Bar. Anabel was out of town. This meant I had been left home alone with no supervision except for the house girl who never asked any questions except if I needed a packed lunch for school and if roast beef would do for dinner. At first, Rob didn't want to go to the bar. He was scared someone might see him. I told him not to worry. Al's Bar was where expats went to pick up *malayas*. Rob and I didn't talk about why he didn't want to be seen with me. Neither of us said the word *underage*.

"What's a *malaya*?" Rob asked.

"A hooker," I said.

"Oh, okay, so no one will be paying attention to us, then."

At the bar, my friends were drunk. Some of the guys from school were playing darts. Some of the girls were dancing on the outdoor dance floor, their bodies sweaty in the yellow light of the street lamps. I would join them after I got some alcohol in me, I thought. Rob ordered us vodka tonics while I watched the *malayas* and the men with whom they would soon get into Jeeps and BMWs. Soon they would disappear into the night, some driving to nearby hotels, others slipping the night watchman in the parking lot a little something to turn a blind eye to what they did in the backseat.

Reggae filled the air. Reggae is perfect for provocative swaying, for hip shaking, for thrusting pelvis into pelvis. Reggae is prelude-to-sex music.

Across the bar, a man who looked about sixty, with white hair and a ruddy red face that suggested a lifetime of drunken nights, stroked the very large breasts of a very tall *malaya*. She whispered something in his ear, and he tweaked her nipple.

I was about to tell Rob to check out the nipple tweaking, when I noticed one of the *malayas* observing me. She was tall and thin but with juicy hips and thighs. Her curly light brown weave fell past her shoulder blades. I stared back at her. Just as Rob handed me my drink, she sidled up to us.

"Hello, sir," she said to Rob.

"Oh, no thank you," said Rob, assuming he was being proposi-
tioned.

"This young girl," said the *malaya*, "shouldn't be here."

"I'm eighteen," I lied, sipping my drink.

The *malaya* dragged her long glitter-polished nails up Rob's arm.
She looked at me as she did this. Her face was round and soft, but her
voice was gritty and hard.

"Are you sure about her?" she asked Rob. "It's foolish to bring porridge to a bar."

Rob laughed and put his arm around my waist.

"I like porridge," he said.

I downed the rest of my drink and took Rob's hand, dragging him
out to the dance floor. The *malaya* was still watching me so I pulled
Rob in and kissed him. I swayed and shook and thrust myself against
him. When he went to get us more drinks, I replaced his body with
that of one of my girlfriends. He came back out and stood watching
us, two glasses of vodka in his hands. I grabbed my friend's face and
brushed my lips to hers. I closed my eyes when I did this, and when I
opened them, Rob reached for my hand.

"You're incredible," he said as he sucked on my neck.

When Rob and I left Al's Bar that night, I glanced over at the *malaya* who had called me porridge. She sat alone, downed a shot. Almost
everyone else was paired up. To all the men in the process of conquest,
she was invisible. We locked eyes. Her face held no expression. I think
I saw her shrug, but I could be wrong about that.

In the taxi back to the Marine House, I let Rob put his finger inside me. I opened my legs wide and put his finger where I wanted it. I
felt powerful. I felt like I had won something. I liked how Rob looked
at me when I came, crying out, not caring that the taxi driver could
hear me. He looked at me like he couldn't believe his luck. It did not
feel creepy, not even that night when I lost my virginity to him on his
top bunk with the dog howling at us from below. It did not feel creepy
until years later when I realized just how young I had been and just
what Rob might have meant when he said he liked porridge.

"Dorothy's story was tragic," Rob said, lying next to my sixteen-year-old naked body. "She was fragile. The world broke her. That won't happen to you. You're tough." After he said that, he laughed.

5. New York, New York, Age 25

"All the black men who don't have wives at our age either have babies or white girlfriends," my friend Toya complained. The guy she had spent an hour talking to at the bar had a fianceé and two kids and had done time for possession of a controlled substance. "Fuck the war on drugs," he said, and we agreed, but that didn't mean Toya was going home with him. We decided to call it a night. The bar was too crowded and too loud, and Toya was now in a bad mood.

Outside, I waited for Toya, who had gone to the bathroom. Across the street, three cops led a line of men, chained together at the ankles, to Central Booking. All the chained men were black. One of them stared at me. He looked like he might say something, but he didn't. He turned his head back toward the inevitable.

I bounced up and down a little to keep myself warm. Toya was taking forever. I wanted to go home to lie in bed with a book of poetry.

"Black women," Toya said as I walked her to the subway, "are the meatloaf at a Greek diner. People sometimes talk about ordering it, but everyone's surprised when someone does, even black men. At least you're light-skinned."

"Hey, *mami*," a man said, sticking his head out of a car. "Yeah, you, *morenita*." He flicked his tongue in and out of his mouth. Getting no reaction, he tried another tack. "You're beautiful," he said. "Beautiful black queen."

Toya and I held up our middle fingers, held them up for a good long time. We held them up at him, and at all of them: all the men who had tried to take our bodies and our names and sell them back to us for less. When we said good night, we hugged fiercely. She smelled like jasmine and palo santo.

"Love you, Toya," I said.

"Love you, Nadia," she said.

My name came out of her mouth and hung, condensed, in the cold air. My name from her mouth was hot and potent. It was visible. As I walked away from her, I said my own name quietly. I watched it take shape.

THE BLUE CHAIR

New York, New York, Age 28

Day Three

I am shipwrecked on a blue chair island. It rises, just barely, above sea level. It is a small pyramid of jagged rock, formed from collision, subduction, eruption. A volcano grew on the ocean floor, magma flowed and became lava. It solidified in salt water. Gasping for air, I washed up onto it.

I wonder if this rock is hospitable. A two-inch cockroach skitters across the floor. It stops and waves its antennae, detecting sound. Or is it smell it senses? Does it know I'm here?

In the next room, my roommate is on the phone. Earlier, he knocked and asked if I wanted pizza. I did not respond, and he gave up. I wonder what he thinks I'm doing in here, why he thinks I don't come out anymore, if he's even noticed. Below me—in the apartment below, or maybe two floors down—are other voices, human voices. A man and a woman. *You fucking bitch*, he says. *How dare you*, she says. Their voices rise in the pipes, with the steam heat. My room is humid with it. It condenses and cools inside me and turns to rain. My body shakes in the chair. The chair shakes. The cockroach uses its feet to draw its antennae into its mouth. It cleans them. I stick my fingers in my ears.

The ocean, now, is rough. The land on the other side quakes. There is no solid end to grasp. I will swim again, I hope. But first I must wiggle my antennae. I must listen. I must smell. With my fingernails, I dig into my skin. Fingernails asking questions. The cockroach scurries under the bed, out of sight.

We cannot think another's thoughts, but we can feel their pain. Also, their pleasure, but we focus on pain because pain threatens us. We turn our eyes and block our ears and pretend it is not ours to feel. We let our brains rule our bodies. Our brains tell us we cannot withstand all the feeling, that our bodies are not capable. But we have forgotten—I have forgotten—that we heal, not through logic, not through the brain, but through discharging energy. When we have a fever, we sweat and have fever dreams that make us writhe and cry out. When we eat something rotten, we heave and vomit and shit liquid. We absorb pain and anger through the body, and we must expel it through the body, like a virus, like rot. Can I lick myself clean? Can I scale my skin? Can I molt?

No, no, no! screams the woman downstairs. And my body screams too, but without sound. I am her. I am me. As my body screams, the chair holds me. It holds me and I collapse. The rock softens and smooths, as though suddenly covered by moss. I am cocooned, but still alert. Afraid, but alive. The woman downstairs falls silent. *This is not defeat*, I tell her and also myself. *This is giving in.* And, like seeing a single bright star or satellite in an otherwise dark sky, I know the difference.

Day Four

I am the blue chair island. I rock and the island rocks. I pull at a blue thread on the chair's arm. I pull a hangnail from the third finger on my right hand.

When I was a child, before I discovered my limitations when it comes to math and science and watching living things bleed, I thought I might want to be a surgeon as well as a writer. The earth, a pretty teacher once told me, is the universe in miniature. The body is a microscopic earth. If I mastered the body, I would know the earth. But I couldn't do that because I could barely comprehend algebra. I don't know what algebra has to do with anatomy, exactly, but I suppose that proves my point. When I was ten or so, I looked through Anabel's sister's textbooks from her medical school days. The pages were covered in numbers and diagrams and equations. There had to be, I hoped, another way to know the earth. I worried I would not discover one.

In graduate school, I studied cities because I wanted to understand how places work, how I might live inside of them, how they might live inside of me. In my studio classes, we drew intricate maps on computers. They showed who lived where and how. On top of those maps, we drew other maps that imagined how we would build the city differently. I chose my graduate school program because it was concerned with how we can make people and communities healthier and happier through the built environment. Other programs were

concerned with buildings for buildings' sake, or for money's sake. We
drew maps with more green space. More affordable housing. A lake!
Better schools. Fewer cars. Light rail. Grocery stores that sold tomatoes that burst with juice when you cut them, instead of chips that
left your fingers greasy; instead of stale powdered donuts in plastic
packaging. I imagined people I knew living in my cities. Their skin
glowed and their lungs filled with fresh air that smelled like spring.
They smiled at one another and at me.

I was fascinated by place because no place had ever belonged to
me; nor had I ever belonged to any place. That was also why, as a
child, I was fascinated by the body. Perhaps, I thought, I could belong
inside my own body. Perhaps I could know the streams of the veins
in my wrists the way other people knew the streams in which they
swam as children. Perhaps I could know the names of the bones in
the back of my hand the way other people knew the names of the back
roads that were shortcuts home. I could know the rhythm of my pulse
like my friend Dan knew the rhythm of the approaching train in his
hometown, the rhythm he woke up to and went to sleep to and hoped
would lead him somewhere else someday. I never did get to know my
body that way.

What will happen, I wonder now, if I cut myself open? I once
dissected a fetal pig. I laughed at its cold, rubbery corpse. I laughed as
I made the first incision. I don't know why I laughed.

I snatch small, sharp scissors from my desk and press the point of
them into my thigh. I cannot bring myself to go deep. I do not laugh.

The earth is reduced to this blue chair island. I rub the soil of my
cheek against the soil of the blue upholstery.

Once, I was in an airport somewhere in Africa, waiting for my father to arrive. It could have been Uganda, Ethiopia, or Tanzania. The
memory is not a clear one. I so often waited for my father at airports.
This airport had big windows that looked out on the landing strip, so
you could watch people get off the plane with their suitcases, cardboard boxes, and plastic bags. Nobody traveling to anywhere in Africa
travels light. Tourists carry giant backpacks full of tents and mosquito

repellent and absurd khaki outfits. Africans carry gifts for everyone they know, and some for strangers.

At the airport, there were no arrival gates. People walked down a ladder and onto the tarmac. They paused and set their luggage down. They took off their sweaters or wiped their glasses. I scanned the crowd for my father, but my eyes landed on a woman with brown skin like mine. She had long cornrows down her back. Her pause was longer than everyone else's. I wondered what she was doing. She got down on her knees and placed her cheek against the tarmac, then kissed it. She stayed there, with her lips pressed to the ground, for a good long time.

"What's she doing?" I asked Anabel, who was waiting beside me, examining her lipstick in the little mirror on its case.

"Greeting the earth," Anabel said, as though it was the most obvious thing in the world. "She's probably been away from home for a long time."

With my cheek against the blue chair, I press my lips against the place in my wrist where my heartbeat whispers. "Hello," I say. Up close, blue veins look like rivers trapped underground. Borders not yet burst.

AFTERSHOCKS

Aftershock:

1. a small earthquake that follows a major earthquake
2. the effect, result, or repercussion of an event; aftermath; consequence

Note:

We know aftershocks are coming, but we don't know when exactly. We don't know how many. And we don't know how long they will last.

Orphan

Before we stopped speaking, my mother told me a story about how easy I was as a baby. When I was just a few months old, she said, she would place me in my carrier on the kitchen counter, at an angle so I could turn one way to watch her sipping tea and reading at the table and the other way to watch her stirring sauce at the stove. As long as I could see her, I wouldn't make a sound. Walking around the room, she would catch me tracking her like a tiny predator.

"Your eyes," she said, "were so much like mine that it startled me. Except they were darker and almost unblinking."

She told this story proudly. I think I know why she told it.

"Even then, you were so self-sufficient," she said. That phrase that is synonymous with independent. That phrase that is the antidote to feelings of responsibility, of obligation. With it, I believe she aimed to soften the glare of all the time I spent longing for her.

As an adult, when I think about the story, I wonder if I tracked her with my eyes because I could feel her, already, leaving me. I wonder if I already awaited disaster. I have felt that waiting in my body for as long as I can remember. It feels like tension, like restlessness, like shaking.

When I was nine, I wrote the story of my life in green pencil on several pieces of unlined white paper. I found those pieces of paper, folded in quarters, between the pages of *Le Petit Prince*, when I was packing to leave for college in New York.

On the first page was a list of places and what I assume to be notes about what they represented at the time, what they meant to me. Of London, I wrote about my aunts and my cousin Laura, about how I missed them. Of Rome, I had this to say: *Sometimes when we lived there we went to the Colosseum and to Pompeii where a volcano erupted and everyone was stuck in lava like statues. I liked my teacher there and I liked eating pizza.* Of Ghana, I wrote about my grandparents' dog being killed by a snake and about my father attempting to take me to an Asante Kotoko soccer game. Even though the rain had stopped hours earlier, we arrived to find an empty pitch.

On the second page: *I do not know where we will live after this. We used to live in Italy. Now we live in Ethiopia in a hotel because there are no houses for us. Maybe when we get a house we will have swings. My sister, baby brother, and I do not have many toys because they got lost in the boxes that went on the boat before we flew here. My father makes me laugh. I do not like it when he goes on missions because that means he is not home to say goodnight. Sometimes he brings me presents like a tortoise or my orange shirt from Pakistan.* I wrote "missions'" with only one s in the middle.

The final sentence in the story: *I have to make sure I don't get left behind when we move.* This sentence was underlined.

Sometimes I think my memories are more about what didn't happen than what did, who wasn't there than who was. My memories are about leaving and being left. They are about absence.

I turned fourteen a month after my father died. A month after, for the last time, my mother told me she would not come for me. For my birthday, Anabel, Yasmeen, Kwame, and I went to dinner at our favorite restaurant in our neighborhood in Rome. Over the years, we had become friendly with the jolly twins with twin mustaches and twin round bellies who owned it. One of them was named Luca, the other one's name I can't remember. Usually, we each ordered our own Margherita pizza. Now and then, I got prosciutto di Parma on mine. For dessert, we always shared the tiramisu and the chocolate tartufo. That evening, Luca and his twin greeted us at the door as they always did.

"*Viene il signore?*" one of them asked as he walked us to our table. Is the gentleman coming?

We hadn't been out to dinner since my father stopped being able to walk, to eat solid food, to know the difference between his daughter and a stranger who had somehow found her way into his bedroom. *Where are you?* he had asked when I brought him soup that would be left uneaten on the tray, cold and curdled. He wasn't looking at me, but rather past me, at nothing, his eyes unfocused. Maybe he meant *who*. Or maybe he was not asking about me at all. Maybe he was asking about someone else from another time and place. Time and place, it seems, become confused in the minds of the dying, or else they just cease to matter. My strong, important father, near dying, cried out for his mother in his sleep as a child would. At the hospital, doctors were forever asking him if he knew where he was. *Timbuktu,* or *The Waldorf Astoria*, he'd say on days when he remembered. *What kind of question is that?* he'd snap on days when he did not. He wrote a poem when he was bedridden, but before words left him. I keep a photocopy of it framed on my bedroom wall: *I was not told / youth makes you grow old / that truth is only a refuge for the lonely.* This from the man who read three newspapers every single day in order to ensure he had a nuanced view of the facts, who read to me from Walden: *"Rather than love, than money, than fame, give me truth."* But what is truth when you cannot be sure of where you are? When you are forced to confront that the end of your place in time, or the end of your time in place, is a *when* rather than an *if*?

"*No, non viene stasera,*" I said because no one else was saying anything, and Luca or his twin needed to know whether or not to leave the extra menu on the table. *He is not coming this evening,* as though he might come again, some other evening, as though his ashes were not in an urn behind a wall of cement and wilting white carnations.

Of the events of that year, after the funeral, I remember scant details. I remember what happened generally but not as specifically as I remember the other years of my adolescence. I remember the pigeons and the starlings. I remember the hack job of a haircut I gave myself because it felt good to be in control of something, anything; to make myself as ugly as I felt. I remember that I wore, almost every day, my father's burgundy sweater. I remember the ticking of his gold watch on my pillow. Beyond that, I don't remember much color, texture, flavor. That birthday, in my memory, however, is quite vivid. I remember the pesto sauce splattered on Luca or his twin's wrinkled white shirt. The woman at the next table's long, pointy red fingernails. The black leather menu with gold lettering. Perhaps I remember that night so clearly because the waiting had ended, disaster had come, and I had denied it: *He is not coming this evening.* Denial has been a driving force of so many of my choices. I have protected denial at high cost.

Six years later, in order to qualify for the financial aid I needed to finish college, I filed papers and presented proof to declare myself independent. As a student under the age of twenty-four, to be eligible to file financial aid forms as an independent, you had to be married, have dependents, be a veteran or active member of the armed forces, or be an orphan. When I tried to put the point of my ballpoint pen in the orphan box, to make a check mark, my hand shook so violently I put the pen down. I sat on my bed picking the pen up, watching my hand shake violently, and putting the pen down, for what seemed like hours, but was probably only a few minutes. On my nightstand were a photocopy of my father's death certificate in Italian and an English translation of it, and an envelope containing a letter signed by Anabel. She had, until then, been listed as my parent, even though we had never actually made that legal. The letter stated that she had stopped supporting me financially when I turned eighteen and that my mother's whereabouts were unknown to me. This was not wholly true, as I knew my mother to be in Sedona, Arizona. The private investigator she had hired to find me a year earlier had told me that before I hung up on him and threw my phone against the wall. I knew where my mother was, but her whereabouts did not have anything to do with me or with my ability to pay for college.

To make the necessary check mark, I took the papers to the bar down the street. I ordered a shot of tequila and then another. It wasn't as though checking that box changed anything. That my father was dead, that my mother left when I was a toddler, that she and I had not spoken in almost a decade—these were all facts that had been true for a long time. But the box, I suppose, formalized their absence, gave it a name. Knowing and accepting the inevitable are two different things.

I had a one-night stand that night—my first. When I woke in a mist of tequila and migraine, I couldn't remember how he had touched me, how he had kissed me, if the sex was any good, if I came, if he came, if he held me afterward. I couldn't remember his name, but I was glad he was there. He was, for a newly official orphan, a minimalist version of intimacy.

For my college graduation, my aunt Freda—my father's younger sister—flew to New York from London. She and my sister and our friend Craig shouted my name from the balcony as I walked across the stage at Rockefeller Center, diploma in hand. But I didn't look up to wave at them because I knew my eyes would seek out the empty seats or the seats filled with the loved ones of others where my father and mother were supposed to be.

I describe myself as conflict-averse, but that is not quite accurate. I am not afraid of the fight, exactly. I am afraid of what comes next. During our final fight, my ex-boyfriend George probably thought my voice was shaking out of anger. But what I really felt was something between panic and penitence. I was certain the end of us was coming, that I had caused it. I was sorry for that. But, again, I was not ready to accept the inevitable. At the first sign of disaster—the chorus of barking dogs, the glass of water shuddering on the table—we scream until the silence is tolerable. We cannot prevent what happens next, but we can forestall feeling the full force of it. We can distract ourselves from the terror with the awful sound of our own voices.

For years, from my fear, I distracted myself by reading studies about orphans. Those studies provided strange comfort. Emotions were reduced to cold science. I reduced myself into them. It was a different kind of denial. Through the studies, I learned that children raised in orphanages often reach out their arms to be picked up, but as soon as they get what they seem to want, they kick and push and wriggle away. Then, once they have escaped, they throw themselves on the floor in utter despair and demand to be picked up again. The first time I read about that phenomenon, I laughed out loud. The story of my life, I thought. Then I curled up on the carpet, closed my eyes, and told myself that reading the studies was enough, that they contained all I needed to know. Into my own soul, I reassured myself, I needn't go deep.

Panic

New York, New York, Age 18

When I was eighteen, I exchanged the sunny thunderstorms of Kampala for the mucky air of New York in August. My father's second cousin John showed me to the room in his apartment where I slept for a week on a top bunk. On the bunk below were bags of African masks and cloth that were what remained of an optimistic but ultimately abandoned import-export business. I did not sleep well in that room. I longed to be able to whisper with my sister in the dark as we always did until one of us fell asleep and stopped answering.

I spent my first days as a New Yorker surrounded by the smells of the world I'd left behind—frying plantains and goat meat. I sat in the window and watched tall, wiry boys play basketball, pounding their chests and pumping their fists with each swoosh of the tattered net. So this, I thought to myself with satisfaction, is the Bronx. I was eighteen and an adult. That my adult life was starting out in the Bronx made me feel cool and competent. What I knew about the Bronx: Somewhere in the borough was the block from which Jennifer Lopez hailed. And, according to Lord Tariq and Peter Gunz, if it wasn't for the Bronx, there would be no rap. I was in the birthplace of hip-hop. I wanted to strut around in my mesh crop top and pleather pants, recently purchased during my summer of clubbing in London. I wanted to be mistaken for a video vixen. Never mind the nightmares of being chased into the Bronx River by men in African masks. Never mind that I ventured outside, in my pleather pants, only to get a bag of salt-and-vinegar chips and a Pepsi from the bodega. Uncle John's nine-year-old son taught me the word *bodega* while lying on the leather couch in his white underpants, luxuriating in the air-conditioning that had me, accustomed only to ceiling fans, wrapped in a woolen sweater. "Get me an orange soda from the bodega." He glanced at his father, also in white underpants, reading the *New York Post*. "Please," he added.

On my last night in the Bronx, the apartment was full of people who had come to see the great Osei's daughter. "Your father was a big man," one woman informed me. "Yes," agreed Uncle John's wife. "And Nadia's mother is some sort of Arab, but American so Nadia is a citizen. She grew up in Europe though." Everyone nodded knowingly. I was both of them and not of them, of this place and not of this place.

Uncle John dropped me off at college in downtown Manhattan in his yellow cab. He pressed a piece of squared notebook paper bearing his Parkchester address and phone number into my hand and told me to come and stay any weekend I wanted. "I'm going to college too," he said. "Next year. The cab is only temporary." I was embarrassed that he felt the need to tell me that, that he needed me to know he was more than the immigrant man behind the wheel of a yellow cab. I was embarrassed by the ease with which I had arrived at JFK with a blue passport and all the rights and advantages that came with it.

I sat nervously on my naked bed in the dorm tower for a long time, unsure of how one went about getting sheets and blankets and towels and too afraid of other human beings to ask one of my fellow residents who were noisily getting to know one another in the hall. I had arrived without those things because my image of college dorms in America was informed by my brief stint at boarding school in England, where all clothing and linens had been standard issue and uniform. One of my American university–educated parents was dead and the other had disappeared, so who was I to ask?

Not long after moving into the dorm in the Financial District, I had my first panic attack, while standing on a crowded uptown bus. I was trying to get to the DMV. Uncle John told me I should get a non-driver's identification card because my passport should be locked away in a secure place. Identities, he said, were stolen in America every day.

I was squashed between two very large people—a couple who argued over my head, their distended bellies contracting and inflating against my chest and back with each breath. I couldn't see above them or around them, and I was certain I would miss my stop and end up in a part of the city full of guns and heroin and people who stole identities. I stuck my hand in my purse and clutched my passport. Sweat dripped from my armpits down my arms. My eyes glazed over and there was a stabbing pain in my heart. The couple, sensing my distress, stopped bickering about whose fault it was that Grandma Jean was not coming to Larry's birthday party.

"You okay, baby?" the woman asked. She took a step back to give me some room. I nodded, felt myself fall backward into her husband's pillowy flesh.

When I came to, I was lying on the sidewalk with my head in the woman's lap. Her husband motioned in vain for someone to stop and help us. He shouted that he didn't have a cell phone. He reached out to grab the sleeve of a well-dressed businessman with a briefcase. The man fluttered his hand and strode importantly on. As I watched the scene from what I was certain was a near-death state, I suddenly became aware of our blackness—the couple's and mine. Is that why no cell phones were offered? Is that why the fluttering hand? A young white woman finally stopped and handed over her phone. An ambulance arrived, lights flashing, sirens screeching. In the emergency room I was told to lie down on a cot that was separated by only a curtain and a few inches from a woman who kept moaning, *I didn't know, I didn't know.*

A baby-faced doctor came in and asked me some questions. He listened to my heart, told me I'd had a panic attack.

"But what about the pain in my heart?" I asked.

"It was in your head," he said. "Try to be less anxious."

Baby Fever

New York, New York, Age 27

In the streaked mirror on my closet door, I search for signs of mother: my mothers, body of mother, me as mother. The clock on the wall behind me clicks. If I don't stop staring at myself, if I don't get my hair in order and mascara on, I will be late for work. Soon my phone alarm will ring. If ignored long enough, it will blare an obnoxious horn. My period is late: eight days and roughly six hours. The blood typically comes right after breakfast.

The month before, to delay George from quitting me, I roused him just before dawn, naked, with my sharpened tongue at his neck. His abs convulsed between my thighs. His eyes snapped open, his hands reached down my back and grabbed fistfuls of ass. He laughed.

"Hi," he said.

We had not had sex in weeks because we were too busy masquerading as unchanged in order to avoid the final fight. We went for walks, watched movies, discussed the news, cuddled and kissed, all without making eye contact, all without inflection or expression, all as acts of diversion. Sex was far too dangerous. It carried the risk of being caught off guard, of being weakened by uncontrollable feeling. But the dissociation produced by abstinence had begun to work against me. I was making of myself a non-factor. George no longer told me he was going to his mother's on Long Island for the weekend. I'd discover he'd left Brooklyn when I'd text to see if he wanted to go to the library or the museum, or if he'd seen Paul's email about birthday drinks. At dinner with me, he'd answer his phone on the second ring, cut me off mid-word without so much as a shrug in apology. Nights, he came over less frequently and usually snuck out before I woke. No kiss on my eyebrow, no Post-it on the door.

"Do we have condoms?" he asked. His voice was hoarse, thirsty.

I jumped up and looked in the usual places: bedside cabinet, medicine cabinet, Darjeeling tea tin. Nothing.

He jumped up, holding his hardness; rifled in jeans, wallet, sock drawer. Nothing. He looked desperate. My chest inflated with sweet recompense. I was desired.

And: epiphany. "I know!" I said. A week before, I'd gone to the gyno for my annual pap. She'd asked me, again, if I wanted children. She'd told me, again, that, on the brink of thirty, now was the time to think about it. At my age, days and eggs were numbered. I said I thought about it often enough, but the thinking resulted only in disquiet. She asked if I was still with the same partner.

"Yes," I said. I hoped this would still be true at dinnertime. George was coming over. I was making sole en papillote. The last time I'd cooked for George, I'd made baked lemon chicken and green beans from a can. George complained about the can, said cans caused cancer. Both our fathers died of cancer, he reminded me. He examined the ceiling and huffed. I would do better, I decided, then immediately felt umbrage, but I chewed on it silently. I chewed it and swallowed it with both my share of canned green beans and George's.

"Are you happy?" my gyno asked.

"Today, yes," I said and raised my eyebrows to signal I was joking, but I wasn't joking. I was lying. George and I were not happy that day, had not been happy for many days, weeks, months before that. And happiness struck me as a ridiculously high standard in the first place. Who in the world was happy? Who in the world was happy *together*? The question was: Would I be unhappier without him? The answer was yes. I loved him. And stronger than my love was fear. Without him, I would have to contend with myself. Against myself, I would make a merciless opponent.

Gloves ripped from her hands, the doctor asked if I wanted to schedule my next appointment, recommended I take a calcium tablet once a day to prevent bone loss, and handed me two condoms in bright pink foil. The calcium tablets went into a brown paper bag in my backpack. The condoms went into the front pocket.

"Condom!" I leapt back into bed, triumphant, brandishing one of the condoms my gyno had given me.

Sex was rough and punitive. This pleased me. *Hate me*, I thought, *hate me*. If there was hate, there was love. If there was hate, there was ligature. There was also, certainly, resentment. But resentment was good. Resentment spoke to a still-unmade decision. Leave me or don't? Leave me and lose me? Stay and hate me?

Hate me, hate me, I begged silently, pretending to tremble from pleasure not pang.

"I love you," he said. "Fuck me, I love you." Was the *fuck me* appeal or resignation? I didn't ask. I will never know. He squeaked, groaned, finished, pulled out. "Fuck," he said again. This time, the meaning was clear. He held up the condom—gashed, dripping, near empty. Semen swam inside me.

"Maybe take a shower," George said. Then, the way I tell the story to myself, he said, "Wash me out of you," but it is more likely he said, "Wash it out of you." Either way, it felt like an answer I didn't want. My sadness did not, I am almost certain, mean I wanted to have his baby. I wasn't particularly worried about the possibility of pregnancy. What were the chances of that? I think I was disturbed by his icy voice, by the fact he did not suggest we shower together. Our nonexistent child was already mine alone. In the shower, tears leaked from me liberally and so did George. I shampooed and soaped, then scoured everything dry with a coarse white towel.

Now, over a month later, that nonexistent child might become real. In the mirror, there are faint lines at the corners of my eyes and deeper ones between them where my brow corrugates. There are small scabs and dark spots peppered across my jaw: pimples I've picked at. Pimples are caused by hormones. Hormone changes?

When Anabel was pregnant with Kwame, her eyelids and nose puffed up. All she wanted was mangoes. When my mother was pregnant with me, the texture of her hair went from straight to wavy. When does that happen? When does a not-yet child start to change you?

In the mirror, I lift my shirt and ponder my belly, wonder if a fertilized seed is incubating in there, absorbing oatmeal and coffee. The horn on my phone blares. I grab my bag and run for the subway.

At work at the restaurant, I am surrounded by pregnancies and children.

"Please make sure my tuna is cooked through," says the woman in what looks to be her final month. Her belly hovers above the table like the top of a hot air balloon. Her boyfriend or husband pokes it with his pointer finger and smiles at her.

"God, I miss sushi," she says.

A mother is drinking Chardonnay and eating halibut two tables away from where her tween daughter and friend drink Shirley Temples and eat spaghetti with just olive oil and parmesan.

"They like to pretend they're grown-ups, so I can't sit with them," the mother tells me. She pulls out a serious-looking nonfiction book. "This is quite a luxury," she says opening to page one. "I used to read at bars all the time when I was single." She gestures toward a petite, thin woman in her twenties who is reading the *New Yorker* at the bar and scanning the crowd. I imagine she is searching for her tardy date. I picture her date as a man in a suit. The woman has on red lipstick and pointy-toed heels even though, outside, it flurries. I am wrong. Another woman arrives. They air kiss. The second woman is also in red lipstick, also in pointy-toed heels, but she is very tall and moderately pregnant. They are seated at one of my tables.

"I'll just have half a glass of the Bordeaux," the pregnant one says. "You can pour the rest in her glass so as to not overcomplicate things." I do not think I react to this. I have no objection, but she explains her Bordeaux anyway: "I'm French."

After my shift, I order the tuna, rare. I sit at the bar with a novel, open it to the first page. I drink glass after glass of whatever red my friend Sam, the bartender, has open. George calls, and for the first time in months, I let his call go to voicemail. I can't focus on the book. I think about my grandmother—my father's mother. She was married at fourteen and birthed my aunt Harriet at sixteen. This was not unusual in Ghana back then. She had three more children after that, the youngest of whom—my aunt Freda—was born when my grandmother was in her early forties.

My grandmother was a bookkeeper, but mostly she was a mother of four. When my cousin Laura was born, Nana was thrilled to add grand to her title. She longs, she tells me every chance she gets, to become great-grand. I once asked her if there was anything else she wanted, or anything she regretted.

"Like what?" she asked. She sounded suspicious. Then her voice turned sad. "I wanted my son to live," she said.

On the subway home, a little boy in an enormous blue coat is nodding off. "Wake up," his father nudges him. "Wake up." When we reach their stop, the father yanks his son up and drags the deadweight of him through the crowd to the door. In the hand not dragging his sleepy son is a paper bag overflowing with groceries. An apple drops and rolls. The father bends to pick it up. The boy, awake and angry about it, sits on the floor to have a tantrum. The father yanks him up again. "Stand clear of the closing doors, please," says the kind robot voice. They don't make it out, miss their stop.

"Shit," says the father, shaking the boy's shoulder a little too roughly. "Look what you've done."

The boy cries louder. The father tells him to shut his fucking mouth. The rest of us sit and stand in judgment.

Where's his mother? I think, before I can stop myself, before I can intercede in the popular, patriarchal, story of mother with the truth of my own experience.

I once designed a Mother's Day card for my father to tell him he was the best Baba-Mama in the world. After he read it, he took off his glasses, rubbed his wet eyes with his fists, said I'd made his day. I did not mail a card to my mother or give one to Anabel.

The father and son get off at the next stop. When they exit, I am relieved.

The next day, at the drugstore, I put olive oil hair lotion, contact solution, and zit cream in my red cart, even though I'm not sure if I'm running low on any of those things. I find pregnancy tests and tampons in the same aisle, grab a box of both. Fear and hope. In the line, I want the female cashier, but the man finishes first. He rings me up, hands me a receipt, tells me to have a good day.

"Next," he says, looking past me. His eyes and voice are bored, which provides strange comfort. He didn't even double bag. *Nothing remarkable*, he seems to tell me. *Nothing to hide.*

At home, before I take the pregnancy test, I make lists:

No:

1. Still in grad school
2. Broke, mostly
3. Live with roommate
4. Already have Yasmeen and Kwame to half-ass mother. Sometimes resent even that.
5. George???
6. Baba dead
7. Genetics and personality
8. Depression/anxiety
9. Don't enjoy playing games with children for longer than an hour
10. Relationships with mothers. One nonexistent, one shaky
11. Lots of other reasons

Yes:

1. Love children
2. George???

After making the lists, I journal about the ways I'd tried and failed to mother my sister and my brother—the ways I was still trying and failing to mother them.

After my father's funeral, Kwame wandered around the house, looking behind every curtain, under every bed.

"Where's Baba?" he asked.

"In heaven," Anabel said.

"But where is heaven?" he asked, peering into the wardrobe in the guest bedroom.

Anabel left the room, her head tilted down and forward, her arms held out in front of her like a sleepwalker.

"Mama!" Kwame cried and started to follow her.

From Anabel's room, sobs.

I scooped him up in my arms and held him even as he tried to squirm away, to get back to his mother.

"No!" he cried. "Let me go." When he said, "I hate you," I gasped and gave up, let him run to his crying mother.

For two years, starting when I was twenty-one and Yasmeen was twenty, my sister lived on the futon in the living room of my one-bedroom apartment in Brooklyn.

I moved her in by force when she dropped out of college. She was supposed to be studying psychology. I was listed as her guardian, so I got a letter stating that she would need to reapply for the next semester as she had not been attending class. Her tuition had been paid out of our rapidly diminishing inheritance.

I went to Seattle to collect her and her belongings (CDs, paints and chalk, a sketchbook, lots of clothing purchased secondhand at Buffalo Exchange, a worn copy of *The Brothers Karamazov*, and a photo album full of memories of us as awkward bespectacled little girls). I told her she had to come live with me in New York and think about what she really wanted from life. I acted as though I knew what I really wanted from life.

Being Yasmeen's safety net made me feel less incompetent at being a grown-up. She didn't put up much of a fight about the move.

She has always surrendered easily when caught. And, besides, she said she had been scared shitless. She wasn't ready to be on her own. Truth be told, I wasn't either. To avoid solitude, I ignored the fact that my aspiring rapper boyfriend was cheating on me with an aspiring *Maxim* model. I hated my short-lived, part-time job at a magazine where I wrote about cuff links and cologne. And I hated my job as a bottle service girl at a smoke-filled club even more. One night, a man got his throat slashed just as I popped open his overpriced champagne. An ambulance was called. He lived. Another night, a member of an actor's entourage pulled me onto his lap and gripped me hard between my legs, wouldn't let go until another waitress walked by and threatened to call security.

Despite the questionable state of my own life, telling another person what to do was no problem for me: *Get up before noon for God's sake. You can't live on cigarettes, whiskey, and egg sandwiches. Get a job. Turn the music down. Pick up your clothes for once. Don't forget your keys and umbrella.*

I also largely didn't mind putting a roof over our heads, filling the fridge with bread and cheese, and telling Yasmeen that everything would be okay even when I wasn't sure it would. Because she was there, I could ditch the rapper.

Every now and then, though—when I'd come home from work to find she'd drunk all the wine, or when the ceiling in the bathroom fell into the tub, or when I just wanted to be left the fuck alone—I resented the responsibility. *We're only fourteen months apart*, I'd seethe, *what the hell? Mothering is for the birds.*

"I'm not your mother!" I screamed at her. Then I felt like a selfish asshole.

Mothering is a verb. It is done out of love and obligation. We approach it with kindness and grudge. I mother, you mothered, we will mother. "You have to take care of your brother and sister," my father told me when he was dying.

"I know you're not my mother," said Yasmeen.

I would make a terrible mother, I decide, and I go to the bathroom to take the pregnancy test. Pee won't come easy. After a couple of minutes, a drop squeezes out. I down two glasses of water, sit back on the toilet. Squeeze, relax, squeeze, relax. This is strange because my bladder is almost always half-full, even when I've just peed. This used to worry me, but my doctor said it doesn't mean anything.

I get off the toilet. On my laptop, I watch a YouTube video about breathing. The instructor wants me to put one hand on my stomach and one on my heart while taking deep, calming breaths. Having my hand on my stomach is not calming. What if it really is in there? My heart threatens eruption. I join my hands in prayer at my rib cage instead.

"Close your eyes," the instructor says. "For just a few moments, there is nothing to do, nowhere to be. Let go of all thoughts."

But my thoughts say that there is something to do, somewhere to go. *Toilet. Stick. Pee on the stick. Why can't you just pee on the motherfucking stick? What's wrong with you? Get on the toilet and pee on the stick.*

"Now, create a quiet place in your mind where you can just observe how you feel. How does your body feel today?"

My body feels like an unauthorized squat. Is there a pre-body in there? If there is, what will it want from me?

All signs say pregnant: unstained underwear, pink plus sign. I throw the stick out, unwrap another. Same answer. Wrong answer.

George is out of town for work. To tell or not to tell is a decision I can delay for five days. In the meantime, I call Planned Parenthood. The verdict, I decide, is not final until blood is drawn.

In a daydream, George and I are married. We live in the building his mother owns in Prospect Heights. Our daughter is brown-skinned and blond-haired. George comes home from work, loosens his tie. A woman who looks like me but is empty of me cradles the girl. I watch from outside.

In another daydream, I am single. I must raise a son. His name is Osei, after my father, and he wears tiny glasses. I read to him in a rocking chair. But when I try to fill in the rest of the room, the surrounding apartment, the rest of a life, the color won't come.

Me as mother is not my story, I realize with some certainty. Not now. Not ever? It is not even, at this moment, a story I can imagine.

In the early days, George and I ran together. He wore shorts that were too short and mine were too long. His career was stalled, mine delayed. We ran side by side, away from all that.

George wanted to be Paul Farmer—that anthropologist doctor hell-bent on saving the world. I didn't yet dare name my heroes—James Baldwin, June Jordan, Joan Didion. *Write one good thing*, I warned myself. *Do one good thing. Until then, keep their names out of your mouth.*

George would heal bodies. I would write stories. I pictured us in a remote village. There'd be a well, a clinic, a vegetable garden, a schoolhouse. Lots of children everywhere. None of them were ever ours.

"I don't think I'll ever get married," George said as though this had nothing to do with me. "I don't see kids in my future."

Once, drunk enough, I asked him where I was in his future, if I was.

"You can come with me wherever I go," he said. Then he added: "If you want." This choice I was granted. It was one I did not want to be given. I wanted us to be inevitable.

I was wrong about the blood verdict. Planned Parenthood tests urine. I say I want a blood test. The nurse says, "not necessary," hands me a cup. She's a heavy breather. Her nose whistles. Heavy breathing has always disturbed me. It is evidence of a body's struggle. When I have a panic attack, air makes sound, entering and exiting through too small a pipe. I smile at her to trick myself into forgiveness.

"You're all set," she says, when I hand her the cup. She has already given me several shiny pamphlets of options.

The test is negative. There is no body growing in my body. Was the choice taken from me before I could make it, or was it always a false positive, a no body?

"She was so young then," my aunt Harriet said once, about my mother, about my birth and subsequent abandonment. She was always trying to convince me to move past my anger, to show some mercy, to let my mother back in. She had always liked my mother.

She didn't judge her harshly for leaving. She never complained about being saddled, for a while, with her brother's two children when she already had one of her own to raise on a nurse's schedule and salary. Of course, my father sent money and clothes, not just for Yasmeen and me, but also for our cousin Laura. But, until my father married Anabel and came to collect me and Yasmeen, Auntie Harriet was the one who got us dressed and brushed and braided in the morning. She was the one who dropped us off and picked us up from school and ballet. She fed us, cuddled us, comforted us, taught us, put us to bed with a story and a kiss; never forgot to leave the light in the hall on.

"You are more like my mother than she is," I argued. "I don't even know her."

"I love you like my own daughter," she replied, "you and Yas, but it's not easy being a woman and your mother was just barely a woman. She made mistakes. I want you to be able to let it go. I want you to be free of the bitterness."

Anabel's sister made the same argument for Anabel at a time when I was determined to add her to my list of banished mothers.

"She just can't stop herself from making me feel like shit," I said, "from the day she came into my life."

Anabel's sister is one of the most elegant women I know. I have never heard her say a bad word about anyone. Her hair is always perfect, her toenails always polished. She dresses like Jackie Kennedy and crosses her legs at the ankles when she sits. She never puts her elbows on the table. She flinched at the word *shit* but didn't reprimand me. Instead, in a kind voice, she said, "She was just a girl. Twenty-two. What were you doing at twenty-two?"

Because I couldn't bear to disappoint this woman I so admired, I talked myself into softening my stance. I re-friended Anabel on Facebook.

I would have been a horrible mother at twenty-one, twenty-two, twenty-three, twenty-four, twenty-five, twenty-six. Anabel was twenty-one when she inherited me. My mother was twenty-six when she left me. What kind of mother would I be at twenty-seven?

My sister claims my mothering saved her. My brother says I make him feel loved. And yet I know I floundered. I often turned away from their needs. My duty as the eldest sibling of a band of sometimes orphans is one I can pick up and put down. I am allowed some measure of stinginess. Everyone will forgive me that. Not too long ago, when my sister texted that she had found herself suddenly homeless and needed a place to stay, I waited an entire day to call her back. I wanted to spend the afternoon drinking whiskey with a man whose girlfriend was out of town. Next to him in bed that night, I withheld sex, wielded power. Once, when my brother needed my help writing a college application essay, I wrote instead a thoroughly hopeless sestina in my journal. It took a pleading, desperate, down-to-the-wire voicemail to get me to do him the small favor. I hated myself for that selfishness.

When I believed I was pregnant, I thought a lot about choice. The decision before me—to become or not become a mother—would be life-changing, potentially life-creating. Now, with the question answered for me, I feel something like relief but heavier. It is like taking off a winter coat in a hot room only to find that I cannot get out of the wool sweater underneath. The question of motherhood is faded but not dissipated. It spotlights other questions, other choices, about love and career and children and tomorrow. I don't have answers and I don't want to look for them.

In my bedroom, days after I learn I am not pregnant, I wait for George to return. Soon, I know, he will end us. There is no cause for alarm. The fault line is dormant. I am still in the *before*. The clock on the wall clicks. It is louder now.

My uterus contracts, my belly rumbles. I close my eyes to the halogen light and questions. When the blood came this morning, it brought with it a fever.

MAINSHOCKS

Earthquake:

a great upheaval

Note:

In an earthquake, the greatest risk to human life is the collapse of man-made structures. Reinforced structures can survive large earthquakes with minimal damage, but even a very small earthquake can destroy structures not built with adequate protection against shaking.

Devices

I have lived in disaster and disaster has lived in me. Between body and environment, conversance. Our shared languages are thunder and reverberation.

My mind has a seismometer inside it. Its job is translation and calibration. And also to signal distress: *Mayday, Mayday, save our souls.* My souls are many and so, I believe, are yours. Some of them are quiet, watchful. Some are ravenous beasts. We need them all. They live behind our flesh. They rumble with one another and with the outside world. Our souls fight for survival.

My disasters, or rather my share of them, were both literal and metaphorical. I list them and summarize them. I contextualize them through the lens of my own experience. Summaries and lists shrink them to a weight I can carry. Metaphor is a privilege, meaning metaphor belongs to those who, like me, came out less scathed. The blighted and broken are left to clean up. They have limited time for abstraction. There is blood on the floor and in their eye sockets.

I have experienced two earthquakes, both negligible. The first struck in Rome in the summer after my father's death. I was fourteen. The magnitude of the earthquake was unknown to me, and the internet yields conflicting answers, but it was low. When it came, I was washing my hands and examining the eruptions on my face in the mirror. So many eruptions from the stress of loss and from adapting to womanhood. There was a groan and palpitations under the tiles. I turned off the tap. I thought I had broken something in the plumbing. My first instinct was to hide. Anabel would be angry. But in the hallway, a framed photo on the wall slanted and threatened to slip from the nail. Yasmeen poked her head out of our bedroom door. We heard screams and pounding feet. My family joined the exodus: Anabel, Yasmeen, Kwame, and me; and Paulina. Paulina was once nanny to us all, even Anabel in her first months as a widow. But now, officially, she was responsible only for Kwame. This did not stop the rest of us from leaning on her. I still went to her for advice and affection and so did Yasmeen. Anabel delegated to her the tasks of making dinner and beds. She was related, distantly, to Anabel; from the same village on Kilimanjaro. Her family was poor, so she had not finished school, though she had wanted to. She loved taking English lessons at a local language school. I'm not sure how she managed, as her Italian was far worse than her English, but she got top marks. She was smarter than me, but she did my laundry while I was struggling through Algebra II.

In the courtyard, the neighbors stood about in their house clothes and bare feet. We all looked up, but nothing fell. Still, I shook for weeks. I was able to openly feel and fear the small earthquake in a way I couldn't feel and fear my own sadness. My grief seemed to make everyone uncomfortable or guilty. My seismophobia, on the other hand, amused people. *Silly girl*, they said, *afraid of a whole lot of nothing*.

My share of terrorism and war: two long, civil (meaning *domestic*, not *amicable*), and at arm's length, and two planes crashing into the twin towers.

"I was there," I've said, about all of them. People's eyes widen. I was there before the partitioning, before the capturing and testifying. I was there before the memorial.

I was there when the children were soldiers; there when Marxism lost. I was there right after the moment of impact, when the towers collapsed. I was there before the metaphors: *Eden before the fall. The hunting of the barbarians. The War on Terror.* I thought I'd witnessed the end times.

The metaphors crept into me. I memorized the stories and forgot much of what I saw. I remember how I felt. I remember being on the periphery. I narrate myself further in, toward center. My memory absorbs what I have been told and what I tell others.

I can only talk about the civil wars in Ethiopia and Uganda from a remove, from a protected place. My walls were high and barbed with wire and cut glass. The walls were warning. The wire and glass were weapon. My body was guarded day and night by men with AK-47s.

In Addis Ababa, where I lived from ages eight to ten, the shift change between day and night guards happened an hour after the driver dropped me home from school. I liked to watch the guards come and go. They gave each other low fives in parting. I wondered who they were outside of their station by the gate. One of them often had a book in hand. One was inclined to pacing. His boots looked too big for him. He didn't look old enough for his weapon. Who was guarding their wives, children, and mothers? If the rebels or the government troops came, would the guards take bullets for us? What did we pay them for their lives? Sometimes my father sent me out to them with blueberry cupcakes we made from American mixes.

My father and his friends drank scotch and tracked the rebels' approach and the dictator's demise. Whatever happened, whenever it happened, the Ethiopian people would suffer and we would leave them to it, at least until the cease-fire. Across the floor, the wives listened in and made contingency plans. Where would we move to? What would we do about school and the furniture? With any luck, our evacuation would coincide with the summer holidays. Our luck was already apparent in the soft glow of the generator-powered chandelier. For this, we swallowed guilt like the abundant seltzer we drank to spare ourselves from the task of boiling bacteria out of tap water. But also, we were glad. This was not our country, not our conflict, not our calamity. My father and his colleagues were here not to occupy or prevent, only to bear witness. They were here to rebuild and replant what was lost and then rebuild and replant when it was lost again.

The baobab trees were dying. The rain had not come that year or the year before. Food didn't always make it through rebel-held areas and roadblocks. Ours was flown in. The lines for fuel and visas were endless. Ethiopians were desperate to get out of the country. There were no lines for us. Measures had been taken. Procedures were communicated. We had only to await special deliveries and telexes.

While stalled in traffic with my father and the driver, I watched a child beggar either faint or die. He wore no shirt and he looked to me like a baby bird. He was so small, younger than me. "Please mother, father," he said, holding out his cupped hand through open car windows. His eyes took up most of the room on his thin face. As he dropped to the ground, the mosque called the faithful to prayer. A woman jumped out of a UN vehicle and crouched over him or his body. There was honking and swerving and the waving of fists out of windows. I don't remember what my father said or did. I know the driver kept driving. I remember crying and hiding it. I felt sick with all my petty complaints. I had so many complaints: the papaya I had been forced by my father to eat for breakfast, the quiz my math teacher popped at us, the power cut that interrupted my millionth viewing of *Annie*. Who was I to have so much and demand even more? Why was I in this chauffeured vehicle with a father who loved me while that child dropped dying or dead in the middle of the road with only a strange white woman to comfort him?

The boy's bird body haunts me. He hovers over me in judgment when I feel sorry for myself, but he cannot stop me from feeling sorry for myself.

In Kampala, the war was, to me, barely discernible. It was a matter of minor inconvenience: the cancellation of gorilla treks or white-water rafting excursions due to safety alerts.

"Fucking Lord's Resistance Army," I grumbled when I was sixteen and had to participate in a bomb drill instead of playing soccer. How easy to forget that people, not so far away, lived in terror. As the light faded, I closed my textbooks and went to meet friends for cocktails. In the North, children filed out of their family's mud huts and walked barefoot on dirt roads. Some walked for ten miles. Every night, they walked to the nearest town: Gulu, Kitgum, or Lira. Eleven-year-olds carried toddlers part of the way. Much of the way was unlit. The children walked so they would not be stolen. Being stolen meant slavery and rape. The Lord's Resistance Army forced children to kill each other in order to poison them with shame. The rebels stormed villages at night.

The children slept on verandas, in bus stations, in hospitals, in the streets, in churches, in the homes of whoever would have them. They woke when the rain came, drenched them through. They woke when cars backfired, and drunkards fought. They woke from the rumbling of trucks in the distance and from fever dreams. When day broke, they gathered for the long walk home, to help their parents on farms and in kitchens or, if they were lucky, to attend school.

Valentine's Day in my senior year of high school in Kampala was on a Sunday. My girlfriends and I had plans to have dinner at a restaurant in Kabalagala. Despite a recent string of grenade attacks in the city, I was not worried. Being part of the kind of international community I grew up in can make one feel invulnerable. Perhaps it was that we were forever being waited on, guided, ushered in, driven about. Perhaps it was the casual availability of everything: burgers, sushi, American television. What was the worst we could imagine while watching *Melrose Place*? Perhaps it was simple entitlement. I did not fear for my life because I knew my life would be protected over the lives of others. I was the child of diplomats, an American citizen. I did not consciously do this calculus. It was obvious.

"I'll call the Canadian consulate," my friend once shouted at a Ugandan police officer who threatened to arrest him for smoking weed in a nightclub. We had been smoking with a large group of people, some expats and children of expats and some locals. People did get arrested that night, all Ugandan. After the police left, my friends and I kept smoking, drunk on shots of whiskey and bravado.

Before leaving for dinner on Valentine's Day, I stood in Anabel's room applying her red lipstick. My friends and I had decided we would all wear red or pink in honor of the holiday. We were going to give one another love letters.

"You're not going anywhere," Anabel said, cell phone in hand. "There has been a bomb in Kabalagala. My friend just called me from Telex Bar. She's fine but there are casualties."

On the radio, we learned that four people had died and twenty-two were injured. Later, someone who was there told me she saw a woman's guts spray out of her body and land on a nearby table. People's legs were severed.

"They're targeting us," a friend said at school the next day. By *us*, she meant foreigners. Telex Bar was an expat hangout. An American aid worker was among the injured, and two Swiss nationals. School was abuzz with fear and drama. We used the word *expat* casually then. We did not question why our parents were called expats while other people were called immigrants or migrants.

"I'm really scared," another friend said at lunch in the open-air cafeteria as she dipped a piece of baguette into tomato sauce. Her boyfriend put his arm around her protectively and pulled her close. She sniffled into his Abercrombie T-shirt. We were surrounded by mango and jackfruit trees. A crested crane watched us; its signature gold-feathered head made it look like a punk rocker. I stared back at it. My friend's sniffling irked me. Here we were in our little bubble, suddenly caring about the war, and only because, this time, the violence had come for people like *us*.

"I need a drink," my friend said. "Want to go play pool tonight?"

"I have to study," I lied. I didn't want to talk about the bomb anymore. Perhaps my friends' fear was real. It seemed performed. I didn't like the role I was being cast in. It was the only one I was right for.

The crested crane spread its wide wings and lifted off, flew toward the guard tower at the top of the steep hill.

I do not need to set the scene for the attack on September 11, 2001. You have read about the clear blue sky, the bright sun. You have seen the video: planes crashing into towers, one after the other. Towers on fire. People on the street staring up at broiling glass, concrete, and steel. Towers collapsing. People running, twisting their necks to watch the pursuing thundercloud of debris. I was one of those runners. Perhaps you were too. Or perhaps you have dreamt you were. I thought the cloud might swallow us all, the whole city. I don't remember fear, only running. My body was charged, electric; my mind benumbed.

I was at Pace University in 2001—a junior. Pace was a few blocks away from the World Trade Center. I lived in Brooklyn, so I took the subway every morning. Usually, I took the N to City Hall, but on September 11, I had spent the night at a boy's apartment so I took the A to the World Trade Center stop. On the subway, I think I heard someone say something about a fire in lower Manhattan. It didn't mean anything to me. There was always something burning in New York.

The boy I had spent the night with and I worked at a restaurant together. Later, I would learn I wasn't the only hostess with whom he was intimate. On the 11th, though, as I got off the train, I gleamed. He was handsome and charming and had a beautiful soft afro. I felt the kind of tired that comes after a night spent laughing, kissing, and drinking cheap whiskey from coffee mugs.

Nobody stopped me from walking up the stairs of the World Trade Center station, from standing under that clear blue sky in that bright sun. We didn't yet know what had happened, what would happen. I noticed the crowd first. Then I heard sirens. I looked up just as everything began falling down. The towers seemed to burst. They roared in pain.

"There are people jumping. Oh my god, there are people jumping" is the last thing I heard before I ran. It might have been my own voice saying it. The jumpers' legs cycled in the air.

In the throng, I saw many other Pace students. I ran into my friend Donyell. I screamed his name. Both of us were covered in gray dust. There were abandoned shoes and purses and shopping bags strewn everywhere. There were masters of the universe weeping on their knees. I grabbed Donyell's big hand. He was on the basketball team.

"Let's go," he said, and he pulled me along. I let him be in charge. It felt right to have someone to run with, away from the end of the world. We ran and walked all the way to Times Square. Neither of us could get cell phone reception, but we picked up news and rumor from other runners and from storekeepers standing outside watching the migration. We were told to keep moving uptown. Someone said there were bombs in parked cars and in ambulances. Someone said nuclear war. A Jehovah's Witness in sensible shoes and a long, prim skirt shouted about the Second Coming. Eventually, Donyell got cell service and called his roommate, who said it was safe to come back. We walked downtown. I don't remember the walk.

I spent that night on the floor in Donyell's dorm room. The trains weren't running, and I didn't want to sleep alone anyway. The dorm smelled like a pyre. The city smelled like a pyre. I was horrified because the dust in our nostrils contained particles of human beings. We were inhaling pieces of fathers and mothers and lovers.

"I love you," Donyell said. He climbed down from his bed and lay beside me on the floor, arms around me. "I've loved you since the day we met."

I said nothing, but I held him back, tight.

The next morning, early, I walked home over the Brooklyn Bridge. I was alone most of the way across. The air was unclean and apocalyptic and so was the quiet. Bits of paper and ash blew about. I didn't know I was crying, but when I got home the ash that caked my face was streaked.

My two roommates—college friends—were watching the news. I spotted people I knew in the footage—running, screaming. I spotted myself. My aunt Harriet called me from London to tell me she had spotted me too. It is hard for me now to distinguish what I saw from the footage of what I saw; to distinguish myself running from the image of myself running. My face in the footage looked blank.

The fear arrived with the next day's newspapers: *War on the World; War on America; Let Us Pray; Armageddon; God Help Them; God Save Us.*

"Our war on terror begins," said President George W. Bush. The word *war* had war inside of it. The metaphor was bloodthirsty.

The walls downtown were plastered with pleas for the missing. Posters begged for any information, any word. I hadn't lost anyone, only my notebook and one red faux-leather glove. Two thousand, six hundred and six people who were in and near the towers were killed. It didn't feel like a war down there, it felt like a graveyard. We covered our mouths when we walked to school and work. Everyone had a cough. I carried lozenges in my coat pocket and tried to avoid looking at the empty space that was a sepulchral thing. It held the shape of skyscrapers. It held the shape of a thundercloud. It held the shape of jumpers, legs cycling. I wanted a ritual, like the women in Rome who made the sign of the cross when passing a cathedral. I left roses and notes in chain-link fences. I gave useless blood. No one was being pulled out of the rubble.

I don't remember speaking to Donyell again after that night. It's possible I did. Much of that year has been worn away. Sometimes, I see photos of him on social media. I've wanted to talk to him about that day, to thank him for his big hand in mine, for holding me, for telling me he loved me when we thought we'd die, but I never have.

The War on Terror became a war in Iraq, a war in Afghanistan, a war in Syria. Stories can be written into being. No story, no metaphor, is innocent of theft, omission, obscuration, or violence.

I have never told anyone that in the days immediately after the attack, even as I grieved a sort of world ending, the loss of life, the launch of war, New York before the terror, I waited anxiously for a boy to call me—the boy I'd spent the night with, the boy who was the reason, or *a* reason, I was there when the towers fell. A tiny piece, but still a piece, of my heartbreak was that he didn't call, not for a week. When he did call, he didn't ask about what happened to me that day and I didn't tell him.

A team of seismologists at Columbia University determined that the planes hit the towers at 8:46:26 and 9:02:54, give or take a few seconds. I must have exited the World Trade Center station shortly after 9:02:54. The impact of the planes produced seismic waves comparable to minor earthquakes of magnitudes 0.9 and 0.7. This felt important, or at least interesting, to me when I read about it in the year after the attack, though no one else seemed to think so.

———

My second earthquake: August 23, 2011. A few seconds in a Manhattan elevator. Magnitude 5.8 when it struck in Virginia. New York only rattled a bit. I was helping a friend who lived in the Financial District with a video shoot for Fashion Week, and she had sent me to pick up pizza. When the elevator jolted, I thought it was a malfunction and that I would plunge to my death. Then the doors opened, and I stepped out and resumed living, heart thumping in my chest. Upstairs, in the third-floor apartment, I'd later learn, my friend collected broken porcelain from under the models' feet. They didn't help her because they were unsettled and had to call their boyfriends and dog-sitters.

On the street, the earth was unmoving. I didn't know yet that others had felt it too. Then someone pointed up. Skyscrapers had swayed or seemed to sway. We searched the sky for a low-flying plane, fire, smoke, a cloud of ash. We found nothing. A woman screamed. Despite the lack of evidence, we ran. We ran for our lives that were not threatened, not that time, but we were not taking any chances. The running felt like repetition because I'd been in the Financial District when the towers fell and because the running took place daily in my head. Things I fled: ghosts, mothers, grief, earthquakes, abandonment, death, thunderclouds, ash, metaphors.

I remember my two earthquakes so clearly because earthquakes are on and in my mind. I think in seismic terms. They are everywhere in my journals. I don't look for signs, I listen for cracking rock. Like an earthquake, the future is hard to predict, but like a seismologist, I analyze risk factors. I feel destabilized, not worried. I don't hide my feelings, I seal cracks.

I did not literally experience the earthquake that inspired my guiding metaphor, my seismic mind. It was the earthquake that struck Armenia on the day my mother came to visit me and Yasmeen in Rome in 1988. Between 25,000 and 50,000 people were killed and up to 130,000 were injured. I didn't know any of those people. I didn't know their families. I watched them suffer on the television news. I appropriated their tragedy and made of it a metaphor in my story. The earthquake came and destroyed their homes, their city. On the same day, my mother came, and her coming toppled me. My mother became the earthquake. I was only seven when I made that leap. It was automatic. It was reflex. My mind ate the earthquake victims' stories. It chewed them into private truths, digested them into memories.

I felt empathy for the victims of the earthquake in Armenia and I felt self-pity. I did not weigh those emotions against each other. They became muddled. I asked my father if we could do anything to help, and he said we could donate money and I could write a letter. He said I was a very special girl, to care so deeply. The letter I wrote, from what I recall, was largely about me: about how I was half-Armenian, about how I was thinking a lot about earthquakes. I stopped short, I hope, of writing about my mother's visit, of putting metaphor on paper next to natural disaster, stamping it, mailing it.

I have lived in disaster and disaster has lived in me. My share of natural disaster was minor, my share of war abstracted. I felt numb during the terror in Manhattan, but my legs carried me. Almost always, I have found a hand to hold.

When I picture an earthquake, I picture an earthquake. And I picture my mother's back as she walks away. I picture my father's tumor and planes crashing into towers. When I picture an earthquake, I picture orphans in Armenia and child soldiers. I picture myself, safe, behind guarded walls. I picture an absence. I hear thunder and silence. An earthquake is trauma and vulnerability: the earth's, mine, yours.

An earthquake is the ground breaking and the heart breaking. It is frictional forces and literary device. A fault is a weakness. A woman's body is a weakness. A wound is a weakness I can't help but pick at. Some wounds never heal.

A story is a flashlight and a weapon. I write myself into other people's earthquakes. I borrow pieces of their pain and store them in my body. Sometimes, I call those pieces compassion. Sometimes I call them desecration.

An American Terror

New York, New York, Age 28

On a Saturday night, some months before I sought asylum in the blue chair, I was terrified my brother Kwame might be in the news the next morning. He might be in the news the next morning because he might end up dead.

Kwame called me from jail. Something about his license. Something about running a traffic light. Something about a woman's purse. I could not understand what he was saying because he was hysterical. I said, "Slow down, slow down," but he couldn't slow down. Then the call was cut.

Kwame had not been in America long enough for his accent or auxiliary verbs to change. He pronounced hard t's and said *shall* instead of *should*. But he had been here long enough to know that, because he was a young black man, the police were to be avoided at all costs. He had seen the videos, read the news reports: Unarmed black man shot forty-one times, killed for reaching for his identification. Unarmed black man killed on the morning of his wedding, leaving his bachelor party. Unarmed black man killed on train station platform for breaking up a fight.

Kwame had his own experience to go on as well. Mayor Bloomberg's New York was one in which the police could stop and frisk anyone they wanted for often vague reasons such as fitting a relevant description, furtive movements, suspicious bulges, casing a location, and *other*. Police stopped hundreds of thousands of law-abiding New

Yorkers every year, and the vast majority of people stopped were black and Latinx men. Nearly nine out of ten people who were stopped and frisked were found to be completely innocent. Kwame was stopped for driving his own car while black, for living on the Upper East Side while black, and for being lost while black.

"It's whatever," he said after each incident, "I'm fine," as something hardened in his bright eyes.

On the phone, when I reached her, Anabel begged me to find Kwame. "What if they do something to him?" she asked. "My son, my only child," she cried. I did not fault her for not counting me.

I waited for the phone to ring again. Every few minutes, I dialed another number I found on the internet. I must have called every police station in New York City. As I waited, my mind filled in the blanks, envisioned the future, wrote a nightmare of a story. Every black mother, sister, and wife in America has written some version of that story in her mind. In that story, our promises to take care of our sons, brothers, and husbands turn into lies. This is a daily heartbreak. For too many, that story has become real. That story is an American terror.

In the version of the story my mind wrote:

My brother was arrested because he was mistaken for a man who stole an old white lady's purse.

Later, I learned the old white lady's purse contained twenty-five dollars, a mini umbrella, and five hard caramels. The old white lady was shaken but unharmed. The man who stole the old white lady's purse looked little like my brother. He was apprehended while stealing another old white lady's purse just a few blocks away. Kwame is short and muscular. The man for whom he was mistaken was tall and lanky. They both had dark skin—dark skin and gaps between their two front teeth.

There was nothing about gapped teeth in the crime report, filed by the old white lady, that led to my brother's murder. There was nothing about my brother's smile or the way he chewed his tongue when concentrating.

The cop who met me at the police station looked into my eyes very intensely when he told me my brother had reached under his shirt for something that might have been a weapon. That intensity infuriated me. I screamed at him to tell the truth. He refused to admit there had been no weapon. I read that in the newspaper the next day, but I knew it already because my brother was a pacifist and didn't believe in weapons.

The journalist waiting for me outside the morgue had a tiny hole in his nose that looked as though it had once held a nose ring. The nose ring made me think about when Yasmeen had a nose ring and Kwame said it looked like a booger.

I did not tell the journalist outside the morgue about this. I told him only that my family would seek answers; that we would take this to the end of time if we had to. I knew there could be no right answers. And who did I mean by *my family*?

On the news, a white anchor said that my brother was a twenty-one-year-old black man. He said he was a college student from Africa. He did not name the country, only the continent. He said Kwame was five-foot-seven. He said he was majoring in business. The anchor reported from in front of a photograph of Kwame I had never seen before. In the photograph, Kwame wore a baggy sweatshirt and looked angry. The anchor said he had marijuana in his system when he was shot. This was likely true but irrelevant. He smoked to not be anxious. The anchor did not say that Kwame often wore tailored suits, like our father. He started wearing them when he was twelve because he wanted to be just like the man he wished he could remember. He was not wearing a suit when he was shot twice by a police officer—once in the chest and once in the back. He was wearing a sweatshirt and baggy shorts because he had been on his way to shoot hoops with the teenage son of his apartment building's security guard. Kwame made friends everywhere. He was one of those people who said *we should hang out sometime* after meeting someone, and meant it.

The teenage son of Kwame's apartment building manager came to Kwame's funeral. He was short and muscular with dark skin. He wore a suit that was too big, borrowed from an uncle for the occasion. When he opened his mouth to say *Amen*, I noticed a gap between his front teeth. A gap between the teeth is called a diastema. In Tanzania, it is considered a mark of beauty. The teenage boy looked a lot like Kwame. The resemblance made me want to take his hand and run, but I didn't know where to go. There is nowhere in America where being a black man is safe.

The story I wrote in my mind was not made real. I was lucky. Luck means my brother, breathing. Luck also means continuing to live with the story in my mind, with the terror. In the real story, at six forty-seven in the morning, my phone rang.

"Nadia," Kwame's tired voice said, "can you come get me?"

As I put down the phone, my hand shook. When I stood, my legs would not hold me.

"He's alive," I whispered. And then louder: "He's alive."

A Heavy Burden

New York, New York, Age 28

There is something black children, especially black girls, are told from a very young age. You know what it is. It has made its way into the political discourse and into television sitcoms. Statisticians have worked to prove and disprove it. Young black people talk about it at happy hours and black student association meetings. We say it silently with nods to one another when we meet in places we are not expected to be: as we take our seats on a panel of experts, for example. Or when we check in with the receptionist at a job interview for a VP position at a big corporation. Our eyes say it when they meet the eyes of other black people at glitzy charity balls. We say it to ourselves as we get dressed and step out into a world that was designed to fail us, to see us fail. *You have to work twice as hard to get half as far.*

It is platitude and truism. It is ubiquitous. It is a persistent whisper in our ears. It is the graffiti carved into the bathroom door.

My father was the first person to say it to me. I was four and had complained about being made to work on my letters and numbers all afternoon instead of being allowed to play outside like the neighbors' (white) children. My father was unsympathetic. After that, he would shake his head and say *twice as hard, half as far* anytime I brought home a less than perfect report card or was given a less than glowing assessment at a parent-teacher conference.

I have heard the phrase repeated by black people in Africa and in America. My Jamaican friend said it when she got passed over for a promotion she felt she deserved. Her eyes were wet. She blamed herself for leaving the office before ten at night "for a month when I had walking pneumonia." My Ethiopian friend said it when I pushed him to skip studying for his bar exam for one night—his birthday—so I could take him dancing. He shrugged his shoulders when he said it, rolled his eyes.

Michelle Obama said it in a 2015 speech at Tuskegee University. She reminded the mostly African-American graduating class that they would be scrutinized harder. They would see their successes attributed to others or dismissed altogether. They would be judged more harshly for their failures.

Black people are expected by the white world to be strong but not angry. Pain must be hidden. Daily slights are to be borne with grace, humility, even gratitude. Weakness is intolerable. Vulnerability must wait until the day is done and the mask can come off in the privacy of our own homes. And by then we might be too tired or too stiff to feel it. This is not just true for black people living in Europe or America. It is also true, in a different form, in Africa and the Caribbean, where black people are the majority. People in former European colonies must see their lives in relation to the lives of white people. As communities, as individuals, we have been told we are inferior. Our economies, our live-lihoods, are reliant on Western economies, white people's livelihoods.

As my seismometer vibrated, as the alarm wailed, I did not stop trying to be twice as good. I would not have known how to stop. We become the stories we are told.

"You are small, black, and female," my father said to me once, near the end, when he was full of warnings. "People will try to cut you down to size. They will think you are weak. They will try to tell you who you are. Never give them the opportunity to think they're right." It was *you have to work twice as hard*, rephrased.

A few weeks before retreating into the blue chair, I was on the third of a triple shift at a restaurant. I also had a part-time job at a nonprofit. A triple shift meant that I worked a night shift, got home at two in the morning, then went back to the restaurant to work from ten in the morning till after midnight. My rent was due in a week and I was still one-third short. I could not afford to give up shifts. It was also finals week. When I got home from the triple shift at one in the morning, I made a pot of coffee and started studying for the next day's statistics exam. I studied and cried. I usually cried when I studied for quantitative tests because I'm very bad at math. Doing things I'm very bad at makes me sad about all the things in the world I will probably never really understand, like electricity and Einstein's general theory of relativity. But this was worse than my typical response to math. I was terrified I would not get an A. Maintaining a 4.0 GPA in graduate school was of the utmost importance. I believed that if I got anything lower than an A on anything, my life would fall apart. I did not, at the time, believe this in an abstract sense. As night turned into day, my crying became more and more hysterical. I was getting problems wrong. Getting problems wrong meant getting life wrong. I worked on one problem for three horrendous hours. Sometime after sunrise, I passed out with my cheek pressed into my textbook. I dreamt of being summoned to an office where I encountered a panel of tall white men who told me I had failed. In the dream, I begged and they laughed and laughed. Even as I begged, I smiled at them.

I woke up with a jolt. I had to be at my nonprofit job in one hour. My exam was that evening. At the office, my boss asked how I was doing.

"Great!" I exclaimed, my smile quivering at the corners. She did not notice.

Looking back on it now, my fear seems absurd. Not a single person, not even when I was interviewing for jobs, asked me what my GPA was. No one asked me about my grade on my statistics final. I got an A minus. To my traumatized brain, it might as well have been an F.

The point of graduate school was to get a full-time job that paid me enough so I wouldn't also have to work at night. I just wanted a job that didn't feel like a slow death. By this point, I had been rejected for more than forty jobs for which I had interviewed. Managers were always super-enthusiastic about me in phone interviews, but when I walked into rooms, they often looked startled. When they called to say I didn't get the job, they sounded sheepish, almost apologetic. They told me how great I was and said they were certain I'd find something soon. In almost every instance, they cited *culture fit* as the reason why the job had gone to someone else. I blamed myself. There must be something wrong with me and how I was presenting. I started straightening my hair again and wearing makeup. Writing and rewriting cover letters and résumés became a compulsion. I didn't have networks to speak of, or networking skills. My introversion makes me hopeless at events designed to help candidates meet employers, but I started going to them anyway which was not helping with my anxiety. I thought I just wasn't smart enough or good enough. I had failed. I was a failure.

The day after my statistics final, I went on yet another job interview, for an international nonprofit that helps refugees fleeing conflict and natural disasters, primarily in the "developing world." The woman doing the interviewing was my age, preppy, white. Her name was something like Brittany or Tiffany. She had on a real pearl necklace and a big diamond engagement ring.

"You lived in Uganda?" she asked.

"Yes," I said. "High school."

"That's great. We do some work there. Our CEO is there now, in Kigali."

I didn't tell her that Kigali is in Rwanda not Uganda.

"I work on our Africa program," she continued.

I didn't get the job. When Brittany-Tiffany emailed to let me down, she wished me the best and told me, just as a heads-up, "to be helpful," that there was a typo in my résumé. She didn't tell me what it was, and I was too embarrassed to ask. I pored over my résumé, became obsessed. A typo. No wonder no one would hire me. Finally, in anguish, I gave up and emailed my résumé to a friend, a professional copy editor at a newspaper.

"The only thing I could find," she said, "is that you wrote *towards* instead of *toward*. But, that's not really a typo. Americans prefer *toward*, the Brits prefer *towards*. Maybe you use *towards* because you went to school in England and Africa." She found the whole thing hilarious. She pointed out that Brittany-Tiffany should have known that *towards* was an acceptable spelling, given that she worked on behalf of African refugees, many of whom were educated in former British colonies. I did not laugh. I did not tell her that Brittany-Tiffany also did not know the names of African capital cities. I deleted the s.

"All of that is going to be a heavy burden to carry," Michelle Obama said in her speech at Tuskegee University. "It can make you feel like your life somehow doesn't matter."

If your life doesn't matter when you are working twice as hard and being twice as good, then it certainly won't matter if you find yourself sitting on the floor in a puddle of your own piss like the woman I saw in the Ugandan hospital, or stripping off all your clothes at a cocktail party, or talking to imaginary people, or being forced into exile in a blue chair by a seismometer in your head. In Ghana, you might end up chained to a tree, covered in paint, waiting for Jesus to save you. In America, you might get shot by the police.

On October 29, 1984, a black woman named Eleanor Bumpurs was shot and killed by the NYPD. The police had been called to her apartment in the Bronx to enforce a city-ordered eviction. Bumpurs was four months behind on her monthly rent of $98.65.

The NYPD had been informed by the housing authority that Bumpurs was emotionally disturbed and that, to resist eviction, she had previously brandished a knife and threatened to throw boiling lye at officers. When Bumpurs refused to open the door, police broke in. In the struggle to subdue her, one officer shot her twice with a 12-gauge shotgun.

I knew about Eleanor Bumpurs because of Hurricane Katrina.

When the levees broke in New Orleans in 2005, I watched hours upon hours of footage of people stranded on rooftops and of people who had just lost everything suffering the indignity of being crowded into unsanitary and inhospitable tent cities in the Louisiana Superdome. "We pee on the floor. We are like animals," said one woman to the *New York Times*. It was impossible not to notice that most of those people were black and poor. It was also impossible not to notice the language being used to describe them: looters, rioters, thugs. By comparison, I saw newspaper stories describing white people who waded through the water in search of food. They *found* bread, the journalists wrote. *Found.* Not stole. Not looted.

America was still a new land to me then and I was still trying to understand it. I was trying to understand what being black meant here, what it meant for me. I was trying to understand the ways in which I had become a different kind of black than I was in England, in Italy, in Tanzania, in Ethiopia, in Uganda, in Ghana. In each of those places, being black meant something different. My particular shade of black—light to medium brown with yellow or red undertones, depending on the season; middle-class; biracial—was valued differently in each of those places as well.

In Ethiopia, people often thought I was Ethiopian until they spoke to me in Amharic and found I could not respond. There, I was unremarkable in appearance. But many Ethiopians don't see themselves as black. Some consider themselves to be of a different race than other Africans, so in Ethiopia, my father was often black and I was often not black. What mattered more than whether I was black, though, was that I lived in the UN compound and that my father was paid in U.S. dollars. In Ethiopia, what mattered was my enormous relative privilege. What mattered was that we had food from the UN commissary while our neighbors starved; that when the war threatened to engulf us, we were airlifted out, business class.

In Italy, being black was unusual enough that diversity of blackness was not a thing people considered. Responses to my blackness ranged from curiosity to rage; from *I want to touch your skin to see if the color rubs off* to *get out of* my *country*.

In Ghana, colorism is one way by which social hierarchies are understood. The lighter, the better, even if lighter skin is achieved with bleaching cream. There, my skin color was often a source of envy. Once, I took a book out into the garden at my grandmother's house.

My grandmother's friend, upon spotting me as she walked up to the house to visit, rushed over to me, waving her arms.

"What are you doing?" she cried. "Get out of the sun! You have such nice light skin. Do you wish to become black like me?" I did, actually. I thought if I were darker, I wouldn't stand out as much, that I would belong. But in Ghana, I also got to see black people running things. In fact, I got to see a president who was quite a bit like me in a surface way: Jerry Rawlings, who was president from 1981 to 2001, was born to a Ghanaian mother and a Scottish father.

In England, race and racism were rarely openly discussed. When racism was mentioned—in history lessons, on television specials—it was relegated to the distant past or to other, "less tolerant" places like South Africa and America. Britain outlawed slavery far, far earlier than the United States did, we were taught at school. Former colonies now enjoy advantages and protections as part of the British Commonwealth, we were told. Curry is a British national dish, we were reminded. Not here, we were told. There is no racism here. And yet, everywhere I went in England, despite the large black population, I was expected to be from somewhere else. "Where are you from?" I was asked incessantly. In my case, it happened to be a fair question. I was not British. But so many black people in England, including my cousins, are. England is the only home they have ever known. And yet, when asked the question, my cousins know that the correct answer, the desired answer, is not London, where they were born and raised. They are supposed to say that they are from Ghana, where their parents were born and raised. The habitual question is a subtle suggestion that they do not truly belong.

In the weeks after Katrina, I learned that, in America, being black and desperate in a disaster could lead to being labeled and treated like a criminal. I turned to Google to learn more about this. What I learned shocked me. What I learned was that black people had been shot, even killed, by the New Orleans police, for trying to survive.

The first of these documented incidents took place on September 1, 2005. Keenon McCann was shot multiple times by SWAT Team

Commander Jeff Winn and Lieutenant Dwayne Scheuermann. The officers claimed McCann was armed, claimed he tried to ambush officers responding to a tip about a band of criminals who had stolen a truckload of bottled water. The criminals, the officers said, used the water to lure thirsty people only to rob them. McCann denied having a gun and sued the city. He was shot to death outside his home in 2008 before that case was tried. Winn and Scheuermann were not accused of a crime.

The day after McCann was shot, Henry Glover was killed by a rookie NOPD officer named David Warren outside a strip mall. Warren's charge was to guard the mall from "looters." To the NOPD, whatever was in the strip mall—packaged American cheese, Twinkies, soda, beer, maybe some deli meat, potato chips, I imagine—was more valuable than the lives of black people. Five officers, including Warren, were charged with trying to cover up Glover's murder by setting fire to a car with his dead body in it. Warren was acquitted.

On September 4, nearly a week after the hurricane, several NOPD officers leapt out of a rental truck and fired their weapons at a group of black people crossing a bridge. Ronald and Lance Madison—brothers—were returning to a hotel where they were staying after being flooded out of their home. Also on the bridge were Leonard Bartholomew Sr., his wife Susan, son Leonard Jr., daughter Lesha, seventeen-year-old nephew James Brissette, and Brissette's friend José Holmes. They had walked to a grocery store in search of food and supplies. Leonard was shot in the back, head, and foot. Susan's arm was partially shot off and later had to be amputated. Lesha was shot four times. José was shot in the abdomen, hand, and jaw. James Brissette and forty-year-old Ronald Madison, who family say was mentally ill, were killed. An officer stomped on Madison before he died. None of the people on the bridge had committed any crime. The police fabricated a cover-up story. The officers, they claimed, were responding to a police dispatch report of an officer down. They claimed they were fired at. All lies, it was later discovered.

After reading those stories and many others, I wondered to what extent the post-Katrina murders were a heightened version of an everyday reality. I googled *black people killed by police*. Eleanor Bumpurs's story came up, as did so many other stories of black women who died for the crime of mental illness.

In the years that followed Katrina, I continued to search for and to read with horror stories about police violence against black people, and particularly black women with mental illnesses. The searches became a strange routine. I visited ex-boyfriends' Facebook profiles to see if they had found happiness without me, hunted for the perfect vintage high-waisted jeans, checked how many more black people had been shot and killed by police.

In 2009, Brenda Williams's mother called the police in Scranton, Pennsylvania, and asked them to check on her daughter's mental health. Her daughter, a fifty-two-year-old black mother and air force veteran, suffered from schizophrenia. This request for help ended with Brenda Williams being shot to death by police. According to the officers, she was naked and disorderly when they arrived. She went into the kitchen and charged out wielding a knife. Considering the officers knew her to be mentally unstable, this behavior should have been expected. Yet Williams was killed.

In my room, before becoming moored in the blue chair, I turned off all the lights and drew the blinds. I called the people who needed to be called in order to cancel my life, length of time unspecified. I was ill, I said, very ill. I was hospitalized. Then my phone and computer were banished to a drawer full of old keys and batteries. I did not trust myself to ask for help. I didn't know if I could trust anyone to help me. Madness was coming, and no amount of working twice as hard could stop it now. My seismometer sputtered. It was spent, kaput. I had finally heeded the alarm. Now I was on my own. I would have to find my own way out. I hoped, despite my blackness, despite madness, despite the rules of race in America, I would make it out alive.

THE BLUE CHAIR

New York, New York, Ages 28

Day Five

In the blue chair, I could no longer stomach the silence. But language felt all wrong—too precise, too polite, too familiar. It was as though I had heard all the words, read far too many of them, and they didn't mean anything—not then, not anymore. What I needed was sound. In an act that was mysterious to me at the time, I turned to my father's music—to jazz.

My father lived to a playlist of Ben Webster, Coleman Hawkins, Wayne Shorter, and Coltrane. Especially, always, Coltrane—the epicenter from which all my father's blue notes rumbled. On Saturday afternoons when I was in middle school and he was dying, his head bald and shiny from the chemotherapy that didn't work, he turned the CD player way up. He studied my face, waiting for me to be moved by Coltrane. It did not happen. The skirmishing horns and keys unnerved me. I put my hands over my ears.

"It's like any other language," he insisted. "You just have to listen, train your ears, let go of self-consciousness, get lost in it."

I told him I would rather get lost in *Madame Bovary* or *Animal Farm*.

Now I wondered if Coltrane—the instability, tension, clash of his most avant-garde stuff, in particular—might not be just the thing. On my iPod, I curated a soundtrack: a soundtrack for unstable body and unstable earth, for madness.

I sat back, closed my eyes, listened to breath blowing through brass, let myself drift on it. As my eyelids grew heavy and the tide of my subconscious rose, a realization washed in. The seeds of jazz were planted in Africa, the flowers bloomed in America. Its roots are long and porous, they burrow deep and wide. Jazz is invented and reinvented, note by note by the musicians who play it. It is a constant process of improvisation, interpretation, blurring the borders between reality and poetry. The written score is a map, a mere suggestion of route.

Jazz requires both remembering and forgetting the past. It was born in a straddled place. Into the tenor saxophone went the rhythms of what are now Ghana, Nigeria, Senegal, and Sierra Leone—the major slave ports of West Africa. Out came a new sound, conjured in a hostile world. It was a stirring sound born of loss, defiance, and dreaming. Little wonder, then, that the music, over time, increasingly rejected order and linearity; that it became so loud and undulating it was off the Richter scale.

In the late 1960s, Coltrane was digging his way out of the dark hole of heroin and alcohol addiction. Music was his trowel. His was a music of searching. It pushed against the already flexible fences of a new experimental form that came to be called *free jazz*, named after the album of one of its pioneers, Ornette Coleman, who once said, "The best statements Negroes have made of what their soul is, have been made on the tenor saxophone." But the sound the soul makes is more cacophony than consonance.

Often, when people write about free jazz, they write in terms of swinging free of constraints: tonality, beat, harmony, tradition. But some argue it is less about swinging *away from* and more about swinging *toward* something new, something unknown. It is about the freedom in plunging fearlessly and without inhibitions, into the great beyond. Perhaps, the plunge will end with a splat, or endless floating in the void. Coltrane was in a place where the risk—of career, of critical acclaim, of his livelihood—was worth it. He was on a quest for sobriety, transcendence. He was trying to save his own soul.

Some fans who were unaccustomed to such mercurial riffing,

abandoned him. His new music, they believed, was too experimental, too intellectual. It asked too much of them. A few times, he was booed off the stage. His music was those things—experimental, demanding, intellectual. It was intellectual in the sense of being engaged with philosophical questions, with the meaning of music, and expression, and life; with advancing thought. I listened to a recording of a live performance in which Coltrane stops playing the saxophone and vocalizes into the microphone, beating his chest, creating vibrato, tremors. The effect is moving and frightening. It is fury, joy, and sadness all at once. Coltrane once told Miles Davis he played so long because he didn't know how to end his solos, and Miles replied, "Take the horn out of your mouth." Even that didn't work. He still had something to say, noise to make.

Coltrane's musical freedom, like most freedoms, was hard-won. He spent many hours a day practicing—rediscovering, investigating, and revising his ideas from the day before. He was determined to keep digging until he hit bedrock—the solid, essential truth at his own core. He wanted to share that truth with others. Music, he believed, was the language through which to do it. "You can't ram philosophies down anybody's throat," he said, "and the music is enough!"

For me, for a few hours in the blue chair, the music *was* nearly enough. In the dark of my room, Coltrane's cacophonous soul spoke to mine. I wept. I wept myself dry, and when I could weep no more, I felt something like a happy rage.

Outside, a motorcycle throttled, a drunk man bellowed something about not giving a shit. Underground, the Q train rattled into the station, shaking the walls of my apartment. The sounds merged, created something that would exist only once, only in that moment, for my ears alone. In it, I heard a message from my father, the gift he had tried to give me all those years ago. I was, in disposition and temperament, his daughter: Ruminative, studious, sensitive. Withholding, controlled. My father knew the time would come when my questions would threaten to overwhelm me, when the answers available to me would be unbearably insufficient, when harmony would be out of reach. He knew that when that time came, the only thing left to do would be to lose control. He wanted to open me to the beauty in abstraction, in complexity, in wild things.

Feral, free, I bounded around my room—crouched down low, arms swinging. Fuck, it felt good.

I should have listened sooner.

Day Six

We begin as a body. That body is ours. It is ours to discover, our dilated eyes still adjusting to the world outside ourselves. We put our tiny feet in our mouths and we laugh. Our laughter is a revelation. The world inside can make its way outside through sound. A meeting place. Our mouths find our mothers' nipples. We suck and slurp and burp. Milk from another body, another world, nourishes the world inside us. We peel at our soft skins with our sharp nails. This causes pain and we scream, and our mother's hands cover our hands in wool mittens. We heave ourselves onto our bellies and try to drag our flesh across the floor. Our brains grow and our explorations expand. We pull ourselves up using the edges of tables. We become upright. We learn to put one foot in front of the other. We learn to fall on our heavily padded asses. Nerves and synapses work together. I touch, therefore I am. No, that's not it. I feel therefore I am. Also not quite right, but closer.

Important questions: If I smack that object hanging above my crib, will it move? Can my body make it move? When my ass is wet and itchy, if I cry, will the body I was forced out of—my mother's body—come for me? Will my ass be wiped and my mouth filled with sweet milk?

Important questions: If I lie upside down in the blue chair island with my feet in the air and my head near the floor, will the blood that rushes to my head flush my adrenal glands and create more positive thoughts? Who told me that? A yoga instructor? My friend Pam? How long can I eat only dry bread, stale cheese, and mushy bananas? We build muscle by ripping tissue from bone, or something like that. What is the equivalent of that for our souls or spirits, or whatever our essence is called? If I squat, will my body show me what to do? It was definitely my friend Pam who said we don't squat enough in Western culture; that squatting eliminates wasteful thoughts and creates calm and openness. My friend Pam is a doula and also an acupuncturist and yogi. I love her and try to believe what she says, though she uses words I understand to make sentences I don't. *We must stay present in bliss and tethered to light*, she says. *When we allow darkness to stay dark, we give it our power and lose our core illumination.*

At some point, as children, we discover how our bodies can give us pleasure. We rub between our legs with small, sticky fingers. Heat is created, fluids ooze; we shudder. Then there is a glorious calm. We don't know what it means. Is it wonderful or terrible? We decide wonderful, and we keep doing it. But most of us know, somehow, to do it on the bathroom floor with the door locked or under the bed on a hot afternoon when everyone is outside eating hamburgers. My friend Luke discovered orgasm very young, too early to know how pleasure must be diluted with shame. He used to rub himself against poles and stick his hands down his pants at birthday parties. His father beat that out of him. Luke tells this story as though it has a happy ending, which I find alarming.

In the blue chair, I am naked. I am the only human body here. Without other humans there is no such thing as shame. Would Adam have covered his manhood if God hadn't made Eve from his rib? Probably not, I think, as I slide two fingers inside myself.

I read in *Psychology Today* that vibrators were invented to treat women suffering from *female hysteria*. Until the twentieth century, doctors did not believe that women could experience sexual desire or pleasure. The only pleasure women got from sex, these men determined, was from satisfying men. Women's bodies existed to bring men's bodies to orgasm. This untruth, unsurprisingly, led to high rates of sexual frustration among women. Doctors called the resulting anxiety, weakness, insomnia, irritability, erotic fantasies, cramps, and wetness between the legs *female hysteria*, from the Greek for uterus. In extreme cases, to cure them, doctors forced women into insane asylums or made them get hysterectomies.

Later, when it was decided by men that women could feel lust and pleasure after all, doctors treated female hysteria by giving women hand jobs. To give doctor's fingers a rest, they invented vibrators, some of which were conveniently powered by sewing machines. Horseback riding was also frequently prescribed. It wasn't until the 1950s that it was decided that female hysteria was not a mental disorder. Today, we do not believe hysteria is unique to women, nor do we believe it is simply an intense form of sexual frustration. But hysteria, now sometimes defined as *ungovernable emotional excess*, is often noted as a symptom of other mental disorders like schizophrenia, borderline personality disorder, anxiety disorder, and conversion disorder. Conversion disorder is a condition in which psychological stress manifests in physical ways: an illness of the mind is *converted* into an illness of the body. Common manifestations include weakness, paralysis, tremors, loss of balance, seizures, loss of vision, and slurred speech. I have experienced all of these "conversions" at some point or another, except for seizures. Often, after I experience them, or even as I am experiencing them, depending on the severity, I also experience heightened sexual desire.

La petite mort is a French expression that likens the weakening of consciousness experienced during orgasm to death—a small death. Sometimes, when I lose control of my mind and body to madness or something like it, I have thoughts of death—of what it might be like not to feel, of unending stillness and quiet. These thoughts, until right before I surrendered in the blue chair, did not extend to how I might get to that quiet, that stillness—to suicide. Perhaps I was saved from those thoughts by my heightened sexual desire, by orgasm, by *la petite mort*.

When I woke up on the floor this morning, on my fourth day

as an inhabitant of my blue chair island, I reached for my glasses as usual. I put them on and crawled up into the blue chair. But the objects around me did not sharpen in shape and color. I took off my glasses, rubbed my eyes, put my glasses back on. Everything was still unclear. I was near blind.

Now my legs hang over the arm of the blue chair. My fingers are between my legs. I point my toes and arch my back. I do not feel shame, not even when I moan, not even when my body begins to thrash. I make more noise than I have ever made about death or madness or orgasm. My body contorts. The blue chair kicks up a fuss. It grumbles and groans and pounds the floor. I make an earth—a small earth—shake. I wait a long time before opening my eyes. When I finally do, I can see.

Day Seven

I dreamt, last night, that a powerful earthquake struck New York and I could not get out of my blue chair. Everything flew about in my room. Things fell and smashed into one another. Some objects—a bookend in the shape of a man reading, a glass bottle full of shells—attacked me. Gravity did not work the way it was supposed to. The bookend and the glass bottle full of shells were boomerangs. I ducked and they flew over my head and then changed course and came back with a vengeance.

It wasn't that I couldn't get out of the blue chair because I was paralyzed or weak. It was because the hardwood floor was an actual ocean and I didn't think I could swim as far as the front door, which was—in my dream—very far away. Then my blue chair began to float on the surface of the ocean. It floated toward the front door. The door opened, and I floated down Mott Street.

The water was clear turquoise on the surface and blue-black in the depths. It was full of thousands of little silver fish. All of New York was water, but everything was all right because everything and everyone was floating. I jumped into the water and let myself sink. It didn't feel like drowning. My mouth open, I let the water gush in until it was all in me, every last drop. I became ocean. Still, then stormy. My tides came and went. I was a liquid body ravaged by nature, man, and self. I was a liquid body ravaging coast. There was another earthquake. My body rose in acknowledgment: a repercussion; a challenge.

TERRAFORMING

New York, New York, Ages 28 to 29

Terraforming:

literally, *earth-shaping*: the hypothetical process of deliberately modifying the atmosphere, temperature, surface topography, or ecology of a planet, moon, or other body to make it habitable

Note:

In *Parable of the Sower*, Octavia Butler wrote, "All that you touch You Change. All that you Change Changes you. The only lasting truth Is Change. God Is Change."

God Is Dead, Long Live God

Loss of faith does not happen all at once. It starts with a crack in the story—the story that guides us. We try to ignore it, but our eyes cannot help but fall upon it—once, twice, ten, twenty times a day. We become obsessed.

I do not remember ever having faith in God—not an unquestioning kind, anyway. When I was four or five, I decided there might be a God because I liked the idea of heaven. I wanted to believe that my tortoise, Thomas, whose head had been eaten by the neighbor's cat, was up there chewing grass in a green garden. But it bothered me that heaven could not be seen through a telescope, that it could not be reached with a space shuttle.

When I was in middle school, church bored me. I found Bible stories to be entertaining and ethically useful but implausible. Yet I took my Communion classes seriously because my father told me it was important to explore religion for myself. "I don't want you to reject Christianity because I don't believe," he said. "It's important that you make up your own mind." In addition to dropping me off and picking me up from St. Paul's Episcopal Church on Via Nazionale every Wednesday night and Sunday morning for six months, my father also instructed me in the study of the Koran and Buddhist sutras. He lay with his head propped up on pillows. His cheekbones were sharp and his eyes sunken. His fingers looked like long, dry twigs. His breath was jagged. Sometimes, so he could vomit or sleep, we had to pause or end our talks. I helped him to the toilet to vomit but he wouldn't let me stay with him: "Shut the door! Shut the door!" Chemotherapy was brutal.

Decency and righteousness, my father told me, were not intrinsic to one group of believers. The Ashanti believed that plants, animals, and trees had souls. Every life was to be respected and cared for. Ancestors watched over the mortal world. They rewarded those who did good with fortune and health. They took fortune and health from those who refused to help others, redistributed it to the needy.

"Ashanti people still honor our ancestors even as most of us pray to a white god," my father said. "The lessons they taught us are treasured. We live because of our ancestors. They are still alive through us." I wonder if, in telling me this, my father was trying to prepare me to live without his body, to know him as an ancestor.

The Ashanti, he reminded me, are guided by, and survive through, the forces of kinship and ancestral linkage. "We take care of each other on earth," he said. "If a family member asks for help, I give it. When a family member needs money for school fees or hospital bills, I send it. And my whole extended family loves you as if you are their child. We take care of each other's children. We raise each other's children. My cousins are my brothers and sisters. My aunts are also my mothers. Your aunts are your mothers, especially Auntie Harriet because she is my eldest sister. You will never be alone in this world."

"And do you really believe our ancestors are watching over us?" I asked.

He smiled. "I believe in the power of remembrance," he said. "And I believe love does not die with the body."

Our Father, who art in Heaven, goes the Lord's Prayer, *hallowed be thy name*. I learned that prayer as a child in a Catholic preschool in England. Later, as a teenager and an adult, I recited it, repeated it, in my head when I found myself on my knees, shaking from fear or grief. I recited it when I could feel the earth seething beneath me. I recited it to hush the sound of my seismometer. I recited it even though I did not call it prayer, did not count myself a Christian.

When it came to faith, I did what my father told me to. I made up my own mind. I might never have believed in God, but I chose to believe in a hallowed father: my father, Osei Owusu. He was my creator. My mother was too, but she was unknowable. My father was, to me, both earthly and divine. When he was alive, I turned to his voice for comfort and guidance. I followed his rules and aspired to please him. Education, family, and justice were three of the most important things to him, so they were three of the most important things to me.

In school, I worked hard, yet math defeated me. Every time I showed my father a bad grade, I felt humiliated, worthless. "You can do better," he'd say. I didn't believe I could. I tried to make up for disappointing him by getting perfect grades in English, history, and French. I did extra-credit projects, wrote long essays about freedom movements in Africa and the Civil Rights Movement in America. I wrote for the school newspaper and tried to read my way through the library, everything from Plato to James Baldwin. My father smiled when we discussed what I read. He smiled when I asked questions. He read everything too. The warmth of his smile felt like being chosen, like being saved.

As my father's cancer advanced, he emphasized more and more my duties to our family, my duty to take care of my brother and sister. When Yasmeen brought home a bad report card, my father summoned me into his room to ask me why I had not done more to help her.

"She looks up to you. She needs you more than anyone in the world," he said. "If she is failing, you are failing. If Kwame is failing, you are failing. Don't ever forget that." I didn't ask what would happen if I was failing so badly I couldn't prevent them from failing. That fear settled silently in my belly.

Once, Anabel punished Yasmeen and me by banning us from eating anything from the fridge and cabinets. We should, she said, eat at school or at friends' houses. I searched drawers and suitcases for foreign currency my father had brought back from trips and forgot. I took the metro to a *bureau de change* in Trastevere and changed British pounds and American dollars into lire. I bought bread, Nutella, cashews, and little packaged apricot jam pies, and hid them in my closet, saved them for weekends when we couldn't eat at school. Yasmeen and I ate our provisions in our bedroom with the lights off. We chewed and swallowed quietly. Once, when we saw the doorknob turn, we jumped under the covers and squished our sandwiches into balls in our fists. Nutella oozed between our fingers. It was only Kwame. We yelled at him to get out and he started to cry. We felt bad for upsetting him, but he couldn't be trusted. He was at an age when he repeated everything he heard, reported everything he saw. We didn't want Anabel to know we were eating without her permission. We didn't want our father to know Anabel had banned us from eating in the house. We were afraid it would break his heart, would kill him. We didn't want to hasten his death. With my hip, I shut the door on Kwame's screams. Yasmeen and I stuffed the balled-up bread into our mouths, licked the Nutella from our hands.

When our home felt too crowded with sadness, sickness, and rage, I took Yasmeen and Kwame on adventures. We went to the Colosseum, where we ate a large container of strawberry gelato, read mystery novels out loud, and people-watched. We went to the Luneur amusement park on Via delle Tre Fontane and rode the teacups and the Ferris wheel, ate cotton candy. I read to Kwame at night until he fell asleep on my chest, let him curl up in my bed when he woke up afraid.

After my father died, I continued to look to his example for lessons about how to live. When I said the Lord's Prayer, I think I was searching for him. Years later, when Anabel screamed at me that the story of his death was a lie, that he had affairs, that he died of AIDS, my conviction shattered. The story of his life—the version I had constructed—was my bible. Now the story had a crack in it. The crack gleamed red and ominous: blood, lava.

My blue chair madness was caused by loss of faith. As I rocked in the chair, I thought about a parable in Friedrich Nietzsche's *The Gay Science*. I pulled the book from the shelf to reread it. In it, a madman shouts, "God is dead. God remains dead. And we have killed him. How shall we comfort ourselves, the murderers of all murderers? . . . Is not the greatness of this deed too great for us?"

Nietzsche was not a believer. When he wrote that God is dead, he was not referring to the crucifixion. He meant that humanity was losing its faith. Without religion, he believed, most of us would lose our way. We would succumb to nihilism. Chaos would ensue. That is why the man in his parable was mad.

My father had been dead for more than a decade, but in the days leading up to and during my blue chair exile, my world seemed a tomb for the questions of his spirit. The questions terrified me.

In Christianity, denominations in which my father (Anglican), Anabel (Lutheran), and my mother (Armenian Orthodox) were raised, faith is a matter of trusting in God, no matter what, without question, without demanding proof. It is the expectation that God, through Christ or grace or fire and brimstone, will fulfill the promises He made to humanity in the scriptures. Faith is undying, unwavering loyalty. It was that kind of faith my father warned me against. I did not realize it until I found myself in the blue chair, but I had not heeded that warning. My worship of my father was fanatical.

As a young man, my father rejected faith in favor of science because his people—Ghanaians, Africans, black people—were colonized, enslaved, and subjugated in the name of whiteness and a white God. The story of Adam, Eve, the snake, and the forbidden fruit was, for him, too simple a fairy tale. He preferred, he told me, the story in which life oozed from the earth in Africa and was reabsorbed into that earth. In that story, there were no chosen people. There was no promised land. No pious right or evil wrong. There was only hope and striving. We were made not by the will of God, but by the forces of carbon and water and lightning and meteoroids and asteroids and gravity and radiation and a ball of fire we call the sun. The quest to understand how all those forces combined to create and sustain life was enough of a quest for my father. He had little use for a book written before we could see microorganisms; before we knew they are in, on, and of us; and in, on, and of every other living thing.

"Everything on this earth is connected!" my father exclaimed. "A better religion, to me, is the practice of noticing that connection, of deepening our understanding of it." In Christianity, there was no need for microscopes or space shuttles or radiocarbon dating. Questions were frowned upon. Everything was already decided. "And that is absolutely maddening," my father said. "If that's the case, why live?"

When it came to my father, I had forsaken questions. I had created a story of him that served my needs. That story was absolute. It was utilitarian. My story of my father lessened the force of my grief, quelled the quaking. My story was sacred. My father was born of a family both humble and royal, my story went. He grew up brilliant, boundless, and black. His brilliance radiated. His blackness radiated. His boundlessness carried him to America, to abundance, to Europe, back to Africa, to fruition. He helped the poor, fed the hungry. He gave me life. He gave life to Yasmeen and Kwame. We were his chosen people. He loved us. He was love, immaculate. His black star rose. It continued to rise, until cancer cut it down.

Anabel had called my story into question. With her story that my father had died of AIDS, she had introduced mysteries. She had suggested that my father had kept secrets from us, his chosen people; that he had strayed from us. I shook my head to silence her story. I drank tequila, straight. I sat in my window and looked up at the dark New York sky, no stars visible. But they were there, I knew. Black star in the sky. Black star father. Black star that wasn't visible but that rose immortal in my heart, in my story.

Yasmeen and I made fun of Anabel and our mother for using God in the same way I used the story of our father. We rolled our eyes.

We pointed out their many hypocrisies. We felt ourselves superior in our doubt.

Anabel, I thought, cherry-picked what she wanted from Scripture, discarded the rest. Bible verses were memorized and recited, used to win arguments. "Thou shalt not lie with a male as one lies with a female; it is an abomination," she said when I asked why she was against gay marriage. "And that's that," she finished before I could try to push our conversation beyond Leviticus.

Yet there were many other issues on which she was willing to cede to science. "It's so obvious we descended from apes," she said when we visited a gorilla sanctuary in Uganda. "Look at his face." She pointed at a male gorilla who watched us thoughtfully, his large dark eyes framed by magnificent long lashes. "I could imagine having a nice cup of tea with him. I've had to stare at uglier men across the table at dinner parties." The gorilla seemed to smile at the compliment.

Anabel did not embrace Christianity wholesale, but she was resolute in her version of it—her story. She made it up as she went along; reconciled it with science and changes in her mood. Church was attended on the important holidays. She prayed for my father to live, for Fendi to have size twelve trousers in their annual sale, for Kwame to grow out of his anger. After my father died, Kwame bit us, kicked his friends at school, stomped his little feet.

"Jesus," Anabel said with her hands clasped in front of her breasts after Kwame threw his bowl of buttered pasta onto the floor in a fit, "please stop my children from behaving like demons. Amen." She bowed her head then got up from the table and poured herself a large glass of white wine. Kwame banged his fists on the table until he tired of it. Then he put his head down and cried. Anabel, Yasmeen, and I ignored him, finished our dinner in silence. As far as I can remember, Yasmeen and I had done nothing to anger Anabel that day, but perhaps including us in her prayer was preventative. Perhaps it was a warning.

For her Somali second husband, my mother converted to Islam. When she was a girl, her family was not particularly religious, though they were regular congregants at St. James Armenian Orthodox Church in Watertown, Massachusetts. They went for the coffee and gossip, my grandfather joked. In Turkey, my great-grandparents were persecuted for their religion. In America, my grandparents' faith was sparing and quiet. It is hard to believe in a god who would allow your family and friends to be massacred in the name of a slightly different god. But being faithless would have been a relinquishment of an identity they had lost so much to preserve. Their family had walked across a desert and crossed an ocean to believe openly. My mother's family found a balance between faith and assimilation. Easter was marked on the Western rather than the Orthodox calendar. They set their Christmas dinner table with Urfa kabob and pilaf, but also roast turkey and mashed potatoes.

As a Muslim, my mother was more devout than she was as a Christian. She prayed five times a day and gave up alcohol and pork. After the summer spent with my mother in Massachusetts when I was six, I reported her daily prayers to my father. In an uncharacteristically unkind voice, he said perhaps there were things she felt she needed to atone for. I sensed he was jealous. I had come back full of stories about my mother and her new life. I didn't tell him about how her husband yelled at Yasmeen and me. I told him instead about how we had BeDazzled sweatshirts at a mall; how we floated in tires in a pond. "Was it *really* that fun?" he asked. "It was all right," I said. "I like it better here."

My mother's new faith widened the distance between us and I resented it. During that summer in Massachusetts, she would follow her husband into their room to pray in Arabic. I did not understand the words or the rituals: the washing of hands and feet, the covering of heads, the bowing toward Mecca. My mother had chosen this man over my father, Yasmeen, and me. She married him soon after she left us. My half sister Wahida is just a year younger than Yasmeen. From this, I assume overlap: an affair. For this man, my mother had converted. He mattered to her more than I did, I concluded. More than I ever would. As a teenager, after my father's funeral, I told Yasmeen our mother worshipped men more than she worshipped any god.

"She'd do anything for a man," I said. "She's not really Muslim."

"But what about Baba?" she asked. "He was a man. She left him."

"Probably because he loved us more than he loved her," I said.

There was no evidence that my mother was not as devout a Muslim as she claimed to be. But the story I told Yasmeen was useful. It fueled my anger, made me righteous. Against my father, against Yasmeen, against me, my mother had trespassed. *Forgive us our trespasses,* the Lord's Prayer continues, *as we forgive those who trespass against us.* But I was not a Christian. I was under no obligation to forgive. Anger dulled pain.

To myself, in the blue chair, I had to admit that I too practiced a faith of convenience and crossed fingers. I too believed fervently in a man-god. I had long prided myself on embracing contradiction, complexity. Now I could see the limitations of my openness. I saw myself dogged, closed-minded. I didn't like what I saw. Even worse, I was panicked because I couldn't see a way forward that wouldn't be a betrayal of my father. I could choose to continue believing my story of him, wholesale, but doing so would be a willful rejection of his teachings: never stop questioning, love questions as much as answers. Or I could examine the questions Anabel's claims had surfaced and uncover things my father had not wanted me to know about his life. And what was I to make of how troubled I was by the possibility that my father had died of AIDS? What did that say about me?

Intellectually, I knew it mattered little what had caused my father's death—AIDS or cancer. I lost him either way. Yet for weeks after Anabel told me my father died of AIDS, I spent three-quarters of every waking hour tormented by questions about who my father shared his body with. Did he have affairs and if so with whom? Did he have a life apart from the one in which he was my father? Did he have a life in the shadows? I was embarrassed by how prudish and intolerant my discomfort with these possibilities revealed me to be. Anabel had forced me to consider—to contemplate—my father as just a man. A man who lusted, who cheated. That was the story of my father Anabel wanted to replace my story with. Why? Why had she chosen that story? I did not believe lust to be a sin, or I did not want to believe I believed it to be a sin. People cheated all the time. What was the big deal? Yet in my story of my father, lust and adultery seemed irreconcilable. Did I think it unforgivable? I did not know. I did not want to find out. I did not want questions. I wanted my faith back.

In the days leading up to my blue chair asylum, I tried to regain my faith by closing my eyes and remembering the year before my father died. I could see him in the hospital. The hopeful poison of chemotherapy dripped from a tube into his veins. Sometimes a doctor came in with scans and explained how the tumors had either shrunk or grown.

When my father had surgery to remove a tumor from his brain, I was in the waiting room. There had been a scar. It turned white then yellow and scabby. It ran across his bald head in the place where some people part their hair—a little left of center. He had cancer. Of that, I was certain. His death certificate confirmed it. For a short time that certainty quieted the questions. But then more questions emerged: Did my father have AIDS as well as cancer? Could HIV cause cancer? If he didn't have AIDS, why would Anabel say he did? Would she lie about that just to hurt me? Could she be that cruel? Why did it matter to me if he had AIDS? Why did I care? How had she known I would care? Was I a prig? *Impossible*, I told myself. I had one-night stands. I wasn't ashamed of wanting men, of my own lust. I had danced topless in a burlesque show. I had a good friend who did sex work to pay her bills while she tried to make it as an actress. I didn't judge her for it. *Did I judge her for it?* Did I think of AIDS as a gay man's disease? Was I afraid that if people learned my father died of AIDS, they would think he was gay? Why should that matter to me? Was I a homophobe? A bigot? *I can't be*, I told myself. I had gay friends, marched in pride parades, supported gay marriage. When one of my cousins came out and some of the elders in our family stopped speaking to him, I was squarely on his side. *I thought we were better than this*, I'd said, *he deserved better from us. I'm not a prig*, I told myself, *not a bigot*. But then the voice in my head said: *Isn't that what a bigot or prig might say? Look at all my gay friends. Look at all my sexually free friends. Look at how I dance with them. Bigot. Prig. Bigot.*

On the internet, I learned people with HIV are more likely to get some types of cancer due in part to weakened immune systems. Some types of cancer occur so frequently in people with HIV that they are called *AIDS-defining* conditions, meaning their presence in an HIV-infected person is a sign they have developed full-blown AIDS. So it was possible that Anabel was telling the truth. My father could have died of both cancer and AIDS. But if it was true, why had she waited all these years to tell me? Why would my father have kept it from me?

I have a memory of a conversation with my father about AIDS. We were living in Kampala, Uganda, then.

In Uganda, I used to ride in the back of my father's pickup truck, standing up, holding on to the hood. In the early morning, the air was damp with mist that would soon clear to reveal the perpetually seventy-five-degree sun. The world was an emerald—sparkling, green, a precious gift. Uganda is one of the most breathtakingly beautiful places I have ever been. And yet, where there was such beauty, there was also the muck of poverty. There were young boys up north with cocaine in their nostrils and machetes in their hands. Those children hacked their neighbors into pieces, burned their own villages to a crisp because their prophet commander forced them to. Young girls were gang-raped, stolen from schoolhouses. Violence against women was endemic. Back then, that violence was only a ghost story to me. I heard whispers of it in the news and saw shadows of it in the eyes of orphan beggars in the street. Their eyes were dead from what they had seen, from the glue they sniffed, and from the death sentence that lived inside of them. Many of the orphans, particularly the girls, were HIV-positive.

When my father and I discussed AIDS, I was twelve. We were listening to the radio in the car one morning as he drove me and Yasmeen to school. I didn't know it then, but he had already been diagnosed with cancer. I don't remember seeing any signs he was sick. *How could you not have known?* demanded the voice in my head as I rocked in the blue chair, *you, who claim to have loved him most of all?*

"Do not drown in the AIDS flood," said a woman's voice on the radio. "Always be on board."

"What's the AIDS flood?" I asked my father as the sound of a traditional drum filled the car.

My father turned the radio down. "AIDS is a deadly disease that is killing hundreds of thousands of people in Africa."

"How do you get it?" I asked, immediately worried for us, immediately tuned in to the buzzing of disease-carrying insects.

My father coughed and stared through the windshield. "From sex," he said, finally.

"Isn't there a medicine for it?" I asked.

"No," he said. "And I'm not sure there will be one anytime soon."

"Why?" I asked.

My father turned off the radio and glanced over at me in the passenger seat. "Because it is mainly poor black Africans who are sick," he said quietly. "And homosexuals."

In the days leading up to the blue chair, I tried to recover small details about that conversation. Had my father's voice sounded worried or angry? What was the look on his face when he said *homosexuals*? That is, I believe, the only time I ever heard him say that word. But I could not extract any clues or meaning from what I remembered. This frustrated me. As my frustration grew, so too did my self-loathing. In the year I was twelve, Sub-Saharan Africa was being ravaged by an HIV/AIDS epidemic. HIV sped along Uganda's pothole-ridden roads. It was carried in the blood of soldiers who, after months of fighting rebels in the bush, hired *malayas*; carried in the blood of refugees returning from overcrowded camps in rural Tanzania, in the blood of truck drivers who had many mistresses along their regular routes. Roughly 15 percent of the Ugandan population was, in the year I was twelve, HIV-positive—the highest rate on the continent. All around me, people were dying. I hardly noticed. My father was dying. I did not know. Why was I oblivious to my father's suffering, to the suffering of so many Ugandans? I was just a child, I reminded myself. But *self-absorbed, unfeeling*, the voice in my head called me. *Bigot, prig.*

When I was sixteen, Anabel, Yasmeen, Kwame, and I moved back to Kampala from Rome. I volunteered at a hospital where I sat with women dying of AIDS. I played cards with them, read to them. Why had I chosen to do that? For school, I had to complete a certain number of hours of community service, but I could have taught writing at a primary school or played with babies at an orphanage. Did I choose the hospital because I thought that's what my father would have wanted?

What had I felt for the women I sat with? Empathy? Pity? I don't remember touching them beyond the brushing of hands during card games, lukewarm hugs when I left. Had I been afraid of their skin? Of their blood? I can't recall. I do remember the smell of their bodies: sour, like pickled onions. It was always very hot in the hospital—too hot. It felt good to tell my friends and teachers about my afternoons in the ward. I liked the approval, the admiration, in their eyes. Every time I left the hospital, the cool evening air tickled my skin. From nearby bars, Lingala music drifted on the breeze. Soon a car would arrive to drive me away from the dying, to the house on the hill where I lived. The UN driver would open the car door for me. At home, dinner would be on the table and everything would smell like wood polish and Windex. A portrait of my father smiled down on me from above the dining table, its frame spotless, dustless. Two Ugandan women, Florence and Joyce, cooked those dinners, scrubbed all the surfaces.

Did I ever ask them if they had lost anyone? I don't think so. I asked them if they had seen my biology textbook; if they knew where my favorite striped crop top was; if I could have half a mango for breakfast instead of scrambled eggs.

Did my father really have affairs? In the blue chair, I racked my brain for any inkling of that, but found nothing except a memory of Anabel telling him he could not come with us to the Miss Uganda pageant. She did not want him looking at bikini-clad beauties. He sulked but did not push the issue. Anabel, Yasmeen, and I went to the pageant and sat in the second row with other United Nations wives and their daughters. None of the husbands had been invited. *Look at her bottom wobble*, Anabel said of a tall, elegant woman who looked a lot like her, only younger. The wives laughed with what sounded like relief.

Yet despite my lack of memories to support Anabel's claims, I know there is much about parents' lives that goes unnoticed by children. Indeed, my father hid his cancer diagnosis from me for a full year and a half. What else had he hidden?

I called my sister to ask if she knew anything I didn't, if she remembered anything differently.

"Anabel told me the same thing years ago," Yasmeen said. "I must have been eighteen, still in high school, after you'd left for college. Anabel and I were fighting about something. She got this crazy look in her eyes and told me our father died of AIDS. I just laughed. I didn't believe her."

"Why didn't you tell me? Why didn't you believe her?" I asked, hoping she could offer me something concrete, something more than internet links and cloudy memories.

"Because I believed our father," she said.

She sounded casual, unshaken. I envied her. I didn't want to infect her with my questions. Quickly, I hung up. That night, from obsessing and trying to resist the obsession with whiskey, I vomited down my shirt. I took the shirt off and threw it on the floor, crawled into bed, slept in the stench of my insides.

Philosophically, my father was what I would now call a feminist, though I didn't have that language at the time. He believed women were as smart and capable as men. He told me I could do and be anything I imagined. His mentor was a woman. In his work at the UN, he often focused on gender equity, particularly to ensure girls in Africa had access to education. These truths were written in my story of my father. But contradicting truths can exist at the same time. My father's marriages to Anabel and, I believe, to my mother were traditionally gendered. My father worked outside the home. My mother and Anabel did not. His wives—my mothers—moved halfway around the world for him multiple times. Our life as a family was shaped by my father's choices. Anabel baked and made homemade ice cream. She planned dinner parties and sewed cuffs into my small-statured father's trousers. During the summer I spent with my mother when I was eight, after hanging up a call with my father, she muttered, "Things must always be done his way." During a fight, Anabel accused him of being impossible to please: he wanted dinner on the table at seven sharp, his shirts pressed just so, his children bathed and in bed by eight thirty.

Growing up, I did not note the contradiction. I did not wonder why my father expected things of his wives that he did not want any man to expect of me. Once, Anabel suggested I learn to cook so I could make dinner for my future husband. "The day my daughter is subservient to a man," my father joked, "I will sell fish." He said this to her as he ate the dinner she had prepared for us.

Against my mother and Anabel, I always took my father's side. Why couldn't Anabel have dinner on the table by seven? What else did she have to do all day? Why should my mother get to make any decisions after she made the decision to leave us?

How little thought I gave to my mothers' desires and interior lives. I never asked Anabel if she dreamed of a career outside the home, never asked my mother about my father's share of the blame for the end of their marriage. I viewed my mothers' lives only in relation to mine. In my life, they were supposed to love, protect, and choose me.

They were supposed to love and honor my father above all others. On those counts, I deemed them inadequate.

During my conversation with my father about AIDS, I asked, "So no one is going to do anything to help the sick people?"

"Some people are trying," he said. "The UN and some other organizations. And President Museveni is trying."

"What is he doing?" I asked.

"He has a plan called ABC," my father said. "It stands for abstinence, being faithful to your husband or wife, and using condoms."

My father had to explain to me what *abstinence* was. I vaguely knew about condoms. I knew that men put them on their penises, so they wouldn't make babies. My father did not make eye contact as he explained ABC to me. Sex was not something we comfortably discussed. I knew the basics. He had signed the permission slip for me to watch a sex education video at school. Anabel didn't have much to say about sex either, and when we did discuss it, it was usually so she could warn me about bad men and what they might try to do to me.

"Who was that boy with his hands all over you?" Anabel asked after watching me compete in a coed track meet, watching a boy scoop me up in his arms after I won a race for our team. "Careful where you let boys put their hands."

In the days leading up to the blue chair, to understand the context in which my father might have been infected with HIV, I read articles and academic studies about AIDS in Uganda. In them, I sought reasons to doubt Anabel's story, to reassume my faith.

Careful where you let boys put their hands, I learned, could have been a slogan for the abstinence part of Museveni's ABC plan. But, to his credit, the president did not stop at wagging his finger at young people, not at first.

Museveni, a civil war hero who helped deliver Uganda from the violent dictatorships of Milton Obote and Idi Amin, decreed fighting AIDS a *patriotic duty* of all citizens. Task forces were created, and the ministries of health, defense, education, and gender were engaged. There were television ads. Daily a traditional drum was played on the radio to remind people of the call to serve their nation by educating themselves, practicing safe sex, and knowing their HIV status. This was the drum I heard in the car with my father.

The ABC campaign challenged male dominance in relationships and society. Women, Museveni said, should take control of their sexual lives. He backed policies that supported women in running for office, strengthened laws against rape, discouraged underage girls from marrying older men. And he launched new school sex education curricula that included messages about gender equity.

In many ways, ABC was about writing a new story. Condoms had long been associated with promiscuity and prostitution. AIDS was stigmatized, was seen by many as a disease caused by moral failing, dwindling faith, a decaying, oversexed society. Some people thought AIDS was a weapon unleashed by white people on Africa—the new colonialism. Those stories were murderous. The new story Museveni's government was writing sought to empower people at risk of contracting HIV and to lift the burden of secrecy and humiliation for those already living with and dying from the disease. In Kampala, HIV-positive public figures were encouraged to come forward to share their experiences, their truths. Uganda's AIDS Information Centers became Africa's first voluntary counseling and testing service. The centers provided same-day results and long-term counseling programs for anyone who wanted them. Museveni called for people to treat people who tested positive with compassion and respect.

These narrative-change efforts were no small thing in what was, and still is, a very conservative country. There is a strong and influential Evangelical Christian movement in Uganda. Even as a preteen, I can remember feeling my sexuality scrutinized. "Cover your thighs!" boys from a local school that shared my international school's soccer field shouted at me and the other girls from my school who played in shorts. "Police your women!" they shouted at the boys who played with us. This was only childish taunting, but it spoke to something in the groundwater.

As Ugandans were getting back the results of their HIV tests, the government was awaiting the results of its own test. Had ABC been effective? The news was good. Young Ugandans reported waiting longer to have sex for the first time. Men reported having fewer affairs. Most importantly, more people used more condoms. The nation's rate of HIV infection plummeted. I remember condom billboards and murals everywhere. They depicted men and women smiling at each other suggestively. I saw a little boy, no older than five, standing outside a grocery shack, blowing into a condom as though it were a balloon. Passersby laughed and stopped to pinch his cheeks. His mother beckoned him over to where she was sitting on a stool in front of her phone card stall. She laughed too and poked at the condom balloon with her finger. Nobody seemed embarrassed or ashamed.

Despite the success of ABC, though, there were many Ugandans who believed God wanted condoms off billboards and out of young people's reach. They wanted sex education in schools to focus only on abstinence. They wanted women to obey their husbands, to stay out of bars and politics. They believed gay people were going to hell and AIDS would take them there. *Fanatics, bigots, prigs*, people like the adult me might have called those people. As a child, I was not aware enough of what was happening to have any opinion, to call them anything. *Hypocrite, bigot, prig*, the voice in my head called me as I sat in the blue chair.

"I don't believe in God," I tell people when asked about my faith. "So much of religion seems to rely on judgment and shame." But religious people do not have a monopoly on judgment and shame. Judgment and shame are used to stop people from poking their fingers into the cracks of sacred stories, from peering into what is hidden underneath. We all have sacred stories, whether we like to admit it or not. The present is a wilderness. The future is a wilderness. The past is a story, is a haven. We build our havens on shaky ground.

Even though ABC was successful, even though the campaign called for compassion and respect, in its focus on individual sexual behavior—on abstinence and monogamy—passing judgment and shaming were present in the policy. And, in November 2004, Museveni signed off on a new policy from the Ugandan AIDS Commission called "Abstinence and Being Faithful (AB)." It was to serve as the guide for all sex education curricula for both primary and secondary schools moving forward. The "C" in ABC—condoms—had been deleted.

It is unclear what led to this dramatic change of heart and policy. Perhaps Museveni sought support from Uganda's growing Evangelical population. Perhaps he did it for money. The replacement of ABC with AB coincided with the launch of the United States President's Emergency Plan for AIDS Relief (PEPFAR) by then American President George W. Bush, which committed fifteen billion dollars over five years (2003–2008) to fight global HIV/AIDS. Bush was an insistent proponent of abstinence-only school sex education programs, even though they had consistently been proven less effective in preventing pregnancy and STDs than programs that included contraception information. Uganda was a recipient of PEPFAR funds.

Museveni has now been in power for more than thirty years. He has angered the world by abolishing presidential term limits and engaging in questionable electoral practices, including detaining an opponent. He has openly criticized condoms as promoting underage sex. He made a speech calling for death by hanging of anyone who knowingly infected another person with HIV. He has called AIDS a disease of promiscuity. He has dismissed homosexuality as a matter of choice, has called gay people disgusting. He signed a bill making gay sex punishable by life in prison.

My research about AIDS in Uganda was aimed at discrediting Anabel's story about my father. I don't know what I had hoped to find. What I found were my own biases. In 2011, the prevalence rate of HIV in Uganda was 7.3 percent, up from a low in 2003 of 4 percent. In the story of ABC, there was the possibility of unity and healing. The story of AB was designed to humiliate, debase, condemn, divide. Stories have consequences. In my story of my father, I set him apart from other people. I made him a god, made myself chosen. As a god, my father couldn't have hurt my mother or Anabel, couldn't have had affairs, couldn't have died of AIDS. But whether my father died of AIDS or cancer, I am connected to the people who live with AIDS and the people who have died from it. In denying that connection, I diminished rather than protected my story of my father. In fixating on the question of whether he had had affairs, I debased our relationship. I perpetrated the lie that cancer is a more respectable cause of death than AIDS. When our stories require us to pass judgment, to inflict shame on ourselves and others, to set ourselves apart, we cause harm. *Bigot, prig*, the voice in my head calls me. And, I must answer honestly. I must answer yes. I want to make it not so. I have work to do on myself. I need a new story.

As a child, what did I believe in? I believed in a father. I believed in his dark, open face. I believed in his gentle eyes behind thick lenses. I believed in his bushy beard, small ears, thick bottom lip that I pulled down with my index finger to reveal bright pink gums. I believed in a round head to hold on to when I sat on his strong shoulders. From those shoulders, I could reach up with both hands to pull leaves from trees. I knew he wouldn't let me fall. At age two, at age three, I didn't always know where my father went when he left the house. I didn't need to know. He always came back. No matter where I hid, he would find me. I knew him, and because I knew him, I knew love. My father didn't believe in a god, but he did believe in humanity, in coalition, in trying.

No doubt, my father hurt my mother and Anabel. Perhaps he had affairs. Perhaps he lied to me. I have hurt people, lied, withheld truths. My father never extolled perfection, so who am I to demand it of him?

"Just try, Nadia," I can hear him saying. He said that often, when I complained that I couldn't do my homework, hold a handstand for more than a few seconds, or be nice to my sister after she had wronged me.

Once, my father punished me for being selfish. The children of one of his friends had come over, had wanted to play with my dolls. I had refused to let them, had ordered them out of my room. After they went home, my father told me to sit on the stairs and think about what I had done.

"Do you ever do anything bad?" I asked him after admitting my naughtiness, after being forgiven.

He laughed. "Of course," he said. "I'm only human. We all do things that hurt other people. The important thing, when we do, is to say we're sorry and to try to do better."

My father—only human—was more than enough for me then. I didn't need him to be a god. He is still enough. I have faith.

Maternal Guidance

In the blue chair, I tried to understand my mothers, myself. What would they say to me, their shaking daughter? From my island, I could not ask. My mothers—Anabel and Almas—were geographically and emotionally beyond range. But their answers, I believed, might offer me an opening: out of the blue chair, out of anger, out of madness, into mercy. I decided to summon their guidance using the forces of memory and divination; extrapolation. *Open*, I told my spirit and theirs as I closed my eyes. *Open.*

———

I saw Anabel in a kitenge-print dress and brown leather sandals, her face bare and dewy, her cornrows tight. She walked toward me. My father walked behind her. She had just picked him up from the airport. It was, I think, the night he told her he'd been diagnosed with cancer. (Years later, Anabel told me he'd gone to see a doctor in England. He told her the bad news in the Entebbe airport, made her promise not to tell anyone.) He wouldn't tell me for over a year.

Yasmeen, Kwame, and I stampeded toward them, our arms wide open. Our father had been gone for weeks. Anabel looked startled. She raised her hand to her chest, moved aside.

"Slow down," she said, "not so rough."

I ignored her, threw myself at my father, arms around his neck. Kwame hugged his knees. Yasmeen his waist.

"Okay, guys," Anabel said, "let him breathe. He's tired from traveling."

"Are you tired, Baba?" I asked, letting go.

"I'm fine," he lied.

Did Anabel wince at that lie? Was she lonely in her new knowledge? Was she afraid?

"Let's eat," she said. "I'm sure dinner is ready. I asked Joyce to roast a chicken."

As we walked from driveway to door, Anabel stopped, snapped a hot pepper off a plant, bit into it. It must have set her mouth on fire. Her eyes filled with tears.

"What are you doing?" I asked.

"I just wanted to taste the pepper," she said. "I've never tasted them."

"Your wife is weird," I said, looping my arm through my father's.

"There is nothing weird about it," she said.

I think I laughed at her, called her crazy—mad. Looking back on that evening from blue chair island, I see she was right. There was nothing weird about how she bit the pepper, nothing weird about how she wanted fire in her mouth. Or if it was weird, if it was madness, it still made perfect sense. It was called for: her madness, mine.

———

I heard Almas's voice raised in protest. She was fighting with her husband. I couldn't make out her words, or I cannot remember them, but they woke me. This was the summer I visited her in Massachusetts when I was eight.

I lay awake until she came into the bedroom where we—her four daughters—slept on two twin mattresses, pulled from bunk bed to floor, and pushed together. Iman—the younger of my half sisters—had one of her legs thrown over mine. Yasmeen's breath tickled my neck. My foot was pressed against Wahida's belly—she lay sideways across the foot of the mattress.

"You're awake," my mother said. She squatted and placed the cool back of her hand against my cheek. "Come, I'll make you breakfast."

In the kitchen, I sat at the table while she scrambled eggs. We were alone, and I wanted to tell her something important, something she would think about when I left; that would make her think about me. But my thoughts were a jumble.

"Here sweetheart," she said, setting my plate in front of me. She sat across from me with a misshapen ceramic mug of coffee. "Are you enjoying yourself here?" she asked.

"Yes," I said.

"Good," she said, "I'm glad." I think I remember her taking a deep breath, opening her mouth as though to speak, exhaling. In my mind's eye, for a moment, time stopped. We were suspended.

The next thing I remember is Almas in the backyard, later that day. She circled the lawn slowly, in a silk dress and house slippers. I ran to her. I wanted to tell her about a game I'd been playing with Yasmeen and my half sisters. The rules of the game, I've long forgotten. Whatever the game was, I had lost and was sore about it. I wanted to play something else. My mother, I hoped, would comfort me, take my side.

She did not stop walking when I reached her. I matched my stride to hers, made my case.

"Don't play, then," she said. "You don't have to do anything you don't want to." Her voice was passionate. It startled me to stillness. She stood still with me. I realized I had been looking at her feet in the grass rather than at her face. When I looked up, through the sun in my eyes, I saw tears glittering on her cheeks. She swiped at them. I thought she was crying about her fight with her husband.

"I'm sorry," she said. She pulled me close, bent her body to kiss the top of my head. Then again: "I'm sorry. The summer's almost over. I wish we had more time."

When she let go of me, I felt satiated. Released but not cast out.

"Go tell them what you want," she said, meaning my sisters in that moment, but maybe also everyone I loved, always. "They'll listen."

The Liminal

One Day After the Blue Chair. On the eighth day in the blue chair, I woke up to the sound of beating drums. I stood up, stretched, and opened the blinds to dark clouds, falling confetti, and dancing dragons. Chinese New Year. It was so obvious, so lacking in subtlety. I laughed out loud. Okay, okay. I opened the door and went to take a shower.

One Week After. I wrote bleak poems about tsunamis and sinkholes. Since I still struggled to sleep, I went for long walks at four or five in the morning. The sanitation workers, hanging off the back of trucks, whistled at me even though I was always in sweats and my hair was unkempt. I liked to give them the finger.

"Come on," they'd say, "that ain't necessary."

"Fuck off," I'd say. It felt good to curse.

Three Weeks After. Gradually, I turned to reading Rilke: *The only journey is the one within.* And Audre Lorde: *Your silence will not protect you.* I took to running at dawn, slow and steady until the first rays broke the gray. I would stop to catch my breath on the path by the West Side Highway and look out over the Hudson River. I'd buy a cup of coffee from the Yemeni man's food cart.

"Good run today?" he always asked. And, always, I said that it was.

"Enjoy," he'd say as he gave me a free banana or an apple.

A couple of years later, after I had moved from Manhattan to Brooklyn, I walked past his cart on my way to brunch with friends. My eyes filled with tears of what I took to be gratitude. I turned around.

"Hello," I said to him, "you might not remember me, but I used to buy a coffee from you very early every morning. Thank you for always being so kind when I needed it."

"You okay?" he asked, clearly having no idea what I was talking about. "You want coffee?"

Three Months After. At the bar, I looked up at a handsome man who had offered to buy me a drink, imagined myself kissing him. When did that happen? I wondered. When did my imagination make room among the catastrophes for kissing? When did I stop only noticing things like the excrement smeared on the walls of the entrance to the Canal Street subway station or the mounds of filthy snow that refused to melt? When did I start seeing, again, the vibrant wildflowers painted on the wall of the bodega in Greenpoint; how the woman in the long, hot pink dress in the West Village looked like a flamingo as she stood on one leg to empty her shoe of a small rock?

"I'll have another rioja, thanks," I said to the man. "After I finish this one."

That night, drunk, I wrote Anabel an email. *I miss you*, it said. She wrote back: *Good to hear from you. Headed to the gym. How are things? Love.*

I sat up for most of the night thinking what to write back. Days later, I still hadn't decided. Then another email from her: *I forgot to say happy birthday.*

A Year and a Half After. As I was making my way out of the fog of my twenties, I called my mother. It was time to end our estrangement, time to try to heal our wounds.

I flew to meet her in Arizona. She picked me up at the airport. I half expected her to bring balloons. The first words she said to me: "Hi, Nadia. Ryan went to pull the car up to the front." She hugged me just for a second. We both stood with our arms crossed. Ryan was the stepfather I had never met—her third husband.

"How are you?" I asked because I could not think of a better, more specific, place to start.

"Oh, you know," she said. I didn't know but didn't say so.

That week, we treated each other like new friends—carefully and politely. We cleaned and chopped lettuce side by side. We watched *Law & Order* and guessed who the killer was. She kept asking me if I needed anything. I kept saying no. In the evenings, I ran alone on the red rock canyon. My legs were shaky even though I never ran more than two or three miles. Sometimes, to steady myself, I stopped, dropped to a sprinter's starter position and stretched—my feet and hands rooted to earth.

My half sister Iman flew in for the weekend. She cried when she saw me and told me she had always loved me even though we hadn't gotten a chance to be real sisters. She wanted to try now. We squeezed each other's hands. This felt strange after the lettuce and the *Law & Order*. The three of us went for a walk, and we ran into a friend of my mother's.

"Is she your daughter?" the woman asked, pointing at me. "She has your face."

"They're both my daughters," my mother said.

"Oh," said the woman, examining Iman's face. "She must look more like her father."

After the woman walked away, I asked my mother if she remembered her conversation with the neighbor over the hedge—the neighbor who thought I must have been adopted from Ethiopia.

"That guy was an idiot," she said. "Obviously you're mine," as though there had never been any question. I thought about telling her I had asked that question too. I was still asking it and would probably ask it for the rest of our lives. But she brushed an eyelash off my cheek and looked into my eyes then looked away, and I saw she already knew that. My whole life, I felt, existed in that instant between my mother looking into my eyes and looking away.

"Come on," she said. "Let's go home."

Libation

I am not supposed to be on the roof. The sign says it might not hold me, suggests I might fall through, into my upstairs neighbor's apartment. But I am not afraid. I am small and alive. I have risen. I must give thanks. I climbed the stairs to pour libation.

Nyame is the Ashanti sky god who created the universe. I take my first swig of whiskey and wipe my mouth with my sleeve. I pour libation to Nyame. I thank him for this warm night, for the black sky of black stars, for this damaged roof, for my blue chair, and for this shaky earth.

Asese Yaa is the wife of Nyame. She is the giver of fertility and upholder of truth. She is the source of every seed in the soil and in the womb. She planted me. She feeds me. I wear her symbol on a bracelet my father gave me. *The earth has weight*, I am reminded, and so do I. I must respect and nurture the earth. I must respect and nurture myself. I drink to Asese Yaa. I pour libation for her.

The caravan from Marash crossed the desert carrying babies and grief. They had photographs of the murdered tucked in their bosoms and holes in the soles of their shoes. Because they walked, I live. *Kenats'y*, I scream to the skyscrapers in the distance. "Cheers" in Armenian. I looked it up on the internet. I tilt my head back, open my mouth wide, pour liquid in, raise my glass. I pour libation.

A queen mother of Ashanti made of my great-grandfather a chief. "You must be a tree and an umbrella," she said to him, laying her large

palm on his shoulder, looking into his eyes so she knew he was listening. "You must offer your people shade and protection." He passed
that message down to his son and his grandson. I was born in the
shade of their tree. I was protected. I pour libation to the Chief. I pour
libation to the Queen Mother. I pour libation to my grandfather.

When I was a child, my mother's parents, Charlie and Laura, sent
me packages every birthday and Christmas: a pink sweater, a green
knitted hat, red ribbons for my hair, and books—so many books, each
one inscribed with love. *We miss you. You are loved. We are with you.*
Did I ever write back? Did I send thank-you letters? I do not remember. I say thank you now. I pour libation.

My aunt Harriet is also my mother. When my father died, when
my birth mother wouldn't come, she came to Rome. Anabel was furious at Yasmeen and me for inviting her and locked us all out of the
apartment. The three of us spent the night huddled together. We sat
on our scarves on the glistening pavement under a crescent moon. Yasmeen and I were not afraid because Auntie Harriet told us there was
nothing to fear. She told us stories, taught us Twi phrases, asked us
to teach her Italian. We talked until the sun rose red, cutting the cool.
The next day, she went to stay with a friend of Baba's, and Anabel let
me and Yasmeen back in. For weeks after Auntie Harriet returned to
London, I heard her voice everywhere. It said the things of mothers:
tie your shoes; *blow your nose*. It said: *Don't run down the metro stairs,
another train will come.*

Auntie Harriet took me and Yasmeen in when we were between
mothers. She is a nurse; a healer of wounds and ailments. She is a
healer of hearts. Auntie Harriet, I pour libation to you.

There were the nannies—Mary, Elizabeth, Paulina—who were
always there after school with tea and sandwiches. They washed and
ironed. They pushed me on the swings and sat on the other side of the
seesaw. Once, there was a small earthquake in Rome, and Paulina, despite being so scared she thought she might piss herself, grabbed nothing of her own as she ran for the twelve flights of stairs. She saved, for
me, my favorite framed photo of my father. I drink to Mary, Elizabeth,

and Paulina. I don't think I ever said thank you. I bow my head. I say penance. I will do penance. I pour libation.

There were the teachers—men and women—who told me I could; who showed me how; who let me eat with them in the classroom when I needed to hide. I pour libation to the teachers.

My grandmother—Nana—worried about my soul enough to sneak me to church. She let me sleep in her bed when the storm sounded like ghosts. I drink to Nana. I pour libation. I pour a little extra.

Anabel's sister has, for years, emailed me every month to recommend books and articles, to remind me to keep reading because she knows that reading has saved me. Baba's sisters Violet and Freda have always been there, arms open, doors open, when I have needed them. We dance together on Nana's porch. When we dance, there is nothing but music and laughter and hips swaying. On the roof, I play highlife on my phone. I pour libation to my aunties.

Yasmeen, my sister, confidante, and closest friend. In your face, I see my whole life. I see reflection, connection, the limits of loneliness. I pour libation to you.

Kwame: Your tiny hand in mine was both plea and lifeline. I drink to the boy you were. I pour libation to the young man you have become.

My father was also my mother. I once made him a card and addressed it to Baba-Mama. Must mother be gendered? M, p, and b are the first consonants babies can sound. They make those sounds ma, ba, pa, as they feed from breast or bottle, opening and closing their hungry mouths. The sounds mean *give me food*. They also mean *I love the people who feed me*. Mama. Baba. Baba-Mama.

I sat across from Baba as he sat at his desk. He drank beer in a tall glass, I drank apple juice with a curly straw. Over drinks, we wrote stories—on paper, out loud. We wrote worlds. He showed me how.

"Aaaaaah," he exhaled after a long gulp. There was foam on his mustache. We were pleased with what we created. We clinked glasses.

For the stories, for the questions, for the beautiful broken places, for the map of my fault lines, for drafting and redrafting, for the certainty of love, for the black star rising, I gulp. I exhale. I pour libation, always, to Baba.

I have two mothers. Almas birthed me. Anabel raised me. A story I could tell is that my mothers drove me mad. But when it comes to madness, there is no such thing as attribution. There is only contribution. My mothers were the sparks that lit the fire, but they cannot be blamed for how it burned. I pour libation to the fire. I pour libation to how it burned.

Anabel, the easy answer to the questions of my aches and pains. Was I the easy answer to yours? We buried the man we loved, and we packed our lives into boxes. We began again. Sometimes, the day after we fought, I woke up to you standing over me. "Shall we go swimming?" you would say. And I took it to mean *I love you, still*. We used to hide from each other to drink in secret. I pour you a drink now, under an open sky. I pour libation to you.

I floated in Almas. I drank her and ate her, and I asked for more. She gave me her lips and her nose and the dent in her chin. She gave me letters on pink paper. She gave me her dreams. She gave me a sound I longed to say, a sound that requires so little to make— two sighs, a parting of lips in between them. Ma-Ma. She gave me almond-shaped eyes and pointed ears. She gave me a wound that was also her wound. Almas, I pour libation to you.

Long live mothers. Long live those who mother. I'll drink to that. I'll pour libation.

Mad black women. Mad black women like me. I pour libation to your ghosts. I pour libation to you.

Home

Let me show you my home. It is the subterranean water body of my mother. I drift in her voice and amniotic fluid. When she steps into the light, I am in the light. When her sun sets, my sun sets. As she moves, I move. I somersault, dive, kick, poke, remind her I am inside her, becoming. Through our placenta, I taste her blood, mingled with Aleppo pepper and mint.

Let me show you my home. It is a city on the Indian Ocean. The fishermen drag their dhows onto white sand at dawn to unload the night's tilapia, squid, and snapper. At dusk, they disappear back into the blue.

Under the shade of a thatched umbrella, I slurp from a straw in a coconut while my father plays soccer with the boys who sell them. We have been here all day, blackening. Tomorrow monsoon season might start, later than in years past. But tonight, live music at Oyster Bay. Women and palm trees will sway and rustle. For me, *mishkaki*—skewered chicken and goat with chili and lime. For my father, *nyama choma* and beer. On the drive home, we will ride in the back of a pickup. We will pass the Aga Khan mosque and the Lutheran church. The smell of bougainvillea and jacaranda trees will come rushing at us on the wind.

Let me show you my home. It is my father's embrace. Strong biceps press into my rib cage, firm hands on my back. My feet are lifted off the floor. I fly, without fear, over my father's head. I know he will hold me up until I land in sheets. "See you in the morning," he says, and I have no reason, yet, not to believe him.

Let me show you my home. It is a country cottage with a red door. In the spring, bluebells carpet the earth beneath the surrounding forest of oak trees. Even on sunny Sundays, just in case, Auntie Harriet makes us wear our Wellington boots and yellow anoraks. We pick wild blackberries along the Cuckoo Trail and stop to smell the daffodils. Sometimes, a shepherd and his sheep are crossing. He whistles and the sheep *baaa* their way to be auctioned at the market.

This used to be a rope-making town, a supplier to yachters, sailors, and hangmen in all of Britain and her colonies. There is still a rope factory, but there are no hangmen. There is a library where we go after school to read Enid Blyton and Roald Dahl.

Let me show you my home. It is built on seven hills. It is eternal: ruins but not ruined, aged but vivacious.

Look around when you walk. Everywhere there is writing on the wall. SPQR is carved into stone (*Senatus Populusque Romanus*, or "The Senate and People of Rome"). Next to it is an alternative series of words to make up the acronym, likely spray-painted by a visiting Milanese or Napolitano: *Sono Porci Questi Romani* ("They're pigs, these Romans").

My classmates ride skateboards into the metro to tag their names in the tunnels. I prefer to ride my bicycle along Via Appia. Among the tombs, I hop off. Grass grows between ancient flagstones. Above: pine trees. Below: catacombs. Let's raise a Pellegrino toast to the dead, and to the still growing.

Let me show you my home. "Would you like chicken or beef?" ask the attendants. We are all wrapped in matching gray blankets. Our feet nest in matching gray socks. The air recirculates. Outside the cool glass, clouds grow heavy. There will be turbulence while we sleep. When we wake, croissants and jam and fresh starts. But tonight my home is a jet-propelled cabin in the sky. My home is moving away and moving toward. On the screen, a dotted line charts our course.

Let me show you my home. Can you smell the eucalyptus? Can you smell the roasting coffee? We make some of the best in the world. The women grind it with their pestles and roast it, making sure to waft the sweet earth of it into your nostrils.

During the Epiphany, we go to Lalibela to watch pilgrims reenact the baptism of Christ. Priests parade in robes of rich velvet. They wave incense. Drums and bells fill the air and lead us to the Fasilides Baths.

In the shantytowns, there is no running water. At our house in the UN compound, we boil cholera out of everything. But today, rich and poor, young and old, faithful Christians and faithless travelers, will jump in with whoops and squawks, and be renewed. Anabel and I hold our breath, hold hands until the splash.

Let me show you my home. It is a family that used to be five and is now four. We are built of love and hurt and rage and silences. We have not yet found the right material with which to patch the roof, to stop the absence from trickling in.

Let me show you my home. Many of the streets have no names or multiple names, but not to worry. You will learn to tell your motorcycle taxi driver to make a left at the mango tree or right at the rolex stand. A rolex is not a watch. It is chapati with eggs, onion, and tomatoes. You won't have much use for watches anyway. Time moves differently here. We meet in Kabalagala for *waragi* and *wolokosso* (loose talk). Join us. As the proverb goes, where they eat flies, eat them.

Let me show you my home. It is my grandmother's porch. We sit here all day and people stop by to say hello and to watch Nana argue with the house girl.

"Are you thirsty?" Nana asks. "I'm thirsty but Afua, useless girl, keeps forgetting to bring my drink."

"Would you like some water, Ma?" asks Auntie Freda.

"Did I urinate in your bed? Why am I being punished?" Nana bristles.

"She wants a beer," I explain. "When she says she's thirsty, it means she wants a beer. I'll get it. I could use one too."

"Finally," says Nana, "a real Jantuah."

Jantuah is her maiden name. It is also her highest compliment. She has never called me a Jantuah before: "American," "sort of Arab," her "precious half-caste granddaughter," but never a Jantuah. Everyone laughs at what was, to them, just typical Nana. But I can barely contain my glee.

In the kitchen, I help myself to a handful of *kelewele*. Then, two cold beers in hand, I go to claim my seat on the porch.

Let me show you my home. The glass and steel grow up and out: towers, sprawl. This city is ever-changing. We must keep moving to keep up. This is why we do not sleep.

You can find me at the bar with a book. The bartender knows my name. He knows my drink. He has read the book I'm reading. He is a poet.

For years, my bedroom had no windows. The cracks in my bathroom grew slimy mushrooms that smelled like chlorine. It was what I could afford. In that apartment, I dreamt of skylights and potted plants. Now my window looks down on a courtyard I don't have access to. It is filled with the garbage that can't be put on the street to be picked up till Thursday.

Any day now, I will make a living. Until then, I pay what I can at the Metropolitan Museum and look forward, all week, to bottomless mimosas at brunch.

Let me show you my home. It is a border. It is the outer edge of both sides. It is where they drew the line. They drew the line right through me. I would like to file a territorial dispute.

Let me show you my home. It is a live fault. The fault is in my body.

Let me show you my home. It is a blue chair. I sought asylum here. I marked my application temporary. For myself, I am writing reconstruction, not elegy.

Look into my eyes. See my glowing skin. My pores are open. I am made of the earth, flesh, ocean, blood, and bone of all the places I tried to belong to and all the people I long for. I am pieces. I am whole. I am home.

Acknowledgements

Parts of *Aftershocks* appeared, sometimes in different forms, in *Catapult*, *Electric Literature*, *Lumina*, the *Rumpus*, the *New York Times*, the *Literary Review*, and *Columbia Journal*. I am grateful to these publications and to the editors I worked with, including Mensah Demary, Nicole Chung, Justin Taylor, Eden Werring, Arielle Bernstein, and Kelly Luce.

I am indebted to the authors, researchers, and editors whose work provided inspiration and information: Toni Morrison, Audre Lorde, Zadie Smith, David C. Pollock and Ruth E. Van Reken, Martin Meredith, James Baldwin, W. E. B. Du Bois, James Schuyler, Geoff Dyer, June Jordan, Cherrie Moraga, Gloria Anzaldua, Toni Cade Bambara, Amiri Baraka, Amélie Oksenberg Rorty, Chinua Achebe, Vladimir Nabokov, William Styron, Rainer Maria Rilke, Zora Neale Hurston, Vaslav Nijinsky, Wole Soyinka, Tsitsi Dangarembga, A. Kyerematen for his paper on Ashanti stools, and Hazel Barrett for her paper about the ABC policy in Uganda. Papers by Kwame Arhin, by Emmanuel Akyeampong, and by Pashington Obeng provided vital information about Ashanti society.

Many thanks to my friends at the Mountainview MFA program who served as early readers of and champions for this book: Ben Nugent, Lisa Janicki, Jo Knowles, Marcus Burke, Wiley Cash, Katie Towler, Lydia Peelle, Robin Wasserman, Chinelo Okparanta, Mark Sundeen, Adam Wilson, Tracy O'Neill, Rebecca Schiff, Rachel B. Glaser, Craig Childs,

Mark Freeman, Dave Moloney, and Dan Johnson. Sarah Eisner read more versions of every chapter in this book than I can count. I am so very grateful. This book could not have been written without Amy Irvine. She coaxed me into the depths and swam beside me the whole way.

Special thanks to my dream-maker of an agent, Meredith Kaffel Simonoff. Draft after draft, her wisdom made this book better. I don't take her belief in me for granted. I would also like to thank everyone at DeFiore and Company, especially Jacey Mitziga. I am grateful to Colin Farstad for his editorial eye.

I am so very lucky that Ira Silverberg saw something in this book. His guidance and generosity have meant a great deal. Thank you also to Cary Goldstein who asked important questions and helped me to wrestle with them.

I am grateful to everyone at Simon & Schuster who worked on and championed *Aftershocks*, including Jonathan Karp, Anne Pearce, Stephen Bedford, Maggie Southard, Julia Prosser, Chelcee Johns, Richard Rhorer, Mark LaFlaur, Chonise Bass, Lashanda Anakwah, Angela Ching, Nicole Hines, Lewelin Polanco, Alison Forner, Ana Perez, Michelle Leo, and Amy Beaudoin. With gratitude to Zack Knoll for his support and for diving right in. Endless thanks to Dawn Davis for being a wonderful editor, guide, and ambassador.

Thank you also to everyone at Sceptre, including Louise Court, Alasdair Oliver, and Maria Garbutt Lucero. This book would not be what it is without Juliet Brooke's partnership and guidance.

With gratitude to everyone at Signatuur, especially Anne Everard; and to everyone at Modernista.

I am grateful to the Whiting Foundation for their generous support, and especially to Daniel Reid, Courtney Hodell, Adina Applebaum, and the 2019 selection committee. Many thanks to Michael Taeckens and Whitney Peeling. Shout-out to my cohort for the ongoing camaraderie: Kayleb Rae Candrilli, Tyree Daye, Hernan Diaz, Michael R. Jackson, Terese Marie Mailhot, Nafissa Thompson-Spires, Merrit Tierce, Vanessa Angélica Villarreal, and Lauren Yee.

I am eternally grateful for my friends and colleagues who inspired me, supported me, lent me their homes to write in, cheered me on, opened doors, covered for me, fed me, and excused my absences, including Jenna Pace, Scott Terry, Kristen Howard, Jeff Gaites, Evelyn Burnett, Gladys Burnett, Tracey Ross, Shlomit Zebersky, Hafizah Omar, Ratna Gill, Sabrina Barrios, Jean Rene Mbeng, Nana Kwame Adjei-Brenyah, Joshua Wolf Shenk, Brittany DeBarros, Marielis Garcia, Brad and Rion Wentworth, Madge McKeithen, Sherrie Deans, Marcus Littles, Natalie Eilbert, Julie Nelson, Glenn Harris, Carter Schwarberg, Bernard and Kate Ayisa, Elodie Baquerot and Mike Lavery, Dave Lafleur, JaNay Queen Nazaire, Ron Chisom, Dr. Kim Richards, Ellen Ward, Elizabeth Reynoso, Ben Hecht, Wade Ekstrom, Devin Vaughan, Rachel Lyon, George Abraham, Julian Randall, Michael Lally, and Nana-Ama Danquah. Too many others to name, but please know that I appreciate you.

Undying love to all the members of my many families, immediate and extended, blood and chosen. I have thanked many of you in the pages of this book. I will continue to thank you. Here, for their support in bringing this book to life, I'd like to name Auntie Harriet, Auntie Freda, Auntie Violet, Laura Barku, Nana Ofaa, Kozi, Mildred, Declan, Aoife, Cathy and Jimmy, Paul and Eddy, Hogie, Iman, Joe, Wahida, Hatim, Catherine, Ryan Smith, Paulina Mamkwe, Yasmeen, Charlie Kessenich, Kwame, Queen Liz, Nana Kwasi, Uncle Leon, Auntie June, Aaron, Gramma Laura, and Grampa Charlie. Mama: I am grateful for where we are and for how much you have celebrated my writing even when it has been difficult for you.

This book would not exist without my partner, Seth Trachy, with whom I am so lucky to move through life.

I open and close with love and gratitude for my father, Osei Owusu.